ALSO BY LES MURRAY

The Vernacular Republic: Selected Poems (1982)

The Daylight Moon and Other Poems (1988)

The Rabbiter's Bounty: Collected Poems (1991)

The Boys Who Stole the Funeral (1991)

Dog Fox Field (1992)

Translations from the Natural World (1992)

Subhuman Redneck Poems (1997)

FREDY NEPTUNE

Fredy Neptune

A NOVEL IN VERSE

Les Murray

Farrar, Straus and Giroux

New York

Farrar, Straus and Giroux
19 Union Square West, New York 10003

Copyright © *1999 by Les Murray*
All rights reserved
Distributed in Canada by Douglas & McIntyre Ltd.
Printed in the United States of America
First published in PN Review *numbers 93, 98, 112, 115 and 118*
First published as one volume in Great Britain in 1998 by Carcanet Press Ltd.
First Farrar, Straus and Giroux edition, 1999

Library of Congress Cataloguing-in-Publication Data
Murray, Les A., 1938–
    Fredy Neptune / Les Murray.
        p.   cm.
    ISBN 0-374-15854-1 (alk. paper)
        1. World War, 1914–1918—Australia—Poetry.   2. Strong men—
Australia—Poetry.   3. Soldiers—Australia—Poetry.   4. Germans—
Australia—Poetry.   5. Lepers—Australia—Poetry.   I. Title.
PR9619.3.M83F74   1999
    821—dc21   *98-48911*

Contents

BOOK 1
The Middle Sea   1

BOOK 2
Barking at the Thunder   47

BOOK 3
Prop Sabres   113

BOOK 4
The Police Revolution   171

BOOK 5
Lazarus Unstuck   213

The twenty sank exhausted to the ground.
'Get up!' The naked swords flickered like snakes.
Then someone fetched a pitcher of kerosene.
Human justice, I spit in your face.
Without delay the twenty were anointed.
'Dance!' Roared the mob; 'This is sweeter than the perfumes of Arabia!'
They touched the naked women with a torch.
And there was dancing. The charred bodies rolled.
In shock I slammed my shutters like a storm,
Turned to the one gone, asked 'These eyes of mine—
How shall I dig them out, how shall I, how?'

—from the Armenian of Siamanto (Atom Ergoyan) 1878–1915

BOOK I

The Middle Sea

That was sausage day
on our farm outside Dungog.
There's my father Reinhard Boettcher,
my mother Agnes. There is brother Frank
who died of the brain-burn, meningitis.
There I am having my turn
at the mincer. Cooked meat with parsley and salt
winding out, smooth as gruel, for the weisswurst.

Here's me riding bareback in the sweater
I wore to sea first.
I never learned the old top ropes,
I was always in steam. Less capstan, less climbing,
more re-stowing cargo. Which could be hard and slow
as farming—but to say Why this is Valparaiso!
Or: I'm in Singapore and know my way about
takes a long time to get stale.

My German had got me a job
out of New York on a Hansa freighter, the Opitz.
That's how we came to be cooking alive that August,
in Messina, plumy undertakers' city.
The first I heard that the War had really come
was a black-faced officer with a target and a church
on his cap, directing sailors to rip
our decks up, for the coal below.

I turned out of my hammock
to fight them—and our bos'un chucked me a shovel:
We're coaling that battlecruiser.
There! The English are after her!
It was like one great bushfire of work,
the whole harbour, under smoke and brown dust,
slings, lighters, big crane-buckets slopping
man-killing rocky lumps, before they poured.

I was sent across to the warship. Up on deck
the band was sweating, pumping Oompa and heirassa
to us below, to encourage our mad shovelling.
A man dropped dead beside me. His face hit the bulkhead bong
as he fell. So when the ship's only clean man
came and nodded Enough, with his Higher Matters expression,
a lot of us sprawled asleep, right on the coal.
When I woke up, we were steaming full ahead, at sea.

Later we heard how the one
British admiral sent after us had been wirelessed
to steam the long way around Sicily
and the other one, racing down the Adriatic, had squibbed
facing our big guns. But I was thinking more
about being shot for a spy, if I protested
or explained myself. So I was off the Opitz
would be enough. A colonial, from the South Sea—

All servicemen are like officers now, but the empires
could be pretty approximate, then, with the lower deck.
You're German, said the Chief. *I'm short two that dropped dead.*
Wear this rig. Come to attention, so! to any officer
and enjoy the Kaiser's dumplings. A warship is a lot less
hard to graft than a freighter. I got used, like the rest,
to being called a sow-lump, a carrion, a waxer,
and soon we were sailing in between dry hills

to a city of bulbs and spikes, Constantinople
where men goose each other and eat off forges in the street.
Soon after, the Kaiser came on board
with crowds of heel-clickers. He wore a resentful snobby look,
electric whiskers in his pink grandpa face, and a helmet like a finial
off a terrace house. We'd to change our caps, he said,
and put on fezes. We were now the Turkish Navy.
Enver Pasha had a haemorrhoid look on him, at that part.

All the women we Turk matlows met we were led to by the touts.
I was ashamed and shy. I was always, round all that:
the tired anger in it, behind the sticky smiles, the contempt
as they stooped over to give you eyefulls.
All I wanted was a girlfriend.
And then, with no Turk orders, our admiral took us to Odessa
and I found myself passing up big silk bags to the gun crews
to make thunderclaps that rang the iron ball the earth's around.

Now Turkey was in, and Russia's last trade lifeline blocked
so she would rot. It was all we'd come to do, I worked out later.
We idled and dressed ship round the City and Black Sea
playing skat, eating goulash.
When Gallipoli came, I thought: I will desert
if I have to fight Australians. But instead
my mates and I, on shore leave up by Trabzon
at last saw women with their faces unwrapped in the open.

[4]

They were huddling, terrified, crying.
crossing themselves, in the middle of men all yelling.
Their big loose dresses were sopping. Kerosene, you could smell it.
The men were prancing, feeling them, poking at them to dance—
then pouf! they were alight, the women, dark wicks to great orange flames,
whopping and shrieking. If we'd had rifles there
we'd have massacred those bastards. We had only fists and boots.
One woman did cuddle a man: he went up screaming too.

We would have been killed but for a patrol from the ship.
Back on board, within days I found out I had leprosy.
I just curled up in my hammock, like a burnt thing myself,
and turned my back. The POs couldn't scream me to work:
Sow-fellow, all you've got's Infaulenza! Acute lazyitis.
When the watch officer saw my white numb places, he
got very serious. And discovered I was a stray.
The Chief lost his rank over it. I was put ashore quick.

So the ship rode the Bosphorus like an iron on shined blue cloth
and I drifted into begging, among the wrestlers and porters
and Dardanelles soldiers in their hessian-bag uniforms
with caked brown rag wrapped round the ends of what
had got shot off them. I drifted between mosques' charity kitchens
Ayasofya, Süleimaniye, the Blue Mosque. And I slept
sometimes for whole days, with my only clothes sticking to me
as they get. No one would touch me, nor my food.

It was chilly at night, about like home
but there were always trash fires to sleep near. I'd wake up
and sit around, half there,
with the carts and dogs and arguments criss-crossing
as if not around but through me. I was at the bottom
of wavery air, the birds' sea-floor, my head alight, and notices
in their running writing saying *jilliby* and *poll-willow.*
A bad place for a Dungog man, waiting for bits to rot off him.

The only one who'd sit with me was a girl-faced man
who'd never shaved. *Alman?* he asked, with his finger
poking up off his head, a helmet-spike. I nodded. And he talked
then, for hours. Poured talk over me like water,
nearly all wasted. *Versteh' dich nicht, mate: I don't savvy,*
but the words tumbled out of him, long words turned up at the ends
as Turkish words are. In between, he taught me the begging words
cüzzamlıyım, dokunmayınız—I'm a leper, don't touch,

sadaka, alms. Allah *rızası için bir sadaka.*
Teşekkür ederim. That's thank you. I learned not to take money,
because I made it unclean, and no one would accept it.
I'd got hold of some lino, for a windbreak. I remember
the *karayel*, the freezing north west wind, was blowing
and I was in my lino, like a rat in a pipe. I was dying,
I realise now, when my mates from the watch,
Heimo and Lutz and Claasen rolled me out of it:

Come on, shipmate: you're for the Berlin nurses,
they'll warm your carcase. The name on this rail pass, that's you!
As we left, the wrestlers in oiled leather shorts were in holts
and a man on the soles of his hands who ended in a board
was bouncing out of shelter, cracking jokes
with his alms-box round his neck.
The no-shave bloke followed us but wouldn't say a word.
Then I got clean new rig, and off to the white-sky countries.

At Berlin, I was carried on a stretcher from the train
through this terrible hall all full of cripples and crying
and racked up in a green motor until I was stowed
in another huge hall of a hospital iced with mirrors
tingling under the lights. The doctors were buttoned and straight
as bayonets, with their guard moustaches, the nurses tight and pink
and all of us Wounded tucked up so trim and square
we couldn't see what shapes each other were.

I was the one from furthest away. The Pacific,
I told them. The colonies. So a smart nurse called me Grocery
and I had to tell her about the zebras and elephants we ate
in New Pomerania. But I still had no spark in me.
'Tuberculoid leprosy' is a heavy sentence out of bearded
Professor Doctors in frock coats. I thought: while I've got feet,
if I can get away, keep my patches covered over
and get a ship, and get to the Pacific,

somehow I'll be right. And home, if I could get right home,
would cure me. Mad. I got as far as a tram
in Lichterfelde. The police came on it, checking papers
and every man not crippled looked haunted and alone
and showed his bits. I stepped quietly off
arse over head on black ice, showed the pyjamas
under my borrowed topcoat, and the police jumped out
into the pointing crowd, with their swords drawn.

[6]

I opened my clothes and showed my islands and countries,
white, with red crust borders. *Lepra. You want to catch it from me?*
The crowd rolled back like potatoes over a floor
but the two soldier police kept pace with me as I stumbled
on that ice. They whistled up more like themselves
and a droll young officer with a blue cross in his collar
who said: *Congratulations. You're holding Berlin hostage.*
What are your terms?—I want to go home, I burbled.

Rather a lot do. And more would have, he answered.
But will home be there? Cigarette? No, I won't seize you.
A lifetime of soup and choral singing without lips
does not appeal. I heard no more of his culture
because from round a corner, a big rope net dropped over me.
Roll him up, said the Leutnant. *Burn the net then, afterwards.*
The nurse who'd called me Groceries, Helga, she was horrified.
She said she'd sneak me out herself, for a walk some Sunday.

For all she knew, she would have been risking death. Unbelievable!
We never had that walk, though. I was shipped
to a walled-in hole on the flats of the Weser River,
the Kaiserly Leprosarium. It was yellow indoor cemetery:
we were there to stay, and things went on there, very slow,
that happen in the grave. From just like a scratchy photo
to bandaged stubs, and earholes, and half faces—
and not stopped, like on cripples in the world, but continuing.

We had a Hauptmann, brought back from Africa by Zeppelin,
from Lettow-Vorbeck's army, that stung the British for four years.
There were lots of colonials in there: I had to be careful,
but he was a wake-up, and soon tipped me a grin:
You're German enough, Sailor, wherever you're really from,
and you won't spy much in here.
That woke me up, it saved me, it made me think escape again.
One thing I'd learned, being crippled was as good as papers,

or old age; nearly as good as uniform. So I waited my chance
and then slipped ashore. I mean, out where there are two sexes,
and children, and grass. I'd been like a long time at sea.
And this time I'd keep the disease wrapped up. No touching people,
but I'd look as if I could. And I'd keep one arm inside
my clothes. And not stride, but trudge like a local subject.
And it worked. Poor love, I'd been a Kriegsmarine sailor
whenever I got lifts, on carts or canals, towards Holland.

I was in Osnabrück outside the Peace Hall this Spring morning
eyeing a couple of other land-rakers like me
and a pretty girl going by with an attaché case,
filling in, I dare say, for some pen-pusher off at the war.
One of the drifters suddenly jumped and tore
the briefcase off her. Really. Because her arm came off too.
I blinked. It was real. She screamed. The veins and muscles
attaching the arm were leather straps. And the thief,

well he was hopeless. He leant his head against the wall
with the case at his feet, still chained to that wooden arm
and the crowd running up—the other bloke had cleared.
The girl was crying, with the sleeve torn off her blouse
and I was the one nearest. I was so stupid-shy,
she was stretching out her hand, her live real hand—
and what do I do but put her wooden arm in it?
If I had got that right, everything would have been different.

She gave me the queerest look, quietly.
And then women were comforting all over her, and police coming,
taking charge, and the robber. I remembered to melt
quick, into the crowd. *What's up?—Don't rightly know.—*
What's that on your face?—Oh, the war—Poor lad! So, on to Paris, eh?
On to Rotterdam, I went.
A few more nights in the hay, or telling about New Mecklenburg
and dodging the deserter-catchers, and I slipped through the bush

into Holland. When the language on signs changed, I grew an arm.
Two years I'd been trapped in the war. Now I could be Australian!
Or North or South American, to speak German and be neutral. Two years!
First thing I did in the Flying Angel, I wrote
a letter home. And cried as I wrote, and cried after.
Then I stuck a chair under my doorknob—this was before showers—
and had a good body-wash. My numb bits were changing,
stinging like burns, and coming off at the rims.

I was terrified. I was coming apart.
Quicker than ever anyone in the Leprosarium.
I had to get a ship. And I did at last, a Dane,
with a huge flag painted port and starboard, bound for Rio.
I was burning in my clothes, sticking to them and ripping free again
shedding like a gum tree, and having to hide it and work.
What I never expected, when I did stop hurting
I wouldn't feel at all. But that's what happened.

[8]

No pain, nor pleasure. Only a ghost of that sense
that tells where the parts of you are, and of needs from inside
so I wouldn't disgrace myself. It seemed I was not to be
a public cripple. And somehow I knew I wouldn't die,
that the leprosy, or whatever it had been, was lifted.
On the other hand, a hatch-coaming dropped on my boot
was supposed to hurt. The blokes were looking at me.
Good, these steel toecaps, I thought to say, feeling nothing.

but hearing bones. I would have to learn quick, and practise
cracking normal, as I call it. It isn't hard to do from memory:
curse when burnt, hunch when you see it's cold, don't hammer fingers
or let your leg bend to the pop! stage. Remember to get tired:
once I worked twenty hours re-stowing a shifted cargo
and then just stopped. Nothing would go. Arms
wouldn't lift, nor tongue lick lips, nor swallow
swallow. I stood there dying. This was later that same year.

I was having all this private life and working my watches too,
not liking to sleep in full dark because of the way
my body, it would fade, and leave me just a self in mid-dark.
Strange to tell that, even now. No one on earth to tell then,
a working man with other men, ashamed of the difference happening me.
I saw men facing worse, though.
We were hove to in the Channel, watching ferries passing
low in the water, with freights of standing men in brown.

You been near that, Sydneyside? the cook asked me.
I said I'd steered clear of it. *Best*, he said. *They going
to camp in the rain in big sewers dug through men.*
I knew not to ask where he'd seen this. *Backbones in rag like gun belts.*
He had a horror-struck, poisoned look. *Maggots eat the ground
up there*, he said. I thought of each man's agony
and how that death mightn't even hurt me, now,
me only, of all my age. *We better on the ships, eh, Sydneyside?*

This is me, and Rosie, and Corbeau, down the Boca
in Buenos Aires. If you could see inside
that new peajacket on Rosie, he'd be every bit as blue.
We'd shipped a prize bull from Galveston. He was in its pen
mucking out, when it took a notion to scratch.
He was between it and the bulkhead, so it simply rubbed him up
the steel and down, looking puzzled it was getting no relief,
and us dragging and jobbing it. *Don't bust with passion there, Rosie!*

The first time I slipped up badly was on that voyage.
We had a deck galley. The cook, a different cook, he was a drunk
and the fire had been doused, in dirty weather. The boy was relighting it
with kerosene, and it blew out and caught his clothes.
He was screaming blind when I reached him, half the galley alight too
and when I got him put out I didn't notice
I had caught, here, all up my calf, you can see it.
They took the boy out, and there I'm tidying up, still burning.

The cook started screaming, I didn't know what at.
One of his blue dragons had come real. I went on burning—
see how deep it goes in? The little silver walls?
The supercargo whopped me out with a soaking jumper
and everybody near was looking. *He devil!* screams the cook
he walk in fire, not hurt. You stay away, you devil!—
You'd know, I said. But the word I was uncanny made the skipper
get rid of me. Or I might have had a midnight flotation test.

There was no pain in the leg, not burning, not healing. It stank
and I used a farm cure on that: metho, poured on neat and smoky.
By the time it healed up, as much as it ever would, I'd lost
my leprosy-thinking. I was young again, becalmed in port, curious,
scratching up dust a bit. A café waitress there noticed
and helped me out. This part is awful to admit.
She had to tell me everything. *Oh yes, you're ready, yes,*
and *Stop, hey, you're finished. I'm flooded. Didn't you feel that?*

I couldn't seem to get a ship through Panama
to the Pacific, but late in '17 I got a job on
a freighter out of New Orleans bound for Cape Town:
from there, I thought I'd sure to get home. Also
our flag was Colombian. But the Yanks came into the war
and the U-boats went for everything. We got sunk, and only
the awful sarcastic tongue of our black Brazilian captain,
João Teixera de Saint-Adroit, kept any discipline

in the only lifeboat. *You believe self-pity to be potable,*
Mr Henshaw? No? Then why share it? They hated him so much
it kept them alive, the ones who could feel their misery.
Mine was more of a knowledge: in two more days
I will die of thirst. Or really, It will die of thirst.
It that I am in. When the Alcázar de Toledo,
our ship, had cracked open, the bos'un ran on deck
screaming *The Huns! The Huns have scuppered us!*

and I had thought the word was simply Hans.
That was the first time I heard it.
The captain said in his cut-crystal English how my *nonchalance*
evaded the fellowship of suffering, but I went to sleep again.
When I woke, they were all dead, except for Saint-Adroit.
He spoke, again in English, but I didn't follow. A pity
not to make what could be your last words simple
for a simple hearer. But some can't get off stage.

Later that day, it must have been, a destroyer,
a British four-stacker, rescued us. I heard a matlow laugh at Teixera
and call out *Where'd thee steal thon officer's hat, Sambo?*
We were put ashore in Malta, that nice stone town in the sea
and my luck was in: leading hand
on a freighter bound for Colombo and Fremantle!
British, with a taffrail gun and Merchant Navy nonsense,
but it was going home. After five queer years, home—

and would have got there but for a wire hawser
that sheared the propeller, off Alexandria.
The company paid us off, and I started trudging
round the offices, in glare that made every shade an island
jammed with poor blowfly kids—*Baksheesh hey Johnny!*—
feet on their shoulders or blind and with even riper sores
than I'd seen layered on with lamb-fat and dye powder
before dawn in Stamboul. Pussing pits, to last for days.

There were soldiers everywhere,
peeling in the sun and taking their whippy swagger sticks
to the beggars. I daresay Egypt was Britain's
Constantinople, but not one where they had to behave.
Any German laying a stick about a Turk would have died!
I was sitting on a bollard, watching the Nile stain the sea
when I heard Australian voices: *Hey! Fred! Freddy Butcher!*
Is it you, you old bugger? And shaking hands all round.

The Rumbels' boy from home, two of the Mudfords from Gloucester,
some of the Relfs—I knew the lot of them:
How are you? Where have you been? What's the news from home?
How are my people? There was just a little hitch there.
Oh, they're good. Or were when we left. Back three year ago.
So you're still a sailor; sly bugger! Seen any of the war?
Man can't blame you, steering clear. But I went back to it:
Last letter I had from home was Easter '14...

They were dragging me away. *Come down to Cairo with us!*
Beer by the bucketful! Heliopolis! Geebung Polo Club!
I didn't follow any of it, but we were in this train
with no glass in the windows, and a bottle in my hand
and soldiers outside stoning shops, or careering on camels
or hanging upside down from water pipes, and men
running in nightshirts, offering them tea.
It was all merry hell, that Egypt.

Next I knew, we were in palatial great stables
at a racecourse. Too good for the horses, they
seemed to be in big holding yards all around
with sun screens of palm on trellises out over them.
I was dizzy with home-talk and home feelings
after so long. Every *whip the cat* and *rybuck!* the boys said
was home. Their saddlesoap was home,
their snake yarns and jokes and tins of Champion Ruby.

Home was the easy stuff to talk about, too.
They were full of the war, the dead mates, and the funny bits
and I had to bite my tongue. When they talked of Gallipoli
I couldn't really say I'd waited for them in Constantinople,
that I'd got there, as they hadn't, and seen the battle's results.
I finally did say I'd been there. Once. *On a ship?*
What's she like? We lost a lot of blokes heading there—
Decent city, on the outside. Sailors don't get indoors much, in places.

What is this place? I asked.—*It's the Remount Centre.*
We come down here for horses and take them back up the line.
Banjo Paterson runs it. I hiccuped on my beer. *Banjo?—*
Major Paterson. All the cracks are gathered to this fray,
says the younger Mudford, laughing.
We're off back Wednesday, with a mob, to Palestine.
Next day we were in the bazaar (*hey Johnny!*) and when we got back
my money belt was gone. Complete ruin. And I hadn't felt it.

Must've used a razor, said one of us. *Mongrel bastards!*
Ar you got to remember, said the youngest Relf, *these people*
don't like us. They're kept two grades below a private
and one below his dog. Robbing us'd be revenge.
It'd be a year's feeds for fifty of them, that roll you had!
Don't come the saint on me, I snarled, *or I'll dong you!*
There was a lot in it, but.
I'm broke, then, I said.—*You'll have to ask Banjo for a job.*

You mean enlist?—A lot have.—
I'm a sailor, not a soldier.—You could see Jerusalem.—
And anywhere else they sent me.—And get shot there too.—
You're not exactly sooling me on.—I don't give speeches.—
I can't enlist.—You mean, you won't shoot Germans?—
No. And nor Australians.—Each man was looking at the ground
Like some of youse, in that. One of them finally said
You get up early and wake up late, in the Army.

This was Banjo. For all that uniform and crupper-strap
over one shoulder, he'd more the way about him
of a bush-town solicitor. Well-made small man, still trim.
As we walked through the yards, there was this grunting heartbroken
pig-squealing, just away. *We're buying up native horses.*
Half of them are entires, and have to be gelded. It's sad
but it's Army regulations. Stallions aren't free like us men
to refuse their passions. And we want them for ours, not theirs.—

More sense than us, sir?—You could be right, young Rumbel.
What chance, Banjo asked, *of a Dungog boy breaking in*
this pepperpot here? It was a tall mad-eyed mare,
grey-black, with narrow withers. *She looks like a mosquito,*
I said, *her head down like that. I'll try her,*
calculating there'd be no job for me if I didn't.
There was no gentling her, nor leading. We went dancing backwards
on the rope, her rearing, tall as cart-shafts, to trample me.

The only safe place was on her back. She fishtailed and I on,
feeling for the other, wild stirrup, booting at bites,
grim death to the pommel I'm gripping, as she'd rocket and reel stiff-leggèd,
pigroot, swerve, bounce high, going *rirr-rirrr*, and jolt-land.
She hit the fence, she switched her bum over her own saddle
so I sat on dusty hair, then a quarter buttock back on leather, leapt
only when she dived, rolling. *Very creditable,* said Banjo.
More creditable than most. I think she's a scratching from this war.

So I was on the strength, as a merchant seaman
in green cord jodhpurs, with a paybook. My drinking mates
had gone north with a draft. I enjoyed the work, grooming, breaking in,
going out with the buying officers to the big estates
with their fat green paddocks that stopped short at bare tan.
The fly-struck eyes of the village kids weren't so pretty
but the war was not to help them. What was it for? Search me.
King and Kaiser. To stop more wars. To show your metal—

I knew not to show mine. Neither show nor tell—
and yet, that Christmas, I did let on, and near died of it.
It was not long after Jerusalem fell.
I was sent up the line, the railway line, to Rafa.
There we unloaded, to drove the mob up through Palestine
through good grass country with pine trees and little quail
and blue olive trees, as we climbed those like Adelaide Hills,
as if we were heading up to Crafers or Norton Summit—

But there was Jerusalem, its towers husked and unhusked on the cob
in its high stone box. That first time, I forgot the mob
and sat my horse and stared.
Other cities, it never mattered that I'd come unprepared
and take them as I found them. But directions seemed to go
up and out from Jerusalem. A freezing rain half snow
had sagged my hat, when Bill Hines our sergeant called me back
to feeling neither cold nor wet, a heavy soul on a droving track.

Jerusalem. There'd be help for me. I was keyed tight with hope.
The paliasse under me—*You sleeping on that straw or eating it?*
my tentmates growled. I went out to pee in the snow, hearing some wit:
You smoke at that end, son? I checked every horse on its rope.
At last it was daylight. Then breakfast. Then finally off
downhill and through the Jaffa Gate. *Halt! Who are you, then?*
An Aussie horse-tailer from Cairo. Let's see. So ye are, a civilian.
Watch yourself in here, boy. They'll rogue you from arsehole to Pentikoff!

I drifted down stone streets like gorges, down alleys of stepped floor
to where I hadn't known I was going: the Holy Sepulchre,
huge awful cave church with cliffs inside, and caverns
and soldier tourists, and glass lamps in front of deathly pictures:
I heard a trooper growl *Easy seen why Christ didn't stop here!*
Black clergy all over, with their hands out. Then one in a hood
said clearly: *Your response to the death of our sisters is good,*
best of all outsiders. If ever you can pray

with a single heart to be free of it, it will leave you that day.
I couldn't find him again; I searched everywhere,
and when I stumbled up, out, they were calling the noon prayer
from all the minars. It was muttering and chanting, that whole city,
it was swarming to God, from one end to the other,
men in fur hats nodding, as they read books to a wall,
women in red wigs, nuns and Muslim nun-wives,
friars and liars and some soldiers not swearing at all.

I walked at random in it; my mind was reeling away
ahead of itself, like picture-slices on a chocolate wheel—
how I'd tried prayer, hard; it always fell dead, felt dead;
did nothing; now though, no, I knew: old good, child-good
versus lone weird good. *Vater unser* and bugger it, there's no heed
to prayer against itself. Laugh, that still feels. But God!
Christmas? I bought a bottle of it. Soon I was on my bum, singing
Marta, Marta, du entschwandest, und mit dir mein Portmonnaie,

and no one picked the lingo. Talk about know their enemy!
I was out the gates by this, in Tsarina Yelena Street
and the stars were like clean spikes—because I was cold!
Cold. And not rubber when I pinched my shoulders. Stung!
Pinched when I pinched. And the bent wrinkly fellow, I could feel him!
The face, and the fingers—I was grabbing all over, putting things
back, remaking myself, re-finding myself. But then people were coming
and I vanished, into numb bulk again. *Fit's wrang, Aussie?*

Ye luke lak ye've loast a croon an foond a penny!—
I'm dead, I screamed. *I was alive. I'm dead again,*
and I bust out crying, in that body,
gulping up up up, tears swamping my sight, tasting salty,
and a crowd collecting round, at a trot. The last, the very
last thing you allow ever: to be caught out both different and helpless.
Humans kill you for less.
But what you can't tell, to anyone, you can howl.

A woman in bonnet and black came swimming the racing crawl
through the mob *What do you mean you mean*
wretches a person weeping is not a spectacle stand away!
So I went back to camp, apologising, between this Sally Army
sergeant major and a Jewish Brigade lance-corporal,
was crimed and fined like a soldier, drunk and disorderly,
and let sleep it off.
And that was the evening and morning of Boxing Day.

Ah dinna lak ye. Ye're no juist richt, ye're eerie.
It was the big Black Watch sergeant who'd heard too much, and me cry
in that street. Now he'd come to our lines to chip me.
Ye're a sookie wean. Fit d'ye say tae that? I didn't say boo
nor: *Today my mouth tastes like what I think of you*
or *Your face looks to me like the wet parts of a dog.*
Both were true. And I might as well have said them.
He was the sort of rooster would anyway attack what puzzled him.

He knocked me down. I got up from that dose
and he knocked me down again. A crowd gathered, packing close.
I started blocking. He hit hard. I heard my arms
smack as he hit them. Odd times, my head or ribs, whack!
as he got one through. But I'd stopped going down.
I just steered him off what did work: eyes and nose,
ears and tongue. I caught him the odd one back
and, to madden him, I murmured *You dab like pussy, pretty Mac.*

O that sped him up, it made him work
and whinny with temper. I'd hit him, he'd stop with a jerk
and I'd say *Hurt me once. Come on, can't you hurt me?*
I can—whack!—*hurt you.*
My price had shortened from tens to five to two:
I overheard the betting. But gradually my interest withdrew
from the butcher's hammer hackwork of his hitting
and I just rode round on the impacts, feeling lonely.

Sharp eyes must have caught me not grimacing enough,
not bothering enough. Voices started yelling *Kill him!*
kill the bastard, Jock! I hurried punches then; he brushed them off
and dropped his hands. *I'll no fecht wir bluidy crankum*
guttiepercha freak ony mair. Ye're no natural, ye jenny-wullock!
All bets were off. My Cairo mates were staring—
Ah'll hurt'm fae'e, Jock! screamed a kiltie, and kneed me in the fork,
and I knew to fall down and writhe, with groans and swearing.

Next morning after a drink of tea at daylight
our Cairo party rode off south. Bill Hines, Yall Sherritt,
Poley Corrigan, myself and the Indian Army man
Loocher Sibley. We were talking dogs, the ones
who caught us out at cricket, the dingo that let Yall pet her,
the curs Poley kept to lick his rheumatics better—
we heard like whips cracking, and more and more, back past the windmill,
out north of the city. Chains of sparks dotted off a far hill.

Machine gun, cried Sibley. *And bundooks, lots of them. Dekho that!*
a red star went smoking up the sky from the gully Jehosophat.
Jacko's rode down from Nablus to take Jerusalem back.
Stones kicked. You sensed sizzles in the air. Somewhere went pingg!
Poley's face turned white: he reached around—*Bloody thing*—
and picked a spent bullet out of his tunic like a bee-sting.
You're getting as tough as Freddy, and he's a stature,
said someone. We should have cleared out, but we stared at the war.

So this was battle. Going on, I kept turning round:
battle was strings of riders hell-for-leather in a smoky wall of sound.
There I saw my first aeroplanes. Three came straining over
from down south, rocking, hanging their pony-trap wheels.
In front of those north hills they stopped and braced above ground
on their guns' fumy pencilling. Bigger guns right near
poking out through riveted shields would shorten, and your ear
hurt, round a king gap, then you'd hear the slung case rebound.

My life, keeping out of the human race to stay in it—
I'd have to think back, to separate thoughts that were all one
poem, like, at the brink of what was to happen.
There were no sides for me: both were mine. I'd seen them both.
Better to lie than pick one: better die than pick: and I'd died indeed
flesh-dead, alive in no-life. Not in civvy, not in air,
maybe in fire. Would I re-light there? Feel, feel if only death?
I spurred to a bolt, gravel scattering, back north on my waler—

Blue steep up white rubble, blotch and blotch went bursts in the sky;
harnessed guns, turbaned Indians, Light Horse all yelling Ayy!
men in rags, in their guts, men dead with sheep, butcher's parcels
of floury khaki, near dropped rifles, jump-down terrace walls
and straight lines whippy round me everywhere. My poor horse stopped one,
stopped another one. I spilled off him, left him dying, ran
in behind a stacked wall that was spitting and crying. A man,
a young officer, was kneeling there. Politely he put down his telephone.

Just passing? he asked me. *Er no: my horse bolted.—Oh.*
His phone rang, and he told it numbers. *You're Australian, then?—*
From Dungog way.—Ah. It's said this was the house
of the man who buried his one talent. In the parable.
The hempen chaps with pitchforks across there (lift two hundred)
are the enemy. What else can I show you old chap?
The way to go home, I said shakily.—*Ah, that goes via Damascus.—*
We sat then, not talking. He pencilled a folded map

and rang the artillery. Was I brave? Or an idiot? Did I pass?
because that was the young man's question then
I'd had to find out, without killing, among the killing,
what my human worth would be. The yelling front tore by.
Odd riders sprawled off, asleep, or crawled, or cried.
I looked at the lieutenant. His revolver and he looked at me:
You're not a soldier. Yet you had a rifle. And abandoned it.
Just what are you? A tourist? A spy?

I explained, and he smiled. *A sailor and horse-tailer?*
I showed him my paybook. *Boytcher? Isn't that German?*
A nun-boytchering Hun?—*Damn you, I'm off back*. He cocked his gun:
You may just be innocent, but this isn't civilization.
I can and will shoot you.
This is battle, where bad things are done.
See how I'm dressed in these legal killing clothes?
Foot soldiers were mobbing past. *You! Help me take this spy in.*

From him, I fell into some very horny hands: the Provosts
took me inside their building. I spoke: I was clubbed to the floor,
spoke again, and was booted in the tongue.
Pure angel hide, my next word to them: I bust out laughing.
They drew their truncheons, they started chopping a new me
out of my trunk, not knowing it was dead timber.
They rolled me, for full coverage, cut cunningly at every limb, or
knob bone or joint. And I laughed, without even falsity,

and they hammered away like blacksmiths; it was fair dinkum battery.
I lost bark, a lot, and streamed. Then I got frightened:
to prove their point, to save their world, they would kill me.
I had shared with them what I owned most: a story
they could never tell, any more than I could tell it,
one they couldn't report, nor forget, nor stop wanting to tell it.
God, though, they could stop killing me, and keep me for proof in a cell,
and make a book with other lunatics on who could hurt the unhurtable—

I surged, at this thought, and bowled them aside easily, they
were so astonished. Their truncheons hung down slack
with skin and hair on them. I walked straight out of there
past a sergeant blinded by his cap-peak who screamed HEY!
I sat him flat on his bum, so fierce did I scream back!
I was the wilder ape, and tottered like one out the door
because this horse I rode inside of had started
to float, and yaw. The red sea was coming unparted,

and flooded over me. I vaguely guessed forever.
I came to life near the ceiling of this white room.
A woman was putting a cup to the lips of my body
and directing two men, swarthy, eagle-nosed, who'd boom,
both talking while she talked. I'd never
heard their language before, so I hadn't died at home.
Next mansion I was in was the same room only bed-high.
The woman held me and a bottle as I moaned dark red pee.

Yes, time you were awake. You've missed Sylvester.
Sylvester? New Year's Eve? Had I babbled in German? These
thoughts took half a day to form and fester—
then I came back to the body she was patching up by degrees:
Those two men: did they bring me here?—Nope. I carried you
in a wash basket.—A wash basket?—Yep. On my head.
The same head you talk English with?—Armenian, Arabic, Turkish, English.
I thought if the soldier cops got you again, you'd be dead.

The sun moved the window's double right round the room.
Why come here from Chicago? I was ugly. In the West
sex is the great Calvinist: it prisses, flirts, moralises a lot
but predestination's the reality: you are what you've got.
She fed me more soup. Back then, sex wasn't much discussed
between the sexes, unless to stir it to life.
So I don't shock you? Not into being lewd? Nor prim?
Fine. But now I'm here, I've had to be Armenian. Not a wife.

And then she told me who the burning women had been,
about the lancers checking foreskins, the millions along desert roads
or rag in winter passes, and the awful sound
above fire-roar in churches. Soon she and the men I'd seen
would move up north, closer to the lines, to rescue
stragglers still filtering south, the eyed skulls getting through,
one out of a family, one out of a whole village.
Half of a nation murdered. More than the mind can close around.

Next day I sat the body upright, in a blur.
I was getting back into working it again,
and I asked her for one of those tent-gowns the Muslim women
often wear. *A burqa? For you to travel in?* Horrified
she was, telling me I wasn't fit yet, that it was suicide.
Caught, I'd be shot for a spy, sure, or knifed as an adulterer.
But people in real trouble needed her.—*So you didn't?* she cried
Beaten half to death and warming the snow with your pride.—

Pride? I gaped at her. *Yes, pride, you wooden Indian,*
too boiled to complain of even a little discomfort
when you're beaten to sausage meat!—God help me, I'd neglected
I'd been too stupefied, I'd forgot, to twist and moan—
I do feel, I protested, *grateful. Thankful to you*—
but I was guessing. No ordinary trouble could be real
after the story she and her people were locked in;
my bother ranked nowhere, a hiding I didn't even feel—

The taste of rice and capsicum brings her back,
dark and clever and disgusted. I never learned her name
because I hadn't asked, and then she never came
to the room again. The two grim men brought my paybook,
money and some clean slop clothes as soon as I could walk.
I bought oranges, and followed the scent of them towards Jaffa,
riding on a donkey cart, handing the oranges round
among fellows altogether more cheerful in their moustaches.

Down on the coast it was warmer, and I lost my road a bit,
brooding on what I'd seen but couldn't fathom.
We see just one side of anything. God sees both. It's mostly bearable
but fancy having to stare into an uncovered trench of stories
like the Chicago woman had to be loyal and mother to.
I drifted along dust roads between walls of orange trees
helping myself. *Ahem!* went a voice. *What's this place?*
I asked the man, guilty-like. He smiled and answered *Space.*

He was a chemist, he said, from Manchester—
An Australian and a sailor: then you know space too!
Do you know the eucalypt tree?—I should say I do!
He had a notion to plant the Holy Land with gum trees
and quizzed me about them. I told him the ones I knew best
iron bark and grey gum, box, spotted gum and bloodwood
for gravelly hills, flooded and river gum for wet ground.
There was something in corn, in maize corn, that he'd found.

He was to float a refuge-nation with it: acetone.
But I only learned that later, when the gums were well
along in planting, and fruit trees being wired for water.
That day he gave me dinner, or his farm co-op did. We drank korn.
It was all one in my head: Palestine, the Holy Land, Israel—
I really didn't know his people had ever been gone.
He had, I knew. To Manchester. And I saw him copy me
when I shaped my mouth between sentences and politely

blew the flies (pheg! like that) off my cheek, or nose, or chin.
Telling him those home things made me ache for home,
using words I'd hardly laid my tongue to for years,
the district's English words, was like going there in a dream
but the sort where you're at the house and somehow don't get in,
or you're nearly to the barn and it changes to a street in Leith
with a bad pub called The Eagle Never Heard of America.
I had that dream round then, and woke with my ears full of brine.

What few ships there were in Jaffa had no jobs for me
and I was picked up smartly
by Military Police. Thank God, they'd heard nothing from Jerusalem.
I was a straggler, though, and wouldn't bamboozle them
with my sailor talk. *It's back to Cairo for you!*
You shoulda got ole Weizmann to turn you into a Jew.—
(They're a smarter breed of Orangeman!—Watch it, Deevaleera!)
I went south, unbashed, in an Alvis prison van, with a shearer.

Roads were wheeltracks then, and motors jerked along
at thirty flat out, going Bang! and ear-rear-rear,
so it was a hard long trip. My mate's face looked wrong,
like someone not a barber had shaved him. He licked an odd tear.
It was only the fun some local half-axes were having
with a crying bag-of-bones cur and a red-hot bolt
got him talking, to me but mostly the floor:
I'm a coward. What they say.

I been at it solid for three years. Mates riddled to dogmeat wholesale.
Men screaming like stallions.
Blood and shit blowing out of them in front.
You're terrified, dry-belching, not me Jesus! before a stunt,
running down your legs. After, half fainting glorious! Half of them's mad to fuck.
No after for me but, no more. I stopped calming down.
No energy in me, but no peace neither. My fear's stuck.
Drove in me heart like a stake. I ache all over from.

I boil curry in me guts. I can't find me balls and cock.
Stark empty taste funk has got, pure. Wire straining your spine out.
A coward. A cocktail bastard. Man's better dead than like it.
I can't go home to Natimuk.
We burred on all day and all night across the Canal
and in Cairo they bundled me off.
I tried again to speak to the Shearer, but he didn't look.
Anyway they returned me under escort to Banjo.

He had to reprimand me, tried, and grinned halfway:
You aren't a soldier, though. Not even with your knife and fork
stuck in your shirt pocket. And I'm not one either.
Just keep out of trouble, Freddy. No more Palestine.
He seemed to like me. We had odd yarns together
sitting on the top rail, in the cool after work. *Everyone,*
he said once, *makes up a brief about themselves.*
Health's when they stop pleading it. I wonder how Lawson's faring.

And, a lot clearer to me: *My poems? Of course*
they may be nothing but a long wry farewell to the horse.
The others seemed pleased to see me:
Here's the chabuksowar! Get tired of the burra tamasha,
did you, eh? These hubshee soors deserve a taste of it.
God knows what he meant. His moustache and grin got him
by with everyone. You couldn't help liking the Loocher.
Hines called me an idiot bastard, he was so glad to see me.

Terrible disappointment followed me back, though,
from Jerusalem. Some nights I tossed awake
all night on my cot: was my null numb nothing forever?
Other nights, my body woke as its mind slept:
leaves would brush it, sun sting, water cool it,
it'd meet a girl, somewhere round home way, it'd know her
and we'd have it made up to be together, we'd have kissed and fooled,
and it would all get blocked and lost, among other people—

One time, it dreamed my body was made of fire,
not hurting me, but no flesh human could come near.
It was tough flowing orange, glaring hard gold
out through its buttonholes and gaps; the clothes weren't affected.
Another time, the Army had handed it over to Pilate
but he knocked it straight back
because it didn't eat grass nor divide the hoof.
In the fire dream, I could reach inside it, touch its innards

even trace inside the null bulbs it wasn't worthwhile playing
lonely-games with, awake. Even they were alive from inside,
only from inside. I got through the weeks, that last war-year,
on work, branding, cutting, feeding, watering, training.
I wasn't heavy, but not weightless either, in the day.
I could hear my boots, stamp dust, see things resist and bend,
balance, and talk, and pass for white.
At night I was dark and fell with the dark through the world.

Once, and it felt like no dream, I was facing and falling level
through a tearing red-brown storm. It was the Earth
and I came out of it on our farm. I went into the house.
My mother was screaming and crying, some of the Rumbels and Lauers
were holding her. *Wenn's um die Beerdigung eines «Hunnen» geht*
handelt man schon gern mit uns! Das siehste noch, Agnes—
I realised my father had died. No one saw me. I went in the room.
He'd got so tucked up. His face was liver-black, and so poor.

I woke up yelling, in Cairo. *What bat was you slinging there, son?*
Better kubberdaur, or they'll think you're one of the Kaiser-log.
I guessed he meant I'd been singing out German words.
I dreamt Dad died, I told Loocher. He clucked sympathy.
For days I walked into things.
I cried and prayed, I promised, I vowed
—and a letter came!
after all the years. But strange. Mother, writing in English.

I mean, she barely could. It was a heavy dead letter.
They were well. The farm was going good.
The draught horse Graubart had died. Poor Grobart, old when I'd left,
Potatoes were dear—I devoured it all twice and then
read it over slowly, trying to enjoy it. Something
we weren't used to then had made her nervous. As if others
before me would read her letter. But glorious! It wasn't true that Father
had died at all. He was very well. Like to a stranger. Very well.

He wrote nothing himself, which hurt.
But at least I knew all had been well in October
and my first letter from the Depot had got to them.
None of the other letters? No mention of, what? Forty letters
that I'd sent from Rio and Rotterdam, Miami, Valletta, Bahia—
There wasn't a trace of Mother's eye for a story:
no green tree snake that, falling, stiffened to a pot-hook
blitz-quick and caught a branch, no neighbour lime-washing his fowls,

two of hundreds she'd written me.
No response, either, to my tales of Turkey or numb flesh.
No questions at all to me. Now that was unbelievable!
I walked out on the desert, without the rifle
we were ordered to carry because some thought Turkey the Prophet's side,
walked out towards the moon, upside down to me still, of our ancestors.
Something wrong. Something wrong. Mama was signalling it.
Did I dare to desert Banjo?

Ride fast to Suez, not get a ship, and be shot
for a spy, quite likely? So what could I do but write more letters?
And start, too late, to be cautious in them, in the new way.
What was loose in Australia? What did that word 'Huns' mean for us?
That week, through worry, I picked up a branding iron
by the hot end. Smoke, stench and a shrivelled bubbly palm
I got out of that, and the blokes' eyes out on stalks:
I pretended shock, cuddling it, and Yall took me to hospital.

Don't come the rustic with me, son; you're anaesthetic.
Nothing hurts you, does it? Not anywhere.
And you don't enjoy much either, do you? It's a marvel you're alive:
but you dissemble it so well! You couldn't be more of a find.
I'm going to examine your peripheral nervous system, spinal afferents—
If only you'd been shot in the head; I could look at central ganglia.
You're rarissima avis. You couldn't be rarer pregnant—
I bristled at that. *Don't flinch, it'd make the fortune of both of us!*

Cox was the most barefaced curly-headed rogue medico unhung,
blokes that much still mattered to in the hospital told me,
but that was later. I asked him *Can you fix my hand?*
I can: no one else can, he answered with a grin,
so I took the plunge: *Can you cure me?* I asked him.
Almost a pity, he said. *Don't you think so? Yes you do!*
But in the end, perhaps—
If you bandage the hand I can get back to work, I told him.

Just a minute what is this, soldier?—I'm not a soldier.—
You come under military discipline in the Remount. Like a fool
because his pale black-shaven red face, the Kriegsmarine colours,
made me boil like him, I snapped *I'm a British subject with rights!—*
No, Boettcher, you're my subject. You even pronounce your surname
correctly. So your rights are as wind. You're a British suspect!
One thing for me to know how the land lay, another
for this sawbones to have twigged. I'd need black dark and a start.

For now, though, I had a bed, between stumpy soldier kids
who joked but didn't talk much, staring into their future lives.
In between Cox's tests I hung around the cookhouse
spud-barbering and yarning. It was a little world
that led out into the city stacked round us in the heat
like huge dusty caramels. Some lived there, or had women there
or dealt or worked dodges there. Sam Mundine the Jewish Aboriginal
bait-layer from backblocks Queensland promised me expeditions.

Meantime I was tapped and prodded and written up: Profound neuropathy:
proprioception intact (see? read it) no gross motor deficit:
agnosia frequent in darkness: slight allaesthesia: grossly flattened
cutaneous percept ubiquitous—*Did this loss of feeling start gradually?*
he asked. *I haven't lost feeling!* I snapped. *I've lost*
sensation, damn you. He reddened, changed his mind, bowed:
Your pardon of course. Did sensation leave you gradually?—
As I said, I had like leprosy. I was numb in patches first.—

Then those amalgamated, when the leprosy vanished?—Yes.
I'm not completely blank now. I just feel no pleasure or pain,
and I'm sick of it. Can anybody cure me?—
If I find physical damage to the nervous system, and I haven't,
we probably can't cure you. If there's none, the alienists may.—
Me, an alien! I fumed at that. And then admitted to myself
that it was true. I had become an alien. He was gassing on
about someone Freud, in Vienna. Out of bounds that year.

When are you going to fix my hand? I asked him.
Soon, he lied, *soon*. So I spread it wide open, not a mark
on it. *Like that?* I asked him.
He fairly hissed *O very clever! There's a lot of the malingerer*
in you, Herr Boettcher. He eased a tight collar. *You have*
not nearly enough scars for the injuries you'd have suffered
if you were fully genuine, in three years. Remember, I
can have you strait-jacketed. You're already down as a nerves case.

It had puzzled me too, how I healed now, when I hadn't
back like when I caught fire. Scars from that first part stayed.
When had the change been? What life was living itself
inside my life? The same one that dreamt love
in my sleep, and shamed me? Because that was all the love I got.
The sailor's dream-girl, Nancy of the Overflow—
Enough of that. I hated going back to the ward, though,
because I'd no right to be there.

Cox ordered me back there. I stopped for an hour and cleared
back to the galley for a drink of tea with Sam.
He was saying *Well Mum's people and Dad's uncles live under Law.*
I'd starve, if I kept both koshers! Law people, if they lose
hold of their law, often turn into rubbish, worse
and different from you lot.—Who are we?—The poor in spirit.
In burst two big wardsmen and pulled like a mailbag with sleeves
down over me and buckled it. *Capn Cox's orders, feller.*

Well that was the day I discovered I was real strong.
When effort doesn't reach pain you can take it much further.
I swelled the straps from their stitching,
got my hands in those tears and ripped
the thing into rag, with a big dry busting noise.
They just stood, Sam, the wardsmen, eyes like boys watching Les Darcy.
I gave the wreckage back. *Tell Cox his guinea pig has left!*
Don't know where I was off. I suppose back to the Remount.

I dawdled on the way. Stood about in shady spots—
and a man in a dirty waiter's coat slipped up beside me.
Imshi, Abdul, you clifty bastard! I snapped.
*I not Abdul. Christoforos. Sam Mundine say tell you
not go Banjo. Bad trouble. Bad German trouble you there.*
German trouble. That took my mind off being
amazed at my marvellous strong self. *So? What? Where?*
I asked him these clever questions. *Sam say you go his friends.*

I take. We went by tram
and then by alleys like gangways through a mighty cargo
of flat-roofed houses with odd high iron balconies,
barred windows, soft scraped walls, tiled twiddles of writing, in the sort
of cool gloom that troops were windy of a cut throat in,
and out among loud donkeys, where poor men carried brick walls
built up their backs on a board—*They not live long*—
and women heaved strapped head-loads.

That's how we came to the tailor's shop. *Tea, Mr Buttikher?*
Clap-clap! the boy keeps pouring sugary glassfuls.
Stay as long as you wish. My house is yours. He meant it, almost.
I had his sons' room, all of it, and he, Mr Hanafy,
taught me what I'd been too Australian and damn-all-swells to think of:
invisibility. Through clothes. It's harder now. Those days you just shifted
two classes up or down. So for me not the Sunday cuffs-and-collar,
but the full cream linen, the white boots, pith helmet, blue-striped shirtings—

Not for you the wing collar. Not white. For you always matching collars,
He smiled. *Good you cannot send for your old clothes, Mr Buttikher:
you must become this new man.*—*He won't be rich,* I said—
I will make you a friend's price. Such clothes will draw money to you.
When the first suit was ready, I asked Sam *Won't the English pick my voice?*—
You speak well, like many bush folk, he said. *And they expect the worst from us
so they will indulge you. Especially seeing your clothes speak too
and their accent is impeccable! But only till sundown. Remember!*

Will you come to Shepheard's for support, when I try the water?—
No. I'm a coon. You're a rare bird and hardly notice. But they do.—
Mr Hanafy?—*Alas, I am a Native. Of much too low a grade.*—
Even to be seen with us, outside on Nubar Pasha Street, could trip you.—
So I was a fiddle strung tight with my own guts,
as you can guess, when I breasted the bar in that place—
but it went as if on rails. I was soon that Australian who's in oil.
They confused me with someone, Rothschild's priest. I just smiled.

Well I made some blues, I told Sam. *What's a prefex?*
What's houses, in a school? Blessèd rum school yours,
this major said, and looked me up and down.—The gentry all go to high school.
Most board there, on jail rations. A prefect's a trusty there. Houses?
I dunno houses: I'm a humble blackfellow. You'll decypher it all.
They like to be called gentlemen. Some are. It can restrain others.
Call them sports, too. Never hey sport! or a good sport, though.
Ladies can be sports too—but that's too risky. Don't use it.

Have you ever seen the Nile? he asked then, and we walked
to the Gezira bridge, through quivers of open pleading carriages.
I'd seen the river, yes, the colour of an AIF tunic,
but he wanted to tell me Cox had got the rounds of the kitchen
from Mrs Paterson, one of the mighty Volunteer ladies,
for detaining a man of Banjo's. This was just after I'd stormed out.
So Cox, for spite, had shelved me to the Provosts for a spy.
Yall and Loocher had sent on all they dared, cash, my parents' photo…

Banjo was untouchable, spy or no spy on his patch.
I was sorry he'd think bad of me, though. We never met again.
How do you know so much, Sam?—We are studious people.—
We Jews, or we blackfellows?—Both.—First you're one, then the other.—
And I always will be. Surely you would know about division?—
No. The world's divided. Not me. I won't shoot my left hand, nor my right.—
True: both are white. Is a Jew white? Tell me, Fred.—
He'd get bitter like that, then brighten, like Hobart weather.

You're right to stand aside, Fred. The British stole Australia;
now their grandsons are paying for it. Not paying the owners though.
We'd have charged far less. They gave us plenty: the end of the world
but also the rest of the world. And difficult ancestors, and the clap,
the idea of cuisine, the vision of the tiger—
Why did you join up, Sam?—To get out of Queensland. To die.
You have to, sometimes. Did I tell you I'm staying on, after?
I'm marrying here. Then off to France to learn real cooking.

Back at the Hanafys', I sung out *Ya Satyr!* to warn
the women that a man not part of the family was coming.
The boys were in the family room, on the long wall seats
giggling and smoking green stuff. *This is Father's mother,*
*Umm Mahmud.—How'd you do, Mrs Mahmud?—*More giggles.
She was a solid-built woman with a you-can't-gammon-me look,
a bit like my Aunt Ed, that the girls in trouble went to.
She spoke, and one grandson came sober smartly. Spoke more

and the boy interpreted: *You are not a soldier?*—
No, lady.—*You are Australian?*—*Yes I am.*—
They are dogs of the British. They steal my cousin her shop.—
Looted her shop?—*Yes. And tar with feathers her man.*—
An Egyptian stole my money belt. I daresay he was poor.—
A thief disgraces poor. Should be cut off his hand.—
A dignified little girl brought tea and lollies. *You have*
wife in Australia?—*No. No wife anywhere.*

You travel much? Not stay long in Egypt?—Hey, I thought,
have I worn out my welcome? Fish and guests stink on the third day,
Mama always said. *No, I go soon. I'm in, er, shipping.*—
You have God?—*Eh? Pardon?*—*You Christian, have religious?*—
Well, yes.—*You have God a little and not trust Him?*
That is Christian. She chuckled in her tea-glass.
When she went, the boys lit up the hubble-bubble pipe
again, with the green weed. *You like to laugh with us?*

You have to be somewhere even when there's no story
going on. I lay round Hanafys a lot,
thinking: the nearest neutral ports are in Spain, and such
gloomy trapped thoughts. But I sported my new suits too
in Groppi's and down the Corniche, studying the Tatler
and the Times, to get a line on the folk
who didn't mean a coward when they said 'cocktail'. The Quality.
That was a lot what the papers were for. Social climbing.

Most of Sam's advice was too clever. I spose his colour
was the camel's eye. But for one thing, lots of the Australians
had been made officers in battle. Some were just bush men like me,
others more stuck up. Nearly all were mad for a good time.
The HQ staff officers, much more la-de-da, were having one—
that, now, was a class distinction! So there I am in Groppi's
and a ginger boy captain says *See that old Englishwoman*
with the daughters? When Arab Lawrence was last in,

fearful hot day, fanning herself, she quavers Ninety Seven
today. Colonel Lawrence!—*He barefoot in his robes:*
Many happy returns, ma'am! It's all she's famous for now.
Not in her mind, I thought to myself. One daughter looking back
was giving me the eye. Just a flicker. No. Couldn't be.
I was a civvy. Not a dasher at all.
I'd been sounded, politely, on how I kept out of the strafe.
(The punishment? Eh? Oh!) *Torpedoed. Amidships. I was in the Navy.*

Beecher, come for a spin! Two young officers in a Bentley
and a couple of French Greek girls. We tore around the Valley
scattering donkeys, picnicking among someone's palms.
Coming on dusk we were drinking champagne beside the water
among tall papyrus reed. *You 'ave no girl, Frèdy.* One of them
was flirting to annoy her bloke. It was frantic rooster-sorting
back there, before the guns stopped. Somehow we got pulling reeds
out of the silt and stripping them and flying them

with an odd leaf still hanging, like spears with pennons. They
floated through the air, and hit like touches. Soon we were having
this ghostly fight: huge effort with the javelin
and off it sailed, slow as dreams. You'd pick one from the air
and launch it back, hovering, harmless. The women laughed, then got
bored and quiet. Something important, that they wanted to be boss of,
was getting mocked. And they weren't boss of much else.
We were going to get hell from the flirty one.

But as it was, they drove too quick
on loose corners. The car yawed, climbed a brick-stack
and turned turtle. Steel bit at me. I flew, swam in gravel
with Gia, the lively one. Steam and dust were pouring up
with screaming inside them. I staggered up. I reefed, I
wrenched the car, up, off them. Held it up,
walked it to the side. The one boy was busted. Bubbling and dying.
The wistful girl, Sophie, had a new black knee in her arm.

It got tidied. Gia's father got his daughter back and his car.
The others got mended. The word about me got around,
curse it! I was terrified. Cox was bound to hear.
Fellows and girls gave me looks. Challenges were brewing.
I lay low, for days, prowled the souks where crowds of women
beat prices up and down, through their face-muslins. Then I dropped
to what I should do. A big bet—it would come as a bet—
might save me, if I won it. Might be a passage home,

or a ticket to the gallows, if Cox came to see any circus.
But I put my head back in, very nervous, at one bar,
then another. *Ah Beecher! Young Braine is doing well,
and the, um, dago gels. He says you're prime at juggling stuff
like motor cars about. The HQ set pooh-poohs this rather
but his mess is prepared to back you, if you'll just
hoist some old iron at the sporting club.—What odds
can I get?—Er?—I'll be betting. I'm that sort of horse.*

Being admitted to the club, past immaculate starch
I was bumped by a civilian, formal, greying, accent-free:
Your pardon! My card, he said briskly, patted my hand,
for later. May be useful. In the swirl, I just pocketed the card
as he seemed to want me to.
Then I was in a gym full of gowns and jewels and uniforms,
facing an axle of weights like the big steel wheels
I used to think were cruel on bullock trucks up Stroud mountain.

Very nearly a Bentley's worth, Beecher. Think you can shift it?
I grinned to myself. I'd been expecting worse.
Then I saw Doctor Cox. He was smiling a little bad smile.
I knew which way he'd bet. And how much I could lose.
The talcum smoked on my hands. I gripped, I felt the sit-tight
of that immovable wheel monument. Then in my own emergency,
just like in the car party's, but with better holds, I joined it
to my chest. Stood, tinkling. And jacked it overhead, fully up.

A silly consignment to be stemming aloft in a boiled shirt.
I let it boom and wrangle on the deck.
No more you want lifted? Righto.
And they were all talking and feeling at my muscles. *Olympic*
no man has lifted. A marvel Beecher. Damn me. I never credited—
Three or four women were shining, so near, yet on the moon.
I'd have to run. In hiding, and I'd exposed way too much,
though it was the half of my truth that humans could just stand.

No man has lifted more, says they? Mick Marr at Allyn Brook did,
and Primo on the old Sun Monarch out of Halifax.
For two. Primo did more most days. I was thanking and folding money
and being modest, though. *Beecher, eh? Good for you!* Cox said,
dragging his girl away in what sounded like fair French.
A pink boy who'd had twenty pound against me held it out:
What were you before you got rich, then? Hey? A navvy?
he said. I looked at him. *Don't pay it if you don't want to, son.*

You bloody clodhopping convict oick! he strangled out
in a half-whisper. His silk shirt and red coat were swelling
but I stopped taking notice of him. Australian officers were gathering
as if they hadn't moved, but distilled like, out of the crowd
and another boy was saying *O come on, Charles, do.*
Never ask such a question of a man when you owe him money!—
I'm a member here!—the first boy was near crying. *Indeed you are.—*
Flies of a summer, these poor lads, a colonel mourned.

You, Fred? A rude mechanical? A hewer of wood and drawer
of water? grinned one big hard Australian lieutenant.
Round home they'd think a hewer of wood—I thought of a sideboard in flood—
was a timber prostitute.—Good for you, Freddy. Same again?
I went back to my digs that night in a native carriage,
an arabiyeh, all farty velvet and gold cords.
On the way, I checked the card the man had slipped me.
A Reuters press card. In the name of F.T. Bircher.

It was nearly no surprise, I was getting in so deep.
But next morning I was out after tickets like a guilty thing
and must have looked it. At the shipping office I was queried
and had to show identification. *We get odd deserters, sir!*
at the railway station a big rawboned military detective
screamed *Attention!* at me, then *Sorry, Sir*, but he wasn't.
I went back to Hanafy's on a cloud. Home! On the seventeenth
from Suez! But nervous as a singed fox too.

And that had to be the day the Hanafys gently-urgently
moved me out, to a decent small hotel a cousin owned.
The eldest son opened the batting then. *Is business*
of women. I disobey my father to tell you:
my sister Shahira she has seen you and wishes you.
My father refuses. You are Christian, she is Muslimah
but she is stubborn like Mother. You are of a book, same one God.
She has looked at you from her window when you don't see.

I mean, you are honoured. Someone offers you their life,
because this wasn't an affair that was being offered,
not by her brother. *You will see her?* he pressed me.
It was awful. Curiosity, and being young then, and dreams
in spite of grey dreadful knowledge. Of being cursed.
Tell her, I said, and walked up and down, *tell her*,
tell Sha-kira, is it? I mustered it all in my mind,
that I'm honoured. Truly. But I'm leaving. I am a wandering man.

He nodded. *She has made inquiries. You don't go to women,*
not the Western women, not those in the Wagh el Birket.
Not to boys either. But you shave. You are not harem guard
eh? he giggled. *So, alone. You lose someone one time?*
I grabbed hold of this and nodded. *One time*, I agreed
thinking Why not forget what you can't feel, and be
kind to someone who can? Like, watch happiness. You couldn't watch it
from closer to! But if I see her, I'll have half agreed to

that, and I need to think. Don't rush. It's not real yet. Think.
We agreed I would think. Till the day after next. I asked then:
What does your grandmother say?—Ah, she is all Shahira.
Is beautiful, my sister, he said seriously. *Is sensible, is honourable.*
I didn't doubt it. They'd been honest and generous to me.
Then he added the killer bit: *Men come ask for you, the day you leave us.—*
Oh? *What men?* My heart turned over. *I think soldier police.*
That was the stone end of sweet Egyptian might-have-been. Or so

I thought, panicking. No train, no ship. I didn't dare try either. I
paced the room, in the big September sweat,
lay down, got up, drank water, went out in the bazaars.
I drifted towards the river, towards the Western bars,
hardly knowing where I went. *Still scrimshanking here, Fred?*
a voice asked. I looked. A cousin of the Sternbecks, a Dungog man:
I heard you were with Banjo, but you've come up in the world
by that tog! I babbled, and then remembered I was with Reuters.

He was a pilot with the first Australian squadron,
he told me, as we walked flash coming and going
among the mirror sellers, and fended off the cushion sellers.
He was down on business from Palestine, and sorry
the Fishing Fleet would hardly be coming this year.
The fishing fleet were the English society girls
who came to Egypt to catch smart young Army officers.
I knew most of the British, including my bursting boy subaltern,

had been posted to France. Finishing the Turk was to be
a colonial affair: us, the Indians, black Africans, the Jewish Brigade.
Of course I'd know all this, as a Reuters man. And about
the big push that was about to happen (what was he talking about?).
I say, would you like to cover that from the air?
Great boost for the air arm. I can square it with Colonel Williams.
We'll fly back tomorrow in the late afternoon.
I'd go sooner, but tonight I'm to sport the salt carnation.

The oldest Hanafy boy didn't come alone, the next day.
The girl was with him. All modest, but her veil was mist,
breathed to one side. And Lord, so beautiful; her face as it was
clears all talk from round it. Rose ivory of that big brown city.
Green rose, straight-backed, in the cool of that long room.
Not a word of English, a bit of French, no German—
and not a sign of us misunderstanding each other.
She would be my cure. She would be my death, too.

And yet I started on the road to telling her. I thought:
If I told her how I was, fully, the moment I told her, I'd be healed.
I started with *I'm not this rich businessman.*—
We know, she said through her brother. *You are a German spy.*
She smiled a little, at me sputtering. *It isn't Egypt's war.*
Soon it will be over, and the westerners who care will be gone.
Stay, and we will make you Egyptian, invisible to them.
The moment I tell her, I thought, I'll become able to love her.

I blundered ahead again: *I'm a sailor, I haven't been*
home for seven years, I must see my parents, things aren't
right with them. I have a steamer ticket—first time I ever
paid to sail!—but I'd be caught if I went near the ship.
The ticket's worth money, pity to waste it, here, it's yours!—
How will you go to your country then? she asked.
God knows.—They bobbed their heads. If you will have me,
she said, *I will sail to your country with this.* I nodded,

and it was sunrise, from her face out. It lit up the whole room!
I went to speak again. That nod of mine had just meant 'I see'—
but then I left it nodded. And stood, as if on air
with wonder at what I'd agreed to, had been led into, gained.
From the throttling sharp hum of their talk, I guess her brother
was arguing the toss. No hope.
I stood up. She touched my hand with hers, and left.
Our father too will lose this argument, her brother said, embraced me:

You will be my brother. But remember: first I am her brother!
and followed her downstairs, out.
We discover life, I reckon; we make it up
on the hop, as it strikes us. God knows I'm no thinker, but I
stared, for an hour or more, at this best most frightening thing
I had come in for. I seemed to have blundered right
this time. But now: pack! Jump to it: the jacks are out!
My man was waiting by the airport fence:

Thought you'd changed your mind!
The aeroplane was like tin roofs over wire gates
or a powerful touring car crossways through a Himmelbett,
a what-d'you-call-them: a four-poster.
What's it built of? I screamed. *Doped canvas on a timber frame!*
I'm riding in a kettledrum,
I grinned to myself, as it pounded and then floated away
out of the khaki, up into the blue above the crowds,

the white-eyed kids, the men like rib roasts in their sweat,
the donkey sex shows. You'd be better dead than poor in that country.
Soon we were across the Canal, level with Mount Sinai,
soon there was the Dead Sea, there was Jerusalem!
In the smell of castor oil and acetone and wind
I sat in a leather pit behind a big half cogwheel
high up over Bethlehem, not a thought for Joe Courtney's provosts—
I was flying, and engaged, and twenty-three years old!

My trick was always: learn by shutting your mouth;
people will tell you what you're at, and then all about it.
The air officers knew newspaper talk: coverage, deadlines, scoops—
so, in one day, I did too. Only a journalist would have picked me.
The shy clean-spoken squadron boss with the jerked bare-teeth grin
told me he'd have a treat for me the next day:
I'll send you over in the Handley Page to see Lawrence.
Was I still to wear a tie, I wondered? Apparently, round Colonel Williams.

Less so with the pilot, a Captain Smith—*Call me Hadji.*
We rose and flew off the world, the hills fell down so sharp
into the great brown valley where teams of horsemen were harrowing,
it seemed, at a gallop: dust towered higher than us.
Then we were out over bare furnace ground streamed with thousands
of cameleers and horsemen and flags and puffs of smoke
and when we lit, a small rider in Joseph's coat and bare feet
flashed his bent goldwritten sword at us, barked some words and laughed.

His fellows took us to Lawrence, who nodded at the Captain,
ignored me, and went on staring into
the eyes of an Arab man dragged before him terrified.
The Arab had a point. The Colonel's eyes were a sort
of I-will-forget-you blue,
hot tunnel eyes that said Court me, with superior presents.
He waved the man away. *He cures the Evil Eye for 'em,*
Smith whispered. The whole squadron was in love with Lawrence.

I forgot to say the plane we came in was the biggest
in the whole Middle East. The tough bantam chief we'd met first
banged on its two big engines. *Auda says Truly this is the aeroplane
of which all the others are the foals,* murmured Colonel Lawrence
there, posing in roped white in the middle of miles of hubbub
but I let him look sidelong at me, and said nothing.
I kept him at it all day.
At last he had to speak. *You don't take notes, Mr Beecher?*

I remember what I need, I said. Some stripy-robed hotheads
in that roaring stock-drove of an army
gave me dark looks because I hadn't pleased their idol
but I guessed I'd been meant to ask things and be found wanting,
to play straight man in his theatre. So I didn't want.
I looked at the cartridge belts and carpet saddlecloths, at the tents
with their black wings spread like hens in a dust-bath, and the fires
boiling coffee on a pinch of camel-dung. I was given dates and coffee

at the edge of a space where men were having wrestles.
After I'd looked on a bit, they signalled me try a fall.
I didn't know—but it seemed friendly, so all right.
After I sat a few down, gently, not to hurt, I think the next ones
would have hurt a lot, to beat me. We were drawing a crowd
and men were getting laughed at. I sensed this must bring on
swordplay, any minute, and waved my hands. Enough! No more!
One hurtled from the dust like a tiger, got wrong-footed and sprawled.

Then I saw Lawrence watching. Refusing something the mob cried out for,
refusing it again. Ross—Hadji—was looking at him.
It wasn't at all fair. I'm big; he was a tiny man.
He gave them a speech instead, pointing north, towards the war
and soon had them yelling Aurens! Faisal! Aurens!
Neatly done and sensible. When we were leaving, though,
he had to say: *You might have been a Blue, Mr Beeching,
at Oxford. But of course perhaps you were.*

I might have been a fucking blue tongue, I replied
had I been a lizard. Eh Ross?—Steady on, says Hadji.
The Colonel turned his back with his drapery in a whirl.
You're a rum reporter, Fysh or one of them remarked that night,
not interviewing Lawrence. I shrugged and let it go.
He'd been interviewed enough. But my ears pricked up
when they said he loved to wrestle with his warrior coves
and had beat them all. *Quite a little performer!*

they said. Where I grew up, 'performing' meant
crying in public. Or raging. Anyway chucking the emotion about.
But it doesn't mean that among the quality. This was the Sunday.
On the Thursday following, Hell broke over Palestine
and I was out flying in it. We overlapped valleys and streets,
we shadowed roads, then the plane would hitch and hammer,
sowing dust stalks everywhere among cavalry and bullock carts
till they collapsed or scattered, lorries burnt, tents shivered and went old.

Pilots were freezing in the sun, above the chalked green hills.
I watched a tan cloud with low lightning in it away north:
that was Armageddon, and we were heading into it.
Perhaps that was the Battle. I remember it was a good battle,
that is, not many died. It was mainly Chauvel's horsemen cracking shots off,
ringing and stock-drafting enormous mobs of prisoners—
silly enough to look miserable, some we landed alongside of.
A smaller cloud, out north, was the Indians racing to grab Nazareth.

That night to make it look good I telephoned a number
in Jerusalem and dictated a long screed to it,
while the man at the other end screamed every version of What Gives?
in some language, and hung up. I kept on with the dictation.
It couldn't last, I knew. A day or two,
the redcaps would come for me, I'd face the choking Colonel—
I was right out of plans. Bang! the planes would start, like bigger machine guns,
—because that's what they were. We rode in flying machine guns—

and whirl us away wherever orders and ring-sights
pointed us. God, I'm putting off remembering
or telling this part. Farah Gorge. The Nine Miles of Dead.
In Egypt I'd been spared seeing it. Arrested and hung
I'd have been spared it. The War at last, as I'd avoided seeing it.
The pilots were all sickened. I'm not sure there were orders I should see it
nor permission to take me. They needed me to see it
and not to see it. Two army corps, trapped hopeless in a steep gorge,

a traffic jam made with bombs and guns at each end
then butchered at leisure. The Turks had been retreating from Nablus
down to the Jordan. You can't take surrenders from the air,
so the orders were: Destroy them. Day after bloody day, packed thousands,
anything standing, lay it out, anything still moving, nail it.
The blood-splash of little bombs wet us, perking over the side
at a hundred feet, two hundred. Every rifleman the guns found,
even the parties with their boots off to dig graves got scuttled

in crowding dust-spikes. Guns' scribble made corpses buck
as it raced along the ground. I was there just the once, over this,
but those Australian flyers, day after day they were at it,
the only battle ever won entirely by aeroplane,
some, not the flyers, said. But history has choked on that.
I went once, and came back to a sick shamed squadron mess.
I didn't eat. I packed a bag. I'd made up my mind
my next pilot would be flying a passenger north, not butchering.

Jerusalem was behind us, all the wadis falling east
like tear-streaks through dirt. He was slanting towards the murder-gorge
and I tapped him on the shoulder. *No. Go to Janin*, I said.
What's that, Fred? O Jesus! I had a Mills bomb with the pin out
and the lever clamped shut in my hand.
You know that's bloody murder, I said. *Janin, now. Take a telling.*
That was the captured German airfield. I'd work out what to do next
when we landed there. *Bit late to join the Kaiser now.*

Some had tipped you were his way all along, of course—
Bugger the Kaiser, I yelled back into his wind.
Did he believe I'd really blow us up, that pilot?
Or did mercy get just an edge on duty and orders and
self-sacrifice? Who knows? We lived to land at Janin.
Stop the engine, I ordered. *Now out! Run!* I left the bomb behind
and as we sprinted off, the massacre got docked three machine guns.
No one came to look. No one was about. Deserted field.

I ought to shoot you, Boettischer—Bugger that, I snapped,
and we watched his aircraft turn to rubbish with the porpoise-shaped
and pretty painted other wrecks there. That lieutenant,
young Roper, I think now he might have been glad
to be out of the slaughter job. But he had to act his part:
Fred, it isn't too late. Fritz is washed up. Why go back to him?
Mum's the word, with me. You were covering the wider campaign
and we crashed here, chasing background...

Trap or offer, I ignored him. He hadn't drawn his gun
and probably wouldn't. A beautiful big sand-beige Mercedes
car stood in a marquee, with pumped tires and full benzene tins.
I stacked them aboard, in the rump seat—
then Roper did draw. Sneaked his Smith and Wesson out
was about to give orders with it: I had the crankhandle, I rapped
on the gun so hard it shattered. *Don't be a mug. Take this!*
You crank her, I'll start her, then I'll drop you where you'll be right.

I did, in some town north of there. We cruised through it slow,
he jumped off, almost waved, then remembered, in case his side saw.
I roared on, past clumps of riders, giving them all the big wave,
getting cheered. Winning, happy, still alive, they'd cheer anyone friendly.
Last lot I passed were Enzeds (*Goodayyy!*) in lemon-squeezer hats
way north of Galilee. Then the country got empty and tense
up into the rocky hills. A German corporal flagged me down,
and I saw a machine gun's burnt iron eye looking at me

from higher up. *Halt! Where to then, mein Herr?*
asked the corporal in charge, all peeling ginger burn.
Headquarters North, I said, guessing. *We've all been withdrawn.*
Then I remembered my clothes, and put snap in my voice:
Why are you still here?—To cover the retreat.—You're wasting time.
The enemy's not advancing in this direction. He's turned East.—
How'd you know?—It's my business. Espionage. You can abandon
this position and come with me.—He stiffened. He thought me an officer

or he nearly did, and would have to obey. I improvised:
Oberspionagerat Böttcher, I snapped. *And I order you, dismount this position!*
At your orders, Herr Senior Espionage Counsellor! Greenest thing in Galilee,
he hotfoots it up to the gun-pit and there's an old sweat
who might not have believed me, and a long bloke they had to unchain
from the gun. I swear. They had him shackled to the leg of it.
The word kang *has two meanings,* this said to me, cold sober:
a board fixed around a prisoner's neck in China,

and a Chinese sleeping-stove. He'd an echoey, biscuit tin voice.
Yer see why we hadda chain him, grinned the old soldier.
I shuddered. You think you've got troubles, then you meet
people with worse ones. Then, worst of all, you meet somebody
with absolutely none. *Chuck your gear in the car. Abandon this!*
Bring the gun, sir?—No.—Inactivate it?—Oh, er, certainly!
Hurry up, I muttered to myself, those Enzeds will be on us, hurry!
Dietrich, the tall man said, *is a wire hook for picking locks. A skeleton key.*

I saved a lot of Kiwis' mums from grief that day.
I made the long man dump his weighty pythons of ammo-belts
and bring, like the others, just his rifle and pack.
By good luck, no planes spotted us
and that night we camped under mountain olive trees by a creek.
No one came near. Something howled. I took first watch
with the corporal. He hummed and ha'd his way
half round the world to say he was surprised

at an officer, even in Zivil, driving without gloves on.
Next day we bumped on again over roads like dry creekbeds,
through broken-crockery villages, some with Turk soldiers in them
who looked very dark on us. As if they suspected we
might want to draft them back to the war. The corporal would have.
You want yer throat cut? the Berliner private asked him.
That's the answer you'd get. They've retired from the shit-storm.
By this time we're in Latakia, tobacco land. Big blue-green flannel leaves

shivered in our dust, and the veiled women there had green hands.
Minz, the corporal, was getting cheeky again,
complaining how we seemed to be driving from Pontius to Pilate,
farther and farther from the front.
When I happened to mention how I rode on a Berlin tram
he challenged me straight: no German officer ever,
ever rode in a public vehicle! I stayed calm and thought
what to do. Then I screamed in his face *Atten-shun!*

How dare you question an officer in Kaiserly service, I grated at him.
Down! Flat! Fifty push-ups! And then make order in this car!
Globke the Berliner could hardly keep a straight face
and long Heimann took no notice. All he cared about
was not to be bewildered. To know the Rules got you that.
Every fact was a rule, or felt like one to him. When he was
happy they poured out of him: *Sir Ernest Jones discovered
the Aryan languages helped by Rask and Bopp and Grimm.*

Yeah, said Globke, as we were collecting grass
to stuff a tire holey since the Holy Land,
*Minz is a sit-up doggie, still wetting himself to be an officer
and Heimann's manoly. But you: what mekenke are you working?*
I stared at him. *Doing tulip on me now?* he grinned
and I looked black, and laughed. *You do understand Red Welsh.
You're stacking high! Well, I'll stay peep. I anyway
never was real keen on air with iron in it—*

And I hadn't said anything. This was on the way to Antioch.
More and more Turk soldiers were straggling along the roads home:
some cheered, some shook fists. *Germany lose! Go to Hell!*
There were camels and carts. A foot party stopped us with their guns.
The leaders spoke some German. *Friend sore foots. You give ride.*
He and friends climbed aboard. Minz tried to object and bam!
he flew off and sprawled in the gravel. Left behind: *hey! Comrades heyyy—*
we were let chuck him his pack. And that was the end of my officer turn.

More climbed on later. We wallowed, but the springs held
through Antakya, past a lake, up over high hills
to Alexandretta. I was just a chauffeur now;
Heimann mumbled to himself and looked lost, and Globke
played music on the snout-plane, as he called his harmonica.
We were down to two drums of petrol, the tires were in shreds,
men dropped off, men climbed on. It was late October, khaki
grain country, like our backblocks, but the trees the wrong green.

The Turks would shoot quail, pluck and gut them as we bounced along
and toast them on their bayonets. We lived on tomatoes and quail
and pita bread: not bad. And Heimann kept them amazed
and maybe us alive reciting his encyclopedias. We'd come
in sight of some place, and he'd reel off facts about it:
Tarsus, birthplace of Saint Paul; here Antony first met Cleopatra,
and all the dates and figures. The German-speaking Turk would translate:
some'd groan, some cry Allah! There we broke an axle, and saw Dervishes.

We stopped at an inn, Turks and all, on Globke's piastres.
Our chief passenger came upstairs: *You come*, he said to Heimann,
You come, he said to me, but rejected Globke
who yelled after me, *Leave me yer English suits!*
They took us to a square with crusts of cotton on the cobbles
and men in black robes were praying with their hands cupped
in front of the mosque with its leather flaps for doors
then they started to chant and turn and chant and spin

and their black robes came open on these white concertina-pleated skirts
that widened out from underneath. They spun like parasols, like daisies,
each his own wheel and driving it with his slippers, chanting.
Mevlevieh! cried the Turks and other things with Allah! in them.
The black is shroud, the Turk told me. *White is the soul in Paradise.*
Then I saw Heimann out among them spinning himself
in his flapping yellowy Wehrmacht khaki. *Is holy one*, the Turk said,
recite modern Koran, he laughed, *it have no end!* He tapped his head

but somehow Heimann wasn't ridiculous. A holy one of God,
as old Mrs O'Beirne in Dark's shop at home used to call them
too, I remembered. How had he felt sending men to God
or to the wheelchairs? As surely he had. I didn't ask.
You feel like a virgin asking fellows how does it feel.
A man in a green robe spun out of his whirling near me
and put his book to my forehead, saying words.
He say God touch you.—Must have been with a long stick, I thought.

They wasted our time in Tarsus making axles
on a blacksmith's forge till they got one strong enough.
The army streaming home through town still had its weapons
and, by the look of it, somewhere it meant to go.
I thought of my girl. She was where I wanted to go.
Heimann and I are in no hurry, Globke said,
so what's your rush? Wanna be there when the Fatherland caves in?
I like it out here. I got money. Why not follow al-Shawarma:

a pillar of beef by day and of fat by night?
But then men were coming around and cursing us,
especially the priest-fellows in green. We took off
up the coast road with odd stones flying after us,
The soldiers were better, but still put the arm on us for lifts.
They used to laugh at Heimann, who never looked at them
or anyone, much. He liked the knowledge, not the evidence.
He wore his pork-pie cap and stared past them, past the sea.

It was a bear did for me
and saved me too, perhaps. We saw these two wild fellows
way up the road. Then the stocky one turned out to be a bear
in his collar and chain. I daresay they were performers;
anyway they would have a lift, and the soldiers we had on
thought it a great joke. Up climbed the bear and the man,
down sank the springs, more. He stank, the big-headed fellow,
of bad meat and Painkiller, or so I Muggins thought.

He started to moan and crave, the bear. His owner
played with him, filthy amusements, *he-he-he*, all over half of us
but the bear kept craving till he got a sticky brown pill
to chew and drool. That crossed his little pig eyes.
Next day when he craved and they all laughed at him
I got in his road, and he pawed me. To the bone.
Of course it never hurt. But I shut my fist and hit him
a rosiner in the chops, and another one.

He made his big yawn-noise and grabbed me in his arms
and overboard we went, off that high car. I fell on him.
It busted him inside. He was dying. Poor dumb animal,
I never meant him real harm, poor opium-mad bear.
His owner was screaming and crying, his livelihood, his livelihood!
and maybe his mate too, a lot. Turks and Germans,
all in the car judged I was the human and so
I was responsible. Half my clothes to the owner of the bear.

Poor Livelihood was still bubbling, trying to get up—
I was so wild I lifted him, heavier than a big man
and hoyed him off the road, wallop! Then I gave the suits over.
Come to Berlin, Friend Boettcher, says Globke, *be a wrestler,
I'll make us rich.* But I was sick of them.
Take the car, I said. *Go—Abandon you here?—Yes. Go.
You've got your bear. I'd cost you more than him.—
At your orders, Herr Officer. War ended last week, by the way.*

I was to have wrestles in Germany, had I only known.
Right then I badly needed my Pat Malone
and I'd rather tramp with him than ride with any soldiers.
It was peaceful, having room again,
out on the road with that violet-blue sea on my left,
and when maggots wriggled in the holes the bear had made
in my armour, I bathed them away in that sea
and sat watching it unroll its little lappets on the sand.

There weren't so many soldiers on the road now, nor motors:
mainly just stick-walled bullock carts with pumpkins and hay
and bags of stuff, and men on donkey-back
giving me the time of day: *Merhaba! Ne var ne yok?* How's it going?
and me smiling them off with the signs everybody invents
for themselves when they mean I'm all right, I'm harmless
but I don't want to yarn.
First few nights I camped in the haystacks. I didn't feel it,

but the cold shivered me hard, out in early November. I decided
to fish some gold from my belt and face the humans again.
At the second inn, they asked where I was from
and I thought why not? and said Australia.
Avustraliya? Olada ne yapıyorsunuz? What was I doing here?
The man was dark on me, the woman burst into tears.
It seemed she'd lost sons at Gallipoli. I could manage, just,
to say I was a sailor who didn't have a ship,

not a soldier. The electricity flew,
the woman, she hated me. She'd have been glad to see me dead,
but the others calmed her. Then suddenly she took
a hard grip on her inner handles and spoke
with dignity to me: *You are real. I have hated shadows.*
God has sent you, ordinary man, to burn the hate from me—
God also must have sent me the brains to grasp that much Turkish
but it's what she said. Then *Hoş geldiniz*: Welcome.

Next day, on the road, a big Army car stopped beside me
with a driver and a toff in a beautifully tailored
uniform with gold turk's-head knots on either shoulder,
round beard, amber cigarette holder, and beads
trickling through his fingers. He spoke to me in German,
got a reply, then he spoke to me in English
and got a reply. Then in French, but he drew a blank there.
He was going to İzmir, where he lived. He repeated it, İzmir,

[42]

but first he would stop in a village near, where there was
a conclave of folk poets and players of the *saz*.
He hoped I wouldn't be bored. I promised not,
with a grin, for the lift I was getting. Carts and sulkies
crowded that town, when we got there, pie-carts, halva-sellers,
kebab-men and corn-roasters, bottles of lime and kero-blue,
brass trays of baklava, and people, people almighty
round a sprinkled square with yellow poplar trees.

A wrestler-looking fellow was parting his big black moustache
with recitations in a big black voice, but no one clapped him,
nor the next man. Then a blind man made them sit up
and start yelling out *Allah! Veysel! Allah!*
Why do they say Allah! I asked the colonel. *Ah. Because the poet*
is very good, and everything skilful and good
is of God. He coughed. *This is their opinion.*
Later came a poet who held a cork between his lips

with a needle through it. *That is to prevent him saying*
the sounds b or p or f or m as he improvises.
They have these contests in virtuosity, the Colonel said.
I thought how the needle wouldn't change my speech much.
Half the people I grew up with never move their lips,
I grinned. *Nor open them. How do these keep the thlies*
out oth their 'outh? I could see he was getting concerned;
perhaps I was a coarse fellow, not sophisticated,

not up to my clothes. So I shut up for my lift's sake
and a bit later on, after some pretty wailing tunes
he translated what another fellow was reciting:
    I asked the yellow crocuses
    what do you live on underground?
    Dervish, what are you asking us?
    We live on the Almighty power.
He listened some more, said *This is a very old poem:*

    I asked the yellow crocuses,
    staffs in their little hands
    and Scripture on the tips of their tongues,
    the crocuses are one with the dervishes.
We stayed most of that day. I was fed up, a bit, with so much
well organised ungraspable talk: it makes a cripple of you.
The Colonel was in his glory—but then he snapped sober and modern.
Let us go. I have indulged myself.

As we bowled along, he said *We are between two poems:*
The old one, in which we are the head of Islam
and take Byzantium and butt at the gates of Vienna,
that one is finished. The new poem is steel and dynamo
Ottoman, Gagauz, Turkmen, Kazakh, all of the Turkish peoples
one great secular Turkey from Thrace to the Chinese Wall.
Now that the Russian bear is tearing his own entrails
is time to strike.—The Bolsheviks, you reckon,

aren't one with the crocuses?—We will make them so!
Them and a lot of yourselves and who else? I was wondering.
Do all these big poems burn women? But how would
an Australian ship's officer toff know anything about burnt women?
So I bit my tongue, and felt nothing for my punishment.
Next day, we reached Izmir, a pretty town of balconies.
The dogs, he said, *call this Smyrna. They say it is part of Greece.—*
What do the humans say? I asked. He didn't answer.

The town was flapping with Greek and Turkish flags.
Two into one wasn't going well anywhere that year.
People I couldn't tell apart spat at one another
in the streets. The Colonel offered me hospitality,
but I was headlong hell-for-leather after a ship.
I knocked round the harbour, just starting to be very sorry
I'd turned the Colonel down, and watching a packed Greek ferry
tie up. A bloke on board was yelling *Charlie Chaplin!*

Charlie Chaplin! and holding up big flat tins.
I thought at first—horrible notion!—that those tins
were magazines for Lewis guns.
They were moving picture film cans, of course. For four long years
no one in Turkey had seen hide nor bendy cane of Chaplin
so this fellow was mobbed and clapped and kissed and shoved
till the runners took off with the tins and the crowd streamed after,
yelling and dancing. I told Chaplin about it, years later,

how this Greek from Sydney brought the toddling chestless battler
back into that country in flat round cans the people
took, cheering, like peace and the wide young world given back.
He smiled and guessed what I meant by our word 'battler'.
I was new in Hollywood then.
I found out Takis was from Balmain when I asked
did he speak English, after the crowd had gone. He'd said Chaplin right.
Be buggered, he said. *You win Tatts? I thought you was some Pommy nob.*

Australian Greeks were rare then. It seemed his father had brought
the family back to Smyrna years before
and now Takis had come back too, to help the old man.
Come and meet them! he said. *We can take the ferry to Piraeus*
tomorrow, and get you a ship. Plenty of them there.
But Jesus eh? A black Dago and a Dungog Hun:
we'll both be dodging the heroes for a good while yet!
Good bloke, young Takis, a man to go shaking horses with.

Leaving on the ferry next day, I waved to Turkey
and said goodbye. *Güle güle!* Takis looked at me:
The one staying says that, he grinned. *It means 'laughingly'.—*
Yeah well that's near how I feel, I said.
His Dad had quizzed me close, but Takis didn't ask questions
about my Turkish doings. In Piraeus the day after
it was like as if a door nailed tight for four years
suddenly fell open. I got work on the first ship I tried.

It's not a good idea to go for a deckhand's berth
in a better suit than the Captain owns, so I gave both
my last ones to Takis. Spent an hour getting him to take them:
I never felt right in them.—But Jesus Fred, they're valuable!—
Maybe. I don't belong to the suit world. To the town world.
They're not just clothes. I'm shy of tog I have to keep noticing on me.
I didn't add that I could go like the old blackfellow, asleep
facing his fire with his bare back all sugar-white with frost.

Takis was shot, killed, in one of those suits two years later
and buried, so I heard, at sea
among those purple-white islands just off Smyrna.
As my ship passed the Nile, and called in at Port Said
I thought about sending a letter, a telegram, a card
to Shahira. But I hummed and ha'ed.
She'd just been mistaken. What use was it? Worse than useless.
If I told her how I was, I'd be cured—and she would be cursed.

We went on down to the Red Sea. The lascars in our crew
took a different slant every time they prayed towards Mecca.
I wished I was Charlie Chaplin. He could step back into his own
skin, after a picture. The wind blew and I had stayed like it,
this awful blank secret me, no good to Shahira, to anyone.
Well, wish in one hand, pee in the other, as they said then,
and see which gets full first. I was going home.
Everything might change there. Past Aden, and I was going home!

BOOK 2

Barking at the Thunder

Coming home, I walked into a masquerade.
All the people in Newcastle, all on the train wore these face-masks
of white cotton gauze, some dirtied with tobacco and words.
I had to, too. So there I am riding in a dogbox
through Maitland stewing in that January heat, on through Paterson
between the courthouse and the tall church, above the creek flats,
and all the way so nervous I'm brewing and letting gas
like a great beer-bottle, as I look forward to home.

Then we're at Dungog, all white-whiskered women, muzzled kids
and handkerchief desperadoes. Scared the Black Flu might strike them,
some confused even their families: people singing out *Mum?*
Here I am—
But my family, they aren't there. I'd have known them masked head to foot.
But, maybe it was nothing. The muscular cleared hills looked right.
Smaller, but still home. I'd just hoof it out to the farm
and arrive before my telegram.

Freddy? Fred Beitcher? It was a schoolmate of mine
half-whispering through his rag like a conspirator.
You back? How are you? I shook hands. It made him nervous.
He kept his voice down like that and I didn't know why.
How've you been, Arthur—I started, and he cut in:
Watch out. The Pages, they lost two boys in the war.
The Pages from Main Creek. They never said a cross word to me
in all the years. But I realise, now, that I've been braced for one.

I got no more warnings or welcomes, walking up Dowling Street
and out to the farm. The body sweated hard
but I was cool as ever, hanging from my head
and listening to the boots crunch gravel. Going home!
I'd be there for dinner. Dad would grin his *Na ja.*
Mama might wipe a tear with her apron. Handshakes, hugs, kisses, that.
You see what a flat I was. There was the creek paddock,
there were the sheds, the grapevine wrapped half round the house,

and there were kids there. Oh well, visitors, I thought.
They looked at me, dirty-faced, and when I sang out *Good day!*
they ran like bandicoots to cover, straight up under the house.
I started seeing changes around, and untidiness.
Then out comes a man. Not my Dad, but acting the boss.
Good day, he says, not smiling. *Good day.—What can I do for you?—*
Well I live here. Or my family do. Where are they?
Gone, he spits out. *Where all you Hun bastards belong.*

I was clean hopeless.
King-hit from inside, I stood with my mouth open there.
His woman came out, and looked frightened in the door.
You got it through your head? he snapped. *You're out.*
Get off the place before I sool the dogs on you,
and he hitched his trousers up. I remember he hitched his strides.
The pole barn, the pepper tree,
the trenched tracks down to the cattle crossing. His belt.

I must have wandered round for hours. I can't remember.
I was soaking wet. I woke. The stars were out.
Mosquitoes were singing their good luck in finding me. I went
back into the town, and there weren't many about.
Where's your flu mask, Butcher? I heard a fellow say.
Another: *Sorry about your poor father (no, it's decent!)*
Who they were, I don't know.
I was a ghost. But there were others worse off.

This woman was pushing half a man in a wheelchair
and he smelt noxious. *You haven't pooped yourself again?*
Dear Mother of Jesus!, and he had this awful apology look
on his face forever, as she wheeled him, in his uniform.
I woke up next day in a paddock outside town
and drifted in again. I had to know, but who
did I dare ask? I kept waiting to be told.
Back from the war, Fred? That right you was with Banjo Padderson?

The first cheerful normal voice, it was one of the Maytoms
I'd been at school with. We yarned, and bit by bit
I learned it all. Dad had died, near round when I dreamed it.
Mother had sold the farm. Post Office might know her address now.
A buggerable business. This one was dead, that one crippled:
The district's half buggered, that many wills been tore up.
It'll never be the old happy skylarking young place it was.
Wives and girls in black everywhere. Bet the old 'uns 'll see they keep mourning.

I did try the Post Office. Caused a big silence and got nothing.
Except, I did learn something. A woman, I knew her, got
a telegram while I was there. And wouldn't open it.
Had to have it opened. I only understood a while after.
Later I was over at the bridge, and a cart came by
painted and decorated T.E. Lower: General Carrier
and that was Ted Lauer. *Wie geht's denn, Theo?* I asked
and he went green. *Not much of that Deutsch left in me,*

Fred, he muttered. *You got sense, you'll drop it too.*
So. You been at the war?—*Dodging round it*, I replied,
but he was in a hurry. *It'll all be better in a year or two*,
he reckoned, over his shoulder.
I was starving. I went to have a feed.
I looked such a tramp by this time they made me pay first.
Sensible, except they knew me. Had done since I was a kid.
Yeah, but which merchant's navy? asked somebody out loud, and laughed.

So. Right. I up and walked out of my home district for good.
Goodbye to Green's shop, farewell Walkers Mill.
Slow as I am, I was sure now what had killed Dad.
So goodbye Coorei Bridge, and poor Mrs Khan's waterhole.
I didn't go back or look back for twenty years.
I headed where a duffle bag wouldn't be mistaken
for a swaggie's roll. I was mad to get to sea
but then the thought slowed me: I had a mother to find.

I spent that first night husking in the barn
at my cousins the Thurechts outside Clarencetown.
All them pumped me for sailor-yarns till I ran down like a clock
and settled in, preferring to soak my miseries
in their life of horses and corsets, possum-mooning and floods.
It was cousins and crepe paper, it was the old peace there
as we cracked the rainproof packaging off corn.
The war had never happened. None of them had been fighting-age.

After a bit, half asleep, I dropped down
by giggles and snorts that the eldest girl had been snuggling
up to me. She stormed out the hatch in a huff,
barefoot in one of her mum's old ankle skirts.
I didn't stay on their farm-island
long, though. And leaving, Elise Thurecht the mother
told me she saw Dad not long before the end:
He wasn't fifty but he looked like an old done man.

It struck me, back in Newcastle, how I hadn't gone near pubs
in my home town. Yet here I was down the Terminus,
counting my change, wondering how to finance
a search for my mother, and a fellow drank off my beer.
Whyn't you wear a yeller tie ya poofter cunt?
he asks in a casual voice. Well I'm just in the humour.
It turns out he can't fight. I've got face all over my fists
and men stop me. *Pity to mark him up, he's got a woman*

round in Corlette Street. He picks fights to get his blood up
for her. His name is Oyster Harris.
Oyster staggers off like a man on three legs, grinning,
and one older bloke who held me back shouts me a beer.
We get to talking. I tell him how I've lost my Dad
but not why. He considers. *Yes, they sat on mine,*
he says. *He was having a heart turn. You have to keep them flat.*
His brother and sister, they held him down till he died.

We got along, Cos Morrison and I, half silly and all as I was then.
We talked docks and ports: he'd been to sea a bit,
and about timber, and I listened about his business:
lighters and droghers, moving freight on inshore water.
I listened about how his wife died of typhoid fever:
up here in the hospital. They fought for her, but it got her.
They can't save the goners. She got clear-headed at the end.
She told me to marry again. But I couldn't. I still can't.

We shook hands, parting. I told him my name. He didn't startle,
bristle, ask questions. Funny how quick you sense
what prejudice will be like, how the slurs'll come at you.
It's like as if you know, always. Maybe you turn things round
that you've half-seen done. Now it's your turn. You're the blackfellow.
Seven years she's been gone, he says, still thinking of his wife
and bringing up three little kids he'd mentioned before.
His trouble was more than all the Great War to him.

That weird white gauze summer, Newcastle looked like Stamboul.
The same blue glitter, crowds, women with bandage to their noses,
the same cripples in baggy uniform, with all their wrecked ends masked.
After a day or two, I couldn't stand it in a room
except to work. I had to be outside.
I worked on the wharves a few days but I wouldn't sling the ganger,
so no more pick-up. I lumped beef carcases
at the markets till the foreman called me a black squarehead bastard.

Every night I'd pay twopence to cross the Stockton ferry,
then walk up in the bush, take off my clothes and sleep raw.
I mean, I didn't itch, nor ache, nor feel the weather—
the mosquitoes were welcome to what I didn't feel go.
I'd learned from Dungog how sleeping rough in your clothes
makes you look like a tramp, so I'd wrap my duffel up
in my foul-weather oilskin and sling them in a tree.
I noticed it made me hungry; my fire was inside me and burned fat.

Days I wasn't working I'd look for traces of Mama.
I tried the main post office, I visited our relations up the Valley,
I searched voting rolls, I went to the police.
That was a mistake. *Beotisher?* the sergeant asked:
I wouldn't know anyone like that. That's a Hun name innit?—
No, I said, *it's an Australian name. Won't
you look for her?—If it was to shoot the slut, I might;
one less Hun hoor. And don't you get ideas, Kaiser:*

*if I run you in, the magistrates'll back any charge I lay.
We got 'em trained.* I knew, and he knew by my clothes
and talk that I knew. *Piss off before I vag you!*
I had to swallow this—but it wasn't for being German.
Any Australian man that only wears collar and tie
to funerals and weddings, any unprotected woman
knows what the police are. I'd hoped to crack it for a decent one.
Treat 'em with ignore! as Mo McCackie used to splutter.

And get out of countries where you can't. I found that out later.
Then one Saturday I went up outside Maitland, to my cousins
the Leupolds, that Mama always treated with respect
though they were just farmers like us. We yarned, they pressed me to stay,
I told them my story, except the secret part,
how I'd dodged around the war, how it wouldn't let me go,
but how I'd killed, I thought, nobody. They brought out their boy's letters
that stopped after Fromelles. He couldn't help writing it down,

how men hit in the forehead might run backwards for yards;
hit in the heart, men might leap twice their height like killed fowls;
how men went to sleep running. Shock made him write that way.
I rarely heard returned men talk like it, but I've seen it in other letters.
They'd got over Tom, and never would get over him.
We talked about the new names of things: Alsatian dogs,
Belgian sausage, effervescent powder, Aspros,
and we drank tea. There was no coffee any more, for donkey's years.

Good that Uncle Johann hadn't seen the changes:
I just remembered him, with his eagle's wings of moustache
and talking high bookish German. He died before I went to sea.
We reminisced about him, and they said *Want a surprise?*
Aunt Cathy delved down in her keepsakes box and fished out
another letter, yellow, with New South Wales stamps on it
and addressed in fracture-handwriting, the old German stuff I can't read.
The letter was written over in another big clear hand

Briefannahme verweigert. Receipt of letter refused.
Eh? was my clever question. *His family refused it,*
Aunt Cath smiled. Fifty years before, he'd been a student
sent home for politics. He was a liberal, revolutionist, some such.
While at home, he misbehaved with the chambermaid, got her in the family way.
His people meant to send her away quietly, like normal,
but he was honourable. He'd marry her, he said. He meant it.
When they saw he really meant it, they said he'd be disinherited,

estate, title, uniforms. He married Madi and left Europe,
made good in New South Wales, and wrote home fifty years later,
for the first and only time. *This is that letter,* smiled Cath.
He didn't come to find work, I said. *Oh but yes,* said Cath
They didn't give him one red penny. He and Oma stared bare.
The family guffawed *As you might say!* Cath blushed
but I looked at that letter, unopened still, its expensive
white silk-finish envelope like a dress shirt. It was Johann.

Did I know what firm my parents' insurance was with?
it occurred to old Peter Leupold to ask me.
I didn't. *Maybe go round and enquire by all the firms,*
but get spruced up, or they won't tell you nothing.
I was at the steelworks now, but not working near the smelters. Not game.
If I burned, it mightn't hurt—but I mightn't grow back either.
The money was enough. I soon had a decent suit
packed in my locker, not out on the sandhills where I slept.

It was getting wintertime. The black flu was fading away.
Women wore flowery masks, then no more masks at all.
Faces came out. Girls looked wary again on their own,
or indignant, or sad, for fear of what a smile draws.
The war hadn't improved that.
There was a lot of black about: veils, armbands and ties
and shearlegs in every other park and main street seemed
to dangle a stone soldier over columns of names.

I met Laura that way. I was hanging around the dedication
of one of those memorials. I was picking out the German names on it
and listening to a big man with a gold looped belly chain
get up and speak after the mayor in robes and neck-chain:
Against a barbarous foe these heaped glory on their young nation—
I heard a woman next to me swear
half to herself, half to me: few womenfolk swore much back then:
My poor bugger went because his mates called him a slacker.

She smiled, embarrassed, and it was a good face she smiled from,
honest, blushing around freckles like pale raindrops: *Look,*
there he is: Cope, Private J. I sensed she had to tell someone.
When did he go? I whispered.—*He signed up in the first week*
and was killed on his first day in battle over yonder.
When the speeches were done, and the soldier's boots firming in his mortar
we were still yarning on a bench. And she was grinning
because I'd called the big spruiker a whited elephant.

We got along. We yarned more. I told her about facing clerks
in insurance offices, how often I did it all wrong
and struck a brick wall. *Oh I can handle them,* says Laura,
I know the tune. She volunteered to enquire for me.
They didn't have a chance. I saw later she could purr
or chime like a bell, or draw up like a duchess
and I've seen duchesses. All I know, that day I went
past the docks less keen to chuck Australia and ship out,

as I'd have done already, perhaps with Mama, if I'd found her.
I remember how she used to describe coming out
on the ship in 1890. It was my bedtime story
and helped make a sailor of me. Which she hated,
though sailors had been remote and decent, not like stewards
apt to corner a girl in gangways and breathe offers on her
in their peppermint and pyorrhoea voices.
Laura's enquiries got nowhere; week after week

we'd meet and she'd tell me. I'd wear the suit and yarn
with her in parks, or we'd take scones and tea.
One week she produced a tan Borsalino hat,
and a paper bag for my sailor's cap. *I know you're a sailor,*
but the world doesn't have to. She made a joke of it
but I could fill the rest in: seen with sailors, a war widow—
I tried the hat on. It fitted, near enough,
and was nearly new. Had been for a long time.

Having a friend, my first real woman friend,
not girl friend; no one married was a girl back then—
it kept me stoking coal and stacking bricks
in the BHP coke ovens, which weren't sailing anywhere.
I didn't dare say what pleasure I got just seeing
Laura walk quick with her arms folded, woman-fashion,
or sit on the grass with her toes in their stocking webs.
I knew I should stop. This would crash hard when it crashed.

Funny your mother never left a message for you
with your relations. It was true. I'd been trying not to think it.
Then she asked me about my brother Frank, that died.
He got a cold. Then he started crying with a headache:
Mama my head's noisy! He started screaming, and strained
tighter and tighter. It bent him back like a spring.
The doctor came and couldn't help; they can't.
He was rigid like steel, the baby. Only loosened when he died.—

What did your mother do?—
She was cried—I mean; she cried. A lot. And wouldn't have it
that it'd been a disease. It was her fault,
she insisted. He'd got strychnine somewhere, round the sheds:
strychnine cramps you to death like that.
She hadn't been careful enough. We hadn't been careful.
It was like when Maudie Ackermann burnt her throat out with caustic soda.
Farms are dangerous to toddlers. We kept quiet and she talked.

I was still sleeping rough at this stage. I used to shave dry,
too, but with a mirror, for fear I mightn't feel
if I cut my face—like the Digger in the joke
when his mirror fell down: I get right through the war,
then I'm no sooner home and I cut my bloody head off!
I used to carry my cut-throat in my coat pocket
and one day on the tram in Scott Street some boy said
You a razor gang man? and yelled *Here's a razor gangster!*

They were about then, Snowy Cutmore, Walsh, the Tighe's Hill mob, the Angel,
before Taylor shot him. They stood over sailors and girls:
Can yer mother sew? Let her stitch this up, then!
Anyhow on the tram I yelled *I'm not! I just shave with it!*
and I pulled it out closed. And that caused a real commotion:
the accused is always guilty, when it's violence.
I hadn't flashed the *Klinge*, the blade: I like our word *Klinge*
for how something really razor-sharp clings as it cuts.

I was grabbed from behind. The razor bounced off the tram.
I started to break an arm. Something in his bellow stopped me
and it was my old shipmate Al Rose. Rosie from Texas
that the bull scrubbed the bulkhead with.
He calmed his shipmate, we calmed the tram, we got off
into a nailstorm of rain, into some beers. I paid;
it turned out they were stranded. *The Limeys mainly hire lascars*
now, and these new flag-of-convenience operators

can pay as low as they like, and treat you like crap.
It's all slipping back to the bad old days.
I helped them get on at the steelworks. They stuck it for a week
then an ore ship took them. *Say gooday to Galveston Lil for me!*
The foreman we had on the ovens, Conk Benaud, he was fair
as foremen go, not a crawler. He drove you hard, some days
when he drove himself, I think to quiet war-stuff in his head.
You could chiack him out of it: *Hey Conk, did Essington Lewis*

say he'd make you his heir if we built these ovens in a week?
or: *Hey Conk, ain't this the day you wash your nose?*
Well, suddenly he got dubious about me:
Why did you tell me you was from Dungog, you squarehead fucker?
(Of course he swore. It's a man's sign of feeling cheated.)
What did you do at fucking sea? You aren't just a sailor.
Why do you leave your tog at work? Don't you live somewhere?—
I laughed at him. *Yeah, in a tree with this hot little magpie.*

There was a bust-up coming. I knew the signs.
At sea, that can mean a midnight swim, singing out.
Not often, but it happens.
On land it's a fight sometimes. And always the sack, when he's boss.
It would come suddenly. So. I'd worry only when it did.
Meanwhile I did something out of the ordinary in my life:
I went to the moving pictures. With Laura, in the city.
She laughed, she glowed. It was The Sentimental Bloke.

What struck me was the music playing all through.
A woman in pink at one of those big flat pianos
with a rudder propped up on it played right to God Save The King.
I watched her as much as the story. She galloped the notes
when the larrikins fought the coppers; she played them dreamy and shy
for the romance scenes; she made them teeter and drop clangers
when the Bloke meets Doreen's Mar, but everywhere
she put in lines of songs, gone before you could place them.

One I kept humming after, in between talk,
something about the moon. German. Going 'from western cradle
to eastern grave'. Which is wrong, our side the Equator.
That was the first night we climbed the steep street up
by the cathedral to Laura's family's place.
She held my hand. *It's late, but if you're game*
I'll take you inside. To meet Mar.
I hesitated. *But I won't force you. It's queer to be the daughter again.*

I was lady of my own house—two rooms and share kitchen—
for sixteen months, till Joss' allotment stopped.
I could have kept the flat if I'd started working straight off.
I won't tell you all we said.
When we parted she asked me *Where do you flutter, you queer bird?*
Do you live anywhere?—
My landlady's not respectable. She approves of lady visitors.—
Hmm, Laura sang. *How many lady visitors?*

Conk and the Shop Steward were at it hammer and tongs:
You're a fucking troublemaker!—You're a fucking reactionary!—
You want to make this Russia!—You're so far up the bosses
you can see Billy Hughes!—You want rooting to death with a shotgun!—
Progressive forces will bury cunts like you!—
Progress buries every cunt.—
I went past with Norm Bunt, my mate, both carrying cinder-rakes
to pull out clinker in the burnt-smelling cursing factory air.

Norm had lost his dairy farm. *Missus tried to run it*
while I was overseas, did good, but drought and a flood after beat her,
so we're in the town now, and I'm back to a child.—
A child? I asked him. *Yeah*, he said decidedly:
An adult's their own boss. A child gets told what to do.—
So all employees are kids? I asked him. *Yeah, they are.—*
I've been a kid, on the ships?—Unless you was the captain.—
Do you tell all the blokes this?—Yeah. And it's right. You think about it.

I did. I have often. But it was a wonder Norm
was still alive, I reckoned. In fact, no man said boo to him.
He ran his own job, saw what to do and did it,
invented ways to do it better. Men came to him and deferred to him
in rigging pulleys, in angles of batter, in gas seals.
Conk even deferred to him. I think it was, Norm said his opinions clear
but didn't play on them, like calling men kid names.
He was pretty near an adult. Keeping up with him working'd kill you.

These were the works of peace, that year of the second Armistice Day.
Conk had a down on me, it was bursting to come out.
We were packing coal in the ovens. *Can't you shovel?*
he snarled at me. I looked at him.
He'd been shifting less than I had. *You bastard you wouldn't know*
if your arse was on fire! No, I thought. I of all men wouldn't,
and you've noticed something that has scared you. *Conk*, I said
sometimes you're a dog—What? he raved—

without a leg to piss on.—He snatched his false teeth out
Geth your thime! he frothed. *Go andh hollect your wageth!*—
What about this? I asked Cockrill the Shop Steward,
as I came back later to collect my duffel. *Not relevant,*
not relevant, Kaiser. You're a lone wolf, few mates, there'd be no
agitation value in you. I was dealing with a cultured gent
who had a big dictionary. So I tipped him a wink
and he whanged at me *This isn't a kid's game, Comrade!*

But it was, to me. With no one to answer to or keep
I was so free I was dangerous.
Here's me around then in the hat that Laura gave me.
We'd have been going to the theatre that night
and for beer and oysters after.
At the theatre we saw a lady get sawn in halves
and a man eat soap, which is more dangerous,
and all suchlike stuff I learned the secrets of later.

The next thing, well, I was taught it's low down to boast
about the next thing. Say we walked for hours
because we had nowhere to go, and sat for hours
because we had nowhere to lie. But finally
we went to my landlady with the useless roof
and the little twigs under you. And there were laughing and tears
and things felt, and sensations had and given—
and things not told, too. It's not just the privacy of one.

I hoped what I'd kept quiet would stay quiet,
even get buried, under loving-stuff and living-stuff.
What tipped me over into daring with Laura, at the last,
was how she was glad that I was happy to be
shot of my stuck job, aground there in the steelworks.
I remember explaining the best side of Conk Benaud,
how he'd told us he couldn't bear life getting different
from what his mates killed in the war would recognise:

I can't bear them turning strangers, back there, all out of date.
I don't want anything they never got. Might be silly
but that's me. He said this over smoko one morning.
Laura dabbed her eyes, listening, and said roughly *You're the world's*
clumsiest suitor, aren't you? You're hardly a masher at all!
Then she got sober. *I see women living just for them, in remembrance.*
Men too. Half the country. Perhaps for the rest of our lives.
It frightens me. Loving you's like deserting a funeral.

A lot of my days just then were spent in the pub.
I could have gone that way. After all, I could feel a drink:
not just how it tasted, but how it wound coldly down me
tingling gas, if it was beer. And because my flesh was already
where blind drunk takes yours, I caught up with myself
odd afternoons, as men put pencilled bets
on Eurythmic and Calligraph and Windbag and Come Outside
Protestant Dingo—I'm not sure all bets were on horses.

But every day was getting to be Saturday.
I took a pull the day Oyster Harris reappeared
in front of me, grinning: *Want a rematch, birdshit?*
I looked up. *No. I'd just put you through again.*
Let's chin the bar. That rafter. The one hangs longest by his hands
will be the winner. He hummed and ha'ed, then *Yah!*
He leaped and hung. Me likewise. I wouldn't overdo it,
and be noticed. And the Oyster wouldn't get hammered.

For me, it was nothing. I could have gone to sleep like it,
but he hung on with all the guts and pain
and wildness and gameness there could be in a man.
He hung, he clung, he drooped, he drew back up;
he shuddered and wound, he bent and straightened, he flexed,
his fingers burnt red and white, the nerves were kicking in his skin.
He looked flogged, he looked bursting—and then he crashed and howled
and I wished I'd fought him. I dropped beside him and got cursed:

Get away from me you unnatural jiujitcha bastard!—
You've made an enemy there, Cos Morrison said to me.
He liked you when you fought him. How did you hang there so long?—
Just science, I said, grabbing a word that boxers use a lot.
Did he come to town with you?—He mostly does, said Cos
I was bringing a woman back.—
Bringing a woman back?—
Housekeeper. I sacked her. She was squaring the potatoes.

Ever since his wife died he'd been hiring housekeepers,
widows and station cooks and servants who hadn't caught a man.
I dunno, he said. *I pay 'em right, I don't make them palaver*
Yes Sir No Master, I don't put it on them for a ride
but the good ones don't stay and the no-hoping ones I sack them.
The last one shook the sheets and this one she squared the potatoes
peeling them, and burnt the kettle; got through a month's flour in a week.
Poor old Ruby from England she fell in the fire she was eighty.—

What happens the good ones?—Fellers marry them on me.
Changing the subject, he said then: *You miss the salt water?*
I did, I admitted. *And the money's running low,*
but I've got a mother to find, if she's alive and in Australia.—
It's not far, he said, *just up the other side Port Stephens,*
they're looking for a drogher hand.
And so by service car and boat, by Salt Ash and Lemontree Passage,
I got to the deep sea port called Winda Woppa

which sounded like its name, as they winched great slings
of girders and sleepers thundery into ships' holds.
Timber-stain and briny glare, and creamy in the blue of channels:
suddenly I liked the world again
as I hadn't been liking it since I'd lost my place in it.
Also Laura's face was in my head.
I landed, and walked past a steaming black-rafter palace
called Birdsville Mill, with blades singing big logs flat-sided

under rollicking drive-belts. There were ribby hulls chocked up on ways
all along the foreshore, and fellows adzing tea-tree-wood knees.
I met the boss and got on
and was sent to learn the river and the work,
wrestling, or coaxing, a fifty-foot sternwheel drogher
under tons of logs along channels never deeper
than two fathom, out of bays and crevices,
and swimming ashore with a line when the crabbing bitch

went aground yet again, and killing snakes in her firewood.
A queer berth for a deepwater man, but you don't get days off
in mid-Pacific. Every lead to Mama still went nowhere, though.
Captain of the punt was Matt Garland, who shot anything eatable:
boom! and three ducks'd drop out of a mob streaming over,
or boom! and three or four would heel over sitting and flap
or boom! and some mullet would turn up their whitewash bellies.
Gwan then! and the boy would swim after them like a retriever.

I had dinner at Garlands'. The wife and old Matt talked
with any guests, but the kids, they weren't let say boo.
They had to signal for things, down under the conversation:
stir without a spoon, strew pinches, pour imaginary milk.
Matt's belt drew a line between human beings and kids.
But that wasn't all the Myall showed me. I soon fell
in love with that tea-coloured two-way river
that flowed to the sea and from it twice each day.

BOOK 2 *Barking at the Thunder* [61]

Palm and tea-tree corridors along the salt channel,
gum forest on the hills that sloped to the saltwater lakes,
it seemed to be the mixture I needed, not to be cured,
but to be real, enough of a living person.
Two or three days' round trip, up, load and back down
from Buladelah or Dirty Creek, or Mayer's Point or Bungwahl
and, in between, cut firewood for the boiler.
I slept on board when we tied up for the night

at Croll's mill, say, or anywhere. Matt stayed in pubs and wouldn't
let me live aboard when we were home. *Damn nonsense!*
Go to the boarding house! So I had to mix, and use rooms.
You coming to the dance, Fred? You want a game of tennis, Fred?
You want to get out a bit. The young crowd drove me mad
with sappy kindness. I said to Laura *Love,*
chuck your job at Winns, and kowtowing at home. Live at Hawks Nest—
Roost on a branch with you? she laughed.

There's another proposal comes just before that one, usually—
Eh? Oh. Er. I'm sorry. Will you marry me?—
Not if you're sorry! She looked down then. *Jokes aside,*
and it's never a joke. But no. I'd live with you,
if you'd have me. In sin. But I said things to Joss
I can't say again. Not and bury him completely.
If the rubber horrors play up and I get pregnant, then
we'll need a license. But not till then. You aren't shocked?

Be a little bit shocked or I'll worry what you thought of me!
I was a bit shocked. Excited by it, too.
I said *Your family would never.* And she agreed *No.*
I thought and said *My father would have told you*
the dead are better in God's hands than our heads.
Better let go. They're not free in our memory
and they have no bodies there. A horrible feeling
crept over me, and stopped my mouth from talking.

Laura looked at me with the concentrated hazel eyes
that made her always strongly there, and decided
to say the next thing: *Some ways, you're the best I ever*
met. Not because you're a desperate caresser,
not because you can be such friends with a woman, although
Lord but that's rare. Joss couldn't. I can't place why I'm mad on you.
But—I don't think you're the father sort. You don't see children.
You're not a family man, sailor. You may never be.

Changing you might spoil you. God you're an adventure, but!
I chewed this over. Grinned. And didn't completely like it.
I wasn't ready for kids—but wasn't I fit to breed from?
Was she saying that? Or did I suspect it of myself?
Marriage, she said into our silence, *isn't what you want*
either. It wasn't the first thing you asked for. Was it?
I sat in the air with my numb bum held to the fence
by gravity; I was terrified I might never get down,

because what she was saying was excuses,
because she had guessed. I had been a fool
to hope that because I smelt and weighed and looked like flesh
and could kid the world I was, good standard flesh,
I could kid a woman, bamboozle her with flesh-tricks
that I judged by guess and yarns. I had never felt experience.
It's not love, she said, *is it, that you feel for me? Not love:*
terror. Of me, but not just me. You're buying me off,

paying and paying. You don't know when to stop.
She tilted her head. *Is it so I won't be scotty about how,*
oftentimes, you've stroked cushions or grass as well as me?
I started to babble. Talk gushed out of me through a smile
as false as one cut in a pumpkin head.
God knows what I said. It was all really Goodbye.
When a tram came, I ran to it. *Love!* Laura sang out behind me.
I waved, I ducked, like a fighter, and rode it the whole way,

and all the way back. She was gone. I was deathly relieved.
I walked towards Carrington, the port way.
It was the time of night when secrets that won't let
people live, or sleep, walk them about, muttering and hunching.
I'd been going to stay in Newcastle all the next day
but what use now? The ferries had stopped, so I swam
and after a while saw I wasn't reaching the far bank.
I was going downstream on a tide that wasn't in the river.

I'd been slowed. I made strokes, but only a quarter
as many as would save me. I couldn't be bothered; I grumped
like a sick man, and wondered, as I picked at the quilt of the Hunter,
at the salt-halo lights stacked so unfairly on one shore.
Nothing would hurt me. I could float to a sandbank and
be a gull-roosting house that crabs walked in and out of
and it wouldn't hurt me. Eels could bite my balls away
and I wouldn't know. Fish could chew off my generations.

BOOK 2 *Barking at the Thunder*

Neither warm nor cold, neither dead nor alive, I was king
alike among the movers and the still;
attacked on the one side of death, I could step through to the other.
I could do fearful things, on either side, and escape
across to the other. I was the secret king
but I'd muddled my laws. I couldn't have, on the having side,
nor let go, on the forgetting side. So then I was king only
while I couldn't rule. And where I couldn't live. Like anyone.

I noticed myself sleeping, I think to get my head under.
A teacher of my Dad's who I'd never met, just heard of,
Sister Mary Theopane, she came to me. She was a window
and I looked through her. There were like gravel paths
but they could have been little long flood-washes.
There was green park country, with trees, but whether it was mowed
wasn't clear. No houses, but crossings of tight cobble in the creeks
just wherever you came to them. There was no one to ask

the name of that lonely country
but I'd belong there. I'd never need to eat, nor talk,
nor walk, nor stop walking. Nothing made a difference there.
I noticed however far the hills were, they never got blue.
Well I wouldn't decide, to go there or not go.
I left it to be decided.
Millions of buttoned fellows had had less time spent on them
before they were snatched away. I'd made a luxury of myself;

next thing, I'd be drinking wine and calling myself sensitive.
So I went to that country
and sat up there. It looked a bit rougher, close to,
with tussocks and odd logs. No houses, though, nor fences.
I still wore my Earth clothes, salty and cardboard brown
and cracking where they bent. I hadn't seen mangrove trees
nor sandhills in that woman-window but
why wouldn't they be there? Queer to be done with meals

and be so hungry. And it seemed there were to be cattle there,
away off, for company. And then I woke up to myself.
I'd floated in my dumb body twelve miles, maybe more,
right up Fullerton Cove and half a mile into the paddocks.
I may be the only man who ever slept through his own drowning.
Anyhow I got up, walked to Williamtown. Ghost Almighty!
the storekeeper said as he looked me up and down
and fed me on big sandwiches for wet money. Ghost Almighty!

Ghost or not, we were off before sunup next day.
I was quietly bumping my forehead against the wheel
just to hear the echoey bone. Matt snapped
What are you at? Stop banging your forehead like an idiot!
and there was soft fire all round his edges, in the dark.
I'd only ever seen that twice before, far at sea.
We were steering through Monkey Jacket, dodging oyster racks
and the boy was whimpering from a flogging with a quince stick from Matt.

Queer, that week; I must have got a long way back
into myself, and vanished from sight. I'd walk past
and people wouldn't see me. In the Plough Inn at Buladelah
a fellow told his brother stuff so private you'd never let
an outsider hear it, not a man outsider, and they sat
on either side of me, eating dinner.
In fact the only person who talked to me at all
was one looking for a yarn in Engels' store in Tea Gardens,

the Pindimar Warden. *You haven't heard of my city?*
It's across from Duck Hole, he said. *Here in nineteen nineteen—*
was you here then?—they had this Admiral Jellicoe,
big stiff Pommy all in feathers, he came and looked the Port over
and reckoned he'd put the whole British Far East Fleet
into Nelson Bay here. The base and headquarters will be
this new city, Pindimar. It's all drawn up: Nelson Avenue,
Collingwood Crescent, Hood Road. Just down here opposite Duck Hole.

Anyway I look after it, the site, till the city is built.
I got my tent in the scrub at One Dreadnaught Road.
You ever been in the Navy? Pompey and Guz
and the Golden Rivet, eh? He brisked off, enthusiastic.
Young Engel's wife winked at me and shook her head.
Is it right? I asked.—*Oh, they drew up plans*, she said.
Then two women beside me started telling woman-details
as if I wasn't there, and I vanished from her attention too.

We were up Mayers Point that Saturday,
me securing the logs on deck where Matt had winched them
when a calabash parted—must have been shoddy steel—
and the chain spewed out, and one log slewing started
all them rolling, and there's me dancing on top
to keep my footing till a flick of the one I was on
threw me away out into the lake and safe from
the rest rolling in, big huge barrels packed with wood.

I had to stay in and get chains round them all
for the bullock teams to snig them ashore for re-loading.
I took some chiack from the drivers:
Was that the schottische you was dancing on them logs?
but an older man roared at them *Behave! Fred mighta got killed!*
I thought that a bit serious, even though it was true,
so to thank the boys for their relief I said
something comical. The older bloke ignored me for a fool.

After, with Matt busting to be off, we drank tea with them.
How long did that biggest stick take yous to fall? I asked—
I rode to the bush just on sunup and started chopping
and I had to whale into him to get him down by dinner:
he wouldn't have been safe to left standing while we eat.—
That bastard that chucked you he kicked back on us as he fell,
sprung back on his limbs and shot between us, said another man
but the oldest still wouldn't talk. He'd been offended.

The young lot at the boarding house were more a crowd than company;
half-axes and flappers. The mill hands round the pubs
were more my age. Even the oldest, I sometimes thought.
But I was slow to make new mates. I was missing the Cairo lot,
Yall, and Bill Hines, the Relfs, and especially Sam.
They were back there in my mind from when I hadn't lost home
and my trust with it.
Now I looked at each person and wondered How did they treat us?

There's a common-human level you can strike with any people
if you don't impose on them, or scare them, or sound strange.
On their own ground works best, and with legs bent if they're men.
It's near impossible not to play up to the other sex
but if you can not, they sometimes forget yours, for minutes:
you can be just human, sharing. Even mad folk and toffs
and others who have trouble getting off stage can be soothed
into it. Outside this, things all slope towards war.

I was always good at it. It was the best I could do,
and it saved me, a few times. I always liked to watch
it gather on a group, or be there between two
and stay—
till a frown hunted it, or a joke against, really, anything.
I've known honest men who thought you could box this
what? solidarity, and have it to share with all people
and dishonest buggers out to corner it for their lot.

The idea of the One Big Union was red-hot back then.
A bloke named Reynolds was preaching it in the pub:
You saw how workers massacred each other in the war
when the High Mucks divided us. We can learn from missing that chance
and stand together next time with pride in the name of Worker—
Hearing this, a mill hand lifted up a face gnawed blue
by the dog Rum and growled out *Fucking work!*
Who's proud of lumping shit at the bottom all his life?

That's a worker.—Reynolds should've known better than snap
If that's how you see yourself—The mill hand stood up and said
Not a man here is proud that this is the best they could do,
donkey work for blacks' wages grafting your guts out till you're old
and life's passed you by and the posh smarties pick you by your hands
your voice, your skin, your cheap tog, your fat old missus.
Work's the penalty for no brains. Dignity of labour
my hairy date. Bullocks don't skite about their yoke.

It shook us all. Some were bouncing up to deny
bits of what others were looking at in their glasses,
or in their hands. Too much had been said, too clearly.
Some would have strung them both up on one rope.
This alienation of yours, mate—Reynolds had no chance.
The other fellow said *This alien world.* And put
his forehead back on the bar in front of all the fighters.
Well I enjoy drawing the beers, said the barmaid Margaret.

Your wife was here after you, said one of the whippersnappers
at the boarding house. *I haven't got a wife.*—
Well somebody's wife was.—*You watch your mouth*, I said
and turned my face to the wall. The painted sketchy curves
the saw had left in the lining boards.
The smell of boiled pumpkin. The trace of sand in everything.
That's where I hit bottom.
What made me think that I'd survived the war?

So Work got up and loaded offcuts on the drogher
for firewood, and raked out her firebox, and oiled gear.
Work thrashed upriver and down, Work talked to fellows
who slogged and yoked and hauled from daylight to dark
for keep, half a crown to spend at cricket on Saturdays
and the promise of a farm in the old bloke's will unless
they fell out with him. Work spliced wire rope, and made bights
and met an old Ridgeway who's dead now and shouldn't be named

but told how the Southern Cross used to live up Black Head
but got killed in battle, then raised to life when two women
agreed to love him; he took them into the sky
from a big myrtle tree out on Seal Rocks where there hasn't
been a tree since the Ark was a dinghy. *Yeah,
them trees all wash away in the flood that time*, he said.
He also reckoned the different languages were a punishment
for trying to follow God. *Each mob got its country then instead.*

I was sent in to Newcastle for a pressure gauge.
*I'm sick of you fussing day and night with that dingo-bait look
on your dial. Go in, get a flapper and flap!
and bring these winch gears when you come back. Go on, get.*
So I trailed round the city with its malt and coal-gas smell
and its different trotting sounds of horses and motor cars,
and tried to keep my mind from climbing up the hill
by the Cathedral, and my feet from following my mind.

Want a knock, Jazzer? a woman muttered near the Customs House.
Take out that brown parcel and part my wet hairs, eh?
But I drifted, and drank
and felt sick at passion. The click-click of kissing, the tart jokes
in gaspy sprinters' voices before the race is run,
the rubbers against a baby—when I was rubber myself,
all over. Full and emptied was all I could feel.
Knowing this would be fire to the knower. It was to me.

I drifted, and drank, and kicked myself about with misery
and then in Hunter Street I saw a woman, my mother!
come out of a picture-house, cross half the street—it was my mother!
and get into a tram, which dinged out my yells of *Mama!*
and ground off west with its roller-sign reading Waratah.
I ran to catch it, car-horns croaked at me, brakes racked,
drivers tore off strings of short swears and pitched them at me.
Back to the theatre I rushed *Who was that lady*

*came out of here just now and caught the tram?
Lady, blonde, greying, with a basket—?* The usher looked me over:
*That's Mrs Boatcher the pianist. Who's asking anyway?
Me, I'm her son. I've been gone, haven't seen her for eight years—
You from Dungog?—Yes.—Farm?—Yes.*—He lit up: *You really her boy, truly?
She talks funny. Some sort of a foreigner, is she?*
I had my chance to be stiffnecked. I nearly took it,
but said *She's European. My father was Australian.*

I got her address. We met and hugged and cried,
and laughed, and I got scolded, and then we cried for Dad.
*No one would deal with us. We couldn't buy seed, or wire
or even groceries. And these were his neighbours, Australians
as he was Australian. He was, you know. He hardly spoke German
when we first met. It came back to him as I talked to him.
I made him German, for me. And they killed him for it.
When I sold the farm, ei for what a price! and left,*

they didn't even forward our mail.—That bit I discovered,
I replied. *But when, how did it start?*—
*After the heavy battles, in nineteen sixteen, it got bad suddenly.
Perhaps I forgot and spoke German in public, in the town.
Perhaps because I was Lutheran and didn't go
to his Catholic Mass. That saved most of his Australian sort,
that, where the bread stays Jesus, all in Latin.*—
You can't blame yourself, Mama.—*Doch. I brought it on us.*

*Reinhardt couldn't bear that his home-place had turned on him.
He grieved himself to death.*
After we sat for a while, I asked when my letters stopped coming.
They stopped bringing our post.—
*Did you get the one where I told you about my disease,
this having no touch?*
Her head nodded. It was only eight in the evening
but she was suddenly going to sleep. *Don't talk of that.*—

*I wrote you how it started. The Armenian women
being burnt. And we couldn't stop it. And my leprosy*—
My mother looked away, anywhere but at me, and drowsed.
These are evil things, she said. *Do not tell this story.*
I felt desperate. I drank tea. From her cup, by mistake.
She was fast asleep. I paced around the room
in her little flat there. The turned-wood stands from home,
the screens, fretwork photo-frames, the padded sewing baskets,

I bumped into half them. But she would not notice.
Never before had I bumped into things in the house
and my mother not chipped me, even from rooms away: Fredy!
Then she woke up and smiled, and asked me about my life now.
I told her. When I came to Laura, her lips tightened.
What I couldn't understand, she'd dozed off like an old woman
but she wasn't yet fifty. She still had the fine yellow skin
of a brown-eyed blonde, not even powdery with down.

Mother wouldn't leave Newcastle. She enjoyed the sport
of keeping up with the flickers, and playing with them:
It's more than vamping. I can pour schmalz, and ridicule,
all sorts of feeling, out of my piano.
I've killed some bad rubbish dead, and the manager none the wiser.
She smiled a wicked smile; *I play for the films, but in them too. It's fun.*
So I would visit on weekends. As before.
I leaped up, healthy again, and gravity hung my boots downwards.

Next time we were at Ireland's mill in Buladelah
loading girders, an old man of the Dorneys
told me about the great Russian order: all the sleepers
for the Transsiberian railway. Twenty-five years' cutting.
There's a lot of miles come from just my broadaxe. Hundreds was cutting.
He was so proud. It reminded me how for many people
work is the dragon and they're the heroes, killing and killing him
and laying him down, real and gigantic, on the world.

I wasn't always on the drogher.
Sometimes I'd ride out into the hills to see suppliers,
Newmans, say, at Wootton, McDeans up Rosenthal,
cantering along and scaring goannas up trees.
One day I was heading out of Buladelah to see a family,
the Mitchells, and a fellow in a suit
leant out of his motorcar to ask me how to find them.
Of course I didn't know the way, on good bush principle,

and I really didn't know the car way. I just rode over
through the bush. When I told them, they said
Might have been that other, and nodded round the table, and gave me
the warm edge of several grins. The car never got there.
After wonga pigeon in good gravy, potatoes in cream, and pickles
and geebung jelly, and China pear pie, and a euchre game,
we were round the table. I felt lamed for stories
that night, being barred from my best ones by the Secret,

so I was a listener. Mrs Mitchell, Doris, was saying
Once you got a bush block you wouldn't go back into service.
My boss wasn't too bad: his church had frightened him off girls.
His wife was a middling bitch, not one of the real rank bitches;
still, we had to wear starched caps, like nurses. Here, in Australia.
Her young brother that lived with them was after all he could get,
rubbing up against you, showing you his bulge in the rooms,
froggy hands all over you. He liked the young black girls:

no one to look out for them. This one, Sally Bugg, she was being
sent home up the coast, to have his baby. Much he cared
long as they was out of his road. She asked me:
don't let any of them but Buggerlugs take me to the wharf.
Righto, I told her. I had to think. Then I put it
on the Missus that Sally would do a bunk, not sail
but stay round in town and talk. And I told Bob the driver-gardener
what people'd think of him, seen driving with a young black girl.

He was easy frightened. The boss knew nothing yet.
The missus she spat at her brother that he'd have to be a man
and clean up his own mess for once. They'd had Sally in the house
since she was twelve, and didn't know her, how timid she was.
She would never have run off. His nibs did, straight off to his mates
to offer them favours for a favour, call in debts. All boyos together.
I thought we'd lost, that they'd stick by him.
He looked like a frightened Sebago potato in an egg cup

with that common face of his in a high white collar. I always
reckon that's what cruelled him with the dashers. No style to him.
His mates never come at it. And I reckon they'd have laughed.
The missus made him take the two seater, the sulky,
and he tried the back streets but got boxed. Had to go the main ones.
Sally never said a word. Let him curse at her and talk.
When he strained away the hardest, she smooged up to him
right down Scott Street, past the Customs House. Everybody saw it.

The boss's typist saw it. Sally had a sweet face the colour
of good tobacco leaf, a catch for any honest man.
Him in his spats and coat, with his shirt pinched tight in his bum
and his hat pulled down, till she tipped it back in play.
She never made a scene at the ship. Just quietly spoke to him.
I like the story that comes after the story, so I asked.
The flash white girls sent him burnt corks. And the boss hunted him.
I hear in the end he got a job. And Sally lived with a rabbiter,

later on, that shot her in the hand when he was drunk.
The quacks set her hand-bones best they could, like a kind of hook.
By this time the fire was sighing in its sleep
and settling its reds and blacks, on the big stones of their fireplace.
Reg Mitchell was folding sugar into strips of tobacco leaf
and twisting them tight. *Ever put nicotine on a snake's tongue?* he asked.
Somebody holds his head, you wipe it on, it kills him stone dead.
Did Cos Morrison ever tell you the one about the dog woman?

That's a wicked story, Doris frowned. And Reg nodded.
It horrified Cos. Did he tell you his full name? Cosmo.
He fairly hates it. Cosmo.
I felt at home in the hills there, the bits of selections
with their chisel-shaped iron chimneys that smoked along the edge,
trace-chain hanging in trees, and lawn made by cattle to the door.
I could have forgot myself up in there for forty years
away from comparisons, just being my own human specie.

But if magic had turned me to mettwurst, damn me if I'd run
away from the slicer. If I couldn't drown it, I'd not hide with it.
As I came in off the verandah where my bed was,
Reg was squatted down toasting rounds of bread for his girls,
saying *I showed my boots to my stick horse and it killed him!*
I said *Good morning,* and he agreed to it, *Yeah,* on reflection.
A lot did that.
Then when Doris was away, down at the meathouse, he told

how Cos had advertised in the paper for a housekeeper
and got three replies he didn't go much on
and one that sounded perfect. Up in he said which town.
He'd been caught before, taking on people sight unseen,
so he made a day and rode up there. Hung his horse up,
knocked at the door—and what opened gave him the horrors.
She had fur on her head. Not human hair; real tough fur
like a Kelpie dog. Her eyes were glassy, a dog's eyes,

with slits for pupils. And the fur came right down her forehead.
She had no brow. Otherwise she was a nice woman, like
her sister, that was normal. He'd have hired the sister all right.
He had to go in, for politeness. They gave him tea and biscuits,
and pleaded with him. She needed the job, the dog woman.
Cos could hardly speak: *He couldn't look at her: he kept*
thinking her mother must've been frightened with a dog
like my sister Em. She don't know but she was born

with a bullock's tail between her shoulders. A mad Durham bullock
had bailed Mum up when she was expecting the baby.
The doctor come out in his buggy and cut the thing off her
and they burnt it. So Cos is there shuddering in their parlour
till he could get away. Nearly broke the hallstand getting out.
The girls were pop-eyed. This was better than school. This was their school.
They reckon he hires his housekeeper women to sleep with
but I don't believe it. He might do better if he did.

As I rode back that time I saw the longest
team of bullocks I ever saw. Eighteen pair stringing out
through the timber, empty trucks bumbling along behind.
One was a bull, sawing at his yoke. Two were heifers.
I thought about it, on the way back to our boat
and had the sense to keep quiet till I told Matt.
Are Soameses at that again? he laughed. *The brands'll be healed
and trucks left in the bush, when they load that lot on the train.*

Never do the impossible near where you like living.
I'd taken to the Myall, but timber is dangerous work
and throws terrible emergencies.
Up at Dirty Creek, at Crolls' mill there, we were loading slings
of telegraph poles in wet weather. They were slippy. One slid
in the loop, and kicked up. Its butt end caught a mill hand
by the Oxford bag trousers he was wearing out at work.
This other one was sliding to stub him with its butt.

I leaped, and stopped it. Stemming it back and up
as Matt slacked off the winch, letting the other end down gently.
I had a good look up that dirty-skinned ironbark monster,
soapy from the rain and its juice-froth. Oh it wanted me!
The mill bloke never said boo. *I'd gave myself up,*
he told me later. *This was it, the big bayonet.*
After, all the hands were staring at me like Mitchells' girls
and Matt was stepping round me: *You dumb Fritzie bastard!*

but it wasn't an insult. It just ran out, till his mouth shut.
All the blokes were breathing in *Jesus!* like Moslems breathe out *Allah!*
and I knew I'd put my pot on. Nothing was going to be the same.
Just luck, I grinned. *It hung up in the loop—*
Sailing back through the bush, I had only the wheel
and the usual sea-eagles that worked the river to talk to.
Matt tinkered with the engine, which didn't need it, the boy
forgot to make tea. Rain spilt off the swamps and stained the river.

I felt the sack coming, and couldn't fly like the snipe
that Harry Legge's barrister guest tramped two hours back
to Legge's Camp to get his snipe gun for. *Why didn't you shoot 'em
with the gun you had along?—But that was my Greener duck gun!*
The hours went by. It would come when we got in
but it didn't. Days passed. We went on more trips
and then, off old black Becky Johnston's at Boolambayte,
Matt, not looking at me, asked: *You know the Double Island shallows?*

Yes, I said.—*And the bad bit near Dee's Mill, don't you?*—
Like I know my waistcoat pocket.—*Hm.*—It gradually
made sense. He was telling me I was too valuable to sack
but his manner had already told me he was frightened of me.
They were fighting times. Men threw off their coats at a word
and got into it. No dance was a dance without it. But Matt,
he only fought children, with pants belt, buggy whip, quince stick.
All right, Captain, I said to myself. If you're windy of me, that stops too!

Maybury, Motum—I never can remember the man's name
I saved that day. But soon after, a miracle happened. Dolf Engel
jumped across from their store boat and gave me a letter. From Sam!
Blue paper, French stamps. *Dear Fred, you dodgy matlow*—
he hoped I was alive, he was happily married, they'd stuck
in Oran for a while but he was now *apprenti saucier*
in the grandest place in Vichy that would take a Jew.
Why hadn't I gone back for Shahira? *I wouldn't have thought you*

afraid of colour. You know she tried to sail out and find you
but the captain refused her, because Australia would refuse her
entry? Even though she's quite wheatish, as the Hindus say.
She was heartbroken. She went into a decline, but is married now
under family orders. Young Braine, that you heaved the motor off,
actually married Panaghia, after the war. He had
to jack in his commission. Greek is colour, to the British Army.
Yall Sherritt writes that he's starving on a brigalow block.—

Lord God, I had so few. A mother and two friends—
and one of them lost to save her from learning the truth.
No more women friends. My running away to spare them
hurt them undeserving. But knowing me would kill them.
I had to live near the human race, and be mates
with lots of it, shallowly. It, my body, walked me
to the engine room, to sit and bawl for myself
and Shahira, and Laura, and Dad, and God knows who all.

Crying still had a taste, and jerked the breath, and flooded seeing.
Nothing I'd done for the first time since Trabzon
felt like anything. No feel or quality to it.
Things I'd learned before could work by memory:
Being tired, that slows and gets heavy. Being on fire though
only smells, and frightens onlookers, if you're in my tribe,
and what you call love, that comes to a laundry-smelling salt point—
with kindness before and also after, if it's real love.

With babies after, too, love or not. Would they be numb like me?
Was I the start of a new race, without its own females yet?
Like the first human, having only apes to sleep with,
if religion was wrong.
That one must have felt queer, all warm and muzzy with its relatives
but upright in secret, not satisfied with gibber, and too bare.
All right, I pitied myself,
but I was the only one to know I needed pitying.

My mother flew into me over Shahira. *I'm not proud*
that you would bolt like a hare from an honest girl.
Were you afraid people here would scorn such a marriage, to a native?
A real sow-act, your encouraging her then, giving her your ticket.
Idiotic. You should have at least written
that you had changed your mind, not let her sit in hope
till it turned to shame. Have you often done such piggeries?
She was dark, and nibbled her anger like knots in a string.

I slept over in the flat as usual, and had bad sleep.
No dreams I remembered, waking, but I'd been dreamed, sour and hard
and woke with the webby grey browns of it still in my mind,
had the breakfast Mama cooked, kissed her and hit the road,
weightless but feet downward, like always. To cross the river
and catch the service car to Salt Ash, I always
had to pass Winns in Hunter Street. I'd slow, and hum and ha,
and feel like death, and drag myself on, away,

but this day I went in. She was selling a nightdress to a man,
Laura. She looked at me, steady, up and down
and asked him *Is your daughter full-figured? As me, say?*
I swear she played him so he drew out the sale, and wriggled
and hitched his trousers. I waited my turn among the drawstrings
and laces and swamis. And she said goodbye to him
with a look like as if she'd picked a tiny feather off his coat.
Then, again, she looked at me steady, up and down.

Did all the half-trousers in that flophouse you live in laugh
about the fool of a woman who came looking for you? she asked.
I looked at my boots. *They laughed at me*, I said,
for missing a prize. Or running away from one. They had.
She went on serving and let me stand about.
My ferry went. I missed the car, too. I didn't mind.
It was madness, I said, *from the war.—*
I lost a man in the war, she said. *But he fought in it.*

And after that *Get! I'll meet you for lunch in the teashop.*
She brusqued in, sat down, ordered. *All right bugger you,*
tell me why you ran off on me that night.
So I told her. The lot. Second person I ever told.
She didn't go to sleep. She looked fascinated. *You feel nothing?—*
Only where things are. She stood up and said *No use*
slapping you. Eh? It's the best get-out I ever heard.
Good on you, sailor! My fault. I picked you up. Fair's fair.

And she was gone. I would have chewed off my hand
to show it didn't hurt, but she was gone.
I would have changed in her eyes from a liar to a pervert,
but Laura was gone. I sang out, and ran into the street
and climbed the hill, and couldn't see her walking—
I don't know how, but I'm on the ferry next
with pins and needles all over me. Coming right.
Feeling my toes, my knees, my bum and shoulders:—

I must have prayed the right way. With a whole heart.
I must have prayed, down under my knowledge of it, for her sake.
It's gone! I said out loud, and people looked at me.
I still had to be careful. But: gone. No more loveless, freak, nor strong,
no more numb, or light, or never tired, or safe.
I tell you, gravity was driving my legs into my trunk.
Everything slumped, aching. My Hands rose through syrup to my Face,
I Itched, and remembered Scratching, pain changed shape in my Guts.

I bent with my first Cramps in seven years, and spewed.
Then I had to leg it the twenty-odd miles to Salt Ash
on burning ankles, and feel the road-metal through my soles.
Luckily Cos was about, and took me across
to Hawks Nest in his launch. He'd been having strife with officials.
Arguing the toss with fellers paid for tossing
stiffens the mind for jokes and fun, he said
in his mournful voice. *I need a joke, Cos! Tell me one.*

He told me the dreadful stories of the Scotch:
Twa-an-sax tae vulcanize yon French letter.—Aye the Regiment
accepts yer quote! And the grown boy with money flung at him
for the last time by the laird and his mother says *Gang awa back*
an tell him he's no yer faither! and the Scot rejected
at the Pearly Gates: *We're no makin porridge for ane!*
and their brute of a God who sends them to Hell crying out
Lord Goad, we didnae ken! and in His infinite mercy He

roars down *Well ye ken noo!* No wonder they fight
and scream as they're fighting. I was trying not
to interfere with myself till I got off on my own:
welcome back, welcome back to a sixteen-year-old's bad habit,
and the sad fun it would be, like the razor-scraped boys
who made bedspring music and fo'c'stle smells late at night
in the boarding house, and planted their crisp hankies.
But who knew how long I was back for? It was back for?

I didn't get punished. I was still there next morning,
riding the tide up to Tamboy, getting splinters
in my hands, bashing my head sore on the transom
below, from ducking back when I burned them. All jobs were fussy
now, that had been simple. And I still had to keep it all mum.
At that little shack town with no streets and all hung
with nets like hammocks or the cradles of enormous babies
we feasted on prawns from the shot the night before,

picking them out of the kero tin they were boiled in.
I never seen you flinch that much at hot water, Fred,
says one of the Palmer girls. *Did you see Billy Hughes?*
Come through here yesterday with that lunatic from Pindimar
hanging after him. I picked the heads and cellophane bits
off the prawns, and feasted. Politicians, Prime Ministers here or there,
to hell with them. But Cos had been moaning about Billy
too, for sinking, not scrapping our one ten-year-old undamaged

battlecruiser, the Australia. All that bloody good steel!
You going to the dance up Bungwahl? asked the Palmer girl
and for once I caught on. *I am if you'll teach me fancy steps.*
She grinned. I was right. So simple, when you learn.
And a perfectly nice girl. Rough-talking, straight, no fool.
It was no use looking back. So that Saturday
we tied up at the wharf with a crowd from down the Lakes
streaming ashore to the fiddles and powder-burning hall lights.

And soon it was going exactly as they went at Dungog,
the married ones and keen ones dancing, kids and mothers
sitting with the wallflowers, among them some of the prettiest,
that the boys dared not ask—and all the drinkers outside
passing the bottle, yarning and getting fightable
because they daren't ask, and *Off with your coat you bastard!*
and into it, or *Leave him alone: you're safe here, mate,*
we don't pick strangers! I'd heard that was their rule.

I slapped mosquitoes and wondered how I'd go now
that fighting would hurt. I waltzed and progressive barn-danced
with cologne, rubbery points, and jokes about jazz garters
and the accordion was like weatherboards loosened, singing and dancing
and the fiddle sketched its beautiful creak. But the night got later
and the grievance that fun brings with it spat and stumbled
in through the doors, or smoked and drank inside yelling
Fuck em! at warnings *Fuck you too!*—then the urgent cry *Copper!*

A mounted policeman, dismounted in jodhpurs and leggings, was
in the hall shouting *Right!* but working men grabbed his hands
Let go I say! and were spinning him in a ring,
round and round like Phil Garlick's racing car
or a marble in a dish *the King's name!*—*You officious bastard!*
Let's ride the canary cunt! and we dancers stayed shrunk back
out of it as they threw the man heavily, and hauled him
to his hands and knees, and I saw the one who straddled him,

mounting on his back had his spurs on *Gee up Copper!*
and rowelling his ribs through shirt and torn uniform coat.
Giddap you trap Christer! I found myself breaking in on it,
tossing the rider by one leg, stoushing his brother
out through the side door with the strength I used to have
before pain, a last great hit; no one else knew that, nor risked me.
I went the dead-man's carry, the police trooper over my shoulder,
under yells of *Kiss his ring!* and *The Prussians love a policeman.*

Outside he wrestled down, and sat on a log, and made
dreadful strangling sounds, crying. Older men smoking pipes
came over and said *Gawd, look: did they cut him?*—
Oh they cut him all right!—*He'll be transferred to buggery now.*—
Better if he was to stop here: he's broke in.
I eased his revolver off him, like disarming a drunk man
and thanked in my head the Manilaman who taught me the art.
If you want that gun, it's lying deep: you'll need a magnet.

Back inside, the music was going again and I danced
but the man-ride was still there. It was a story. It would never go.
Why did yer spoil the fun? a boy yelled at me:
Shut up Mikey—*You ought to be ashamed*—cried women.
A man dancing swigged from a bottle *Well it was fuckin funny,*
him on the floor with his arse up like a hen—
Nothing a mob does to one person's funny, I told him,
Nothing a mob does.—He held his wife's hand and hanky

high. I saw her chip him. And when he danced near again
he said *Yer right, Kaiser.* But I've never been in the story.
And what I thought later might have been a bad sign,
it seemed round the walls of the hall not ordinary:
the little kids sleeping in blankets down under the seats,
the wives in long old dresses, girls in flapper frocks
with waves ironed into their hair, the odd bloke in a bumfreezer coat
sidesaddle on the bench seats talking to them, the hoots and blushes—

all seemed as it does now, tiny, very long ago
with a queer dead line around it all. I stood, was bumped
and got Jess Palmer bumped. *What's wrong, Fred?* she asked kindly.
None of it's real strong, I think I said. *It don't last. A photo—*
Then colours were back, all too stamping and musical and real
for any more sad distance. And Jess had warm freckles on her bosom.
You was away, she said. *Were you off sailing again?*
I do wish you'd take me: I'd love to see them other countries.

I had some such in mind for when we were sailing home
down the lakes later, but Matt was drunk and turned short
over the Stag Island mudbank and the deepwater end
of the paddlewheel slewed us, as always, and broached us to.
I thought we were set till someone happened by to tow us.
Jess hoped the same. All the crowd did. But Matt would have me
row right over to the mainland with only half enough line
and beg chain off two suspicious fellows camped there

off a steam launch. Detective-looking English fellows.
We arsed about and swore and rove wire rope
to join with chain, and warped her free just on sunup.
Too late for romance. *Ar well you're a working man,* says Jess
and kissed my cheek, going ashore.
Then young Cyril Garland the boy ripped his shirt open
on a cup-hook in the cuddy and I saw long purple stripes
criss-cross on his back, and I was in just the humour.

Who flogged you?—Dad.—What with?—Freezer drive belt.—When?—
Last Sunday.—Right! The kid wore a shirt all the time
and long pants, half mast over oyster-cut bare feet.
I called Matt up from the engine room and other, choice things
like a scab-arsed dingo who didn't deserve kids. He charged me
with a stilson wrench and froth blaring from his mouth. I sidestepped
and he flew overboard *Whae!* just off Cherry Tree
and dragged himself sopping out onto the green native-violet

floor of the palm scrub there. He still had the stilson, and shied it
at me, screaming *Sack!* So ended me on the drogher Mafeking.
And that afternoon, I was rubber again to the knees.
I couldn't bear it. Not again. I cursed, I ran into the scrub
and screamed, and kicked logs with my bare Wellington feet,
but there was no appeal.
I was like the dog who growls and tears off
the verandah to bark at thunder, but can't find it.

I was used to feeling weird in secret, not ridiculous.
I felt like a toff in jodhpurs, artificial from his boot-tops down.
I walked like on stilts, twenty inches above my height.
At times I also felt like the kid who's got away with something
truly bad, and loves the frightening aloneness it brings him.
This was a new feeling on me. Numb, I hadn't had it.
I could just remember it, from way back cursing farms and Dad.
From smoking. From dodging Mass. From things I tried when my stones first
    dropped.

Now, to keep the dumb zone from rising any higher, I chucked
all thoughts of Jess Palmer. Of women altogether, in fact.
I was cursed for women.
I went to Mama's as usual, and stayed
till she knew I was out of work. I did some coasting
in and out of milky rivers. But soon I hit the Myall again,
chopping up burley to go fishing with the Pindimar Warden.
My City is scuppered, he said. *It was a colour in the air.—*

Eh? I asked.—*The little Welshman*, he answered impatiently.
White Australia Hughes. Why did you scuttle our Australia?
Get back to your business.—My business is the Far East Fleet's city:
I'm Warden of Pindimar.—Well, Warden of the Sunk Port,
consider the place yours! And build your own fleet for it.—
Maybe that's what the Japs'll do!
I said. *There were two British drawlers*
along with him, and that made them sit up, in their silk suits—

What did Hughes do then? I asked.—*Ignored me.*
One of the Pommies told a story about Admiral Togo
as the Nip and Russki fleets were closing at Chushima in '05,
first time an Oriental navy faced a Western navy.
Seems Togo's aide reached through between the legs
of his commander to feel if the crown jewels were shrivelled
up with fear, or hanging loose with confidence.—
Didn't the Admiral flinch? I asked.—*Seems he didn't even growl*

Not now! like a real Navy officer. Then Hughes said: Marco Polo
wrote that the Japs were a white people, living on islands
east of Cathay. He never saw them. They knew better themselves,
with that racial equality clause they wanted for the League
at Versailles. Weren't they nettled when I blocked that!
All the same, I preferred them allied to the Empire.—
We'd have to whiten them a good deal for that now, Sir,
to please the Yanks.—Who are keen to squeeze their wedding tackle

and make 'em lash out before they're ready? I put in.
Must we sink our ships as bait, though? They all shut up, and Hughes swore
Duw annol y byd! Which is good Welsh blasphemous swearing,
no sex or dirt in it. My da was a Taff, so I know.
Pa devong, eh Sir? Lisps the other Pom. That's Greek for Watch it.
No, let the people speak, Hughes snarled. And looked at me. Well?—
The boys we stopped you killing for one damn Empire, they
can still father the boys who'll stop the next empire, eh?

I said to him.—And you're off the Commonwealth payroll!
he spat back at me. Heh! I was never on it at all.
The Shire pays me. But my City, it'll never be built.
Goodbye to the wheat port, goodbye to Hood and Prince of Wales
(halfway to their scuppers in sand, I thought privately,
if any of it had ever been true). That must have been when
they cruelled Hughes' independence. He was never Prime Minister again.
I met his longtime secretary once, Miss Mohammed. First rate lady.

Wading in my own madness was worse than being mad all over.
I couldn't bear to float at knee height down the street
so I became a fisherman, camped up a back creek with a boat,
working big cotton nets, boiling wattle-bark to toughen them,
getting ice from the store-boats for my fish-box, selling fish,
steeping choker mullet in honey and brine to smoke them
over a sawdust fire in a black tarpaulin tent,
never doing prawn shots. I didn't mix with people

for two or three years. Let my legs go and I will, I said.
I got more used to Bramble's cattle and God's birds
than to humanity. Visitors to my fire had red eyes.
Sometimes I'd see Harry Legge in his duck canoe
parting the reeds like the sharp beak of a curlew
out ahead of his guest-house coughers.
Other times it'd be the bead of a turtle's nose, just touching
the surface for air, or flathead on the bottom sand.

It's hard to tell about those years. Like peace
they didn't have much words or story to them.
There were instances, like when a king tide brought
porpoises up to the Broadwater. Or the heavy floods
like enormous wire ropes pulling through the channels, or roving
out over the swamps in knotty shortcuts, and carrying
mill logs and rails and whisky bottles and calves
and the fishing spoilt for days, so I'd live on duck and roo.

Talk, that makes times, was like islands I had to visit
to sell and buy stuff. We'd swap the usual blarney:
Got a match, mate? Yeah: my arse and your face!
Or I'd hear the gossip. And forget it as nor'easters striped the water
with long ropes of froth. What started me back to life
was a dazzler of a girl in a flyaway hat in Buladelah.
I roped her motor down for her, where some mug had parked it up a tree.
Aren't you a darling?—I dunno, was my witty social answer.

The bloke who'd hung her car had been an earlier darling,
gossip said. But gossip would.
Perhaps it was just hellery. Perhaps it was her having a car.
Who cares about that? I was smitten, square amidships
and made such a fool of myself that it still stings to tell.
Perhaps it was that I'd been strong truly for the first time,
I mean, without my armour. I had hauled and swung
with my shoulderblades on fire, as the pulleys squeaked around.

I hungered to widen those emerald eyes again, and went,
scrubbed of scales and lake mud, headfirst into introductions
to fellows who looked at her before shaking my hand.
Freddy was so piratical! A sheik-eyed Argentine
with a polo stick turned his back on me
and gazed out over their horse pastures. Meredith tried
to rescue it, drawling fast. Her granny said *He has a well-turned leg.*
You look like young Thunderbolt. Not dark. It will come out in your children.

After that disaster I came down the Valley to Mama's.
I am going home. To Germany. I am forgotten here,
she said, and I hung my head.
Impossible to explain. I decided to go back to sea
and put my name down, paid my union dues and all.
My tackle at the Lakes could rot there, or get shook.
One day I got picked, and thought My God, the boot
is on the other hand now. I went well, but lost, and got kicked

as I crawled in the gravel. Every hit left its hurt,
and I crackled as I breathed, with barked ribs:
a real deepwater man's hiding.
It caused me to miss a freighter job, Osaka and on to Hawaii.
Then comes the day when I'm tight with porridge and eggs
and walking down Laman Street on my stilty heron pins
and I see Laura, coming with a kiddie beside her,
a toddler in his overcoat, with combed hair and my Dad's face.

I stop. I startle back. *Jesus God, why didn't you let on?*—
Not in front of him, please, she says,
looking at him, at the view, looking hugely uninterested.
Where can we—talk? About this? I ask.—*Nowhere. Ever.*—
I flounder about, and then say *I'll come and see your Mar.*
I'll tell them, tell everyone.—*Are you sure you could be the father?*
she says bitterly. *Like with your affliction and all?*
The little boy starts to cry, and my face is running like his.

I hung round in ballast for days, not knowing what to do.
Or knowing very well, but not sure I dared or wanted to.
You're the child so long it's easy to go on being it
when it all goes out of date on you. You've had so much practice.
I pulled myself together, and Mama gave me a long look
as I marched out, on my way. I hadn't told her.
I got just inside the front gate of Laura's people
and the door bursts wide: *Are you the bastard?* screams her father.

Er no, I'm the father, I answered him. He stamped the porch *Christ Jesus!*
and a whole lot more, but it was mostly for show.
I ignored him. All Laura said, even though she'd grinned
at the scene out front was *No.*
I don't want your duty.—*You're not the only one needing it,*
I answered. *What did you call our boy?*—
She looked down the hall, deep into the brown dark there. *Joseph.*
For my husband. She went in a room and shut the door.

I had a few drinks down the hill but I wasn't fit company.
When I got home, Mama had a gentleman visitor.
This had been going on for months. *Herr Volkmar Sietz:*
Friedrich my son.—*Sehr angenehm. A pleasure,*
Not a great pleasure. He was a stiff swollen fellow
in his check suit and waxed whiskers. What was he selling, I thought.
From Paraguay.—*Yes, the Australians, you Australians*
had a colony there too. But our New Germany has outlasted it!

He was selling chemicals. He now lived in the Fatherland
but was in Australia as *Vertreter* for this big firm. And oh,
your pardon, but he was Herr Doktor. A decent Aryan country,
Australia, but slack with honourable achievement-titles.
We mustn't let it become the dictatorship of the proletariat.
Ha ha. Mother glowed at all this.
I glowed with my troubles like a cigarette-end in the dark,
because I went to bed and left them to it.

You can't really pretend our boy is the child of your Joss,
I told Laura, through her window.
She opened it and spoke to me straight:
Can't the dead be fathers? You're one of them. You told me so yourself.
I reeled from that. Me too in the endless white column
of the war's millions.
Have people been bastards to you? I asked her when I could speak,
standing on my knees there. Had my child's mother gone mad?

What made you tell me such a horrible lie?
she asked, a day later. *Surely you knew it was an insult?*—
It might have been my way of crying for my war horrors,
I ventured, feeling the border of nothing at my knee joints,
hoping it wouldn't shift upwards, afraid to provoke it.
My money was near gone, I had to get a decision
from her, quick. To know where I'd be doing what.
So I lied. *Queer, what shock can make a man believe,* I said.

Good day, Joe. I'm your dad. I've been away.
I was the one clumsy with emotions, he was the one
underneath their parlour table, sneaking looks out
through the fringes of the blue Bible-rug that hung down the sides.
Now Mama would see Dad's face again!
What did you say you'd done these three years? Fisherman?
Laura's mother held me out on the end of her questions
as if after I left she'd have to fumigate her voice.

You name isn't Belcher, my daughter says. Blucher, is it?
I've no patience with these Rosenberg-Finkelstein names,
not when they killed her husband, and two of my nephews,
and neighbours of ours' husbands, and boys galore, she said.
I'd heard these lists often, being accused of them. But
you can't wish a woman in Hell, not when you've seen them burn.
I was born at Dungog, I said. *I only ever killed a bear,*
apart from pests round the farm. I'm a virgin in that way.—

No need to be vulgar! she snapped.—*I fell on him,* I said. *It's true.*
I'm sorry about your relatives, I remembered to add then.
I've seen men die in war.—*Her husband was a better man than you.*
He didn't shirk on ships. He did his duty. He enlisted,
fighting to end war.—*Dear God, I hope he succeeded!*
I had to say, even though I was holding myself in.
I had this superstition, while I stayed calm the Nothing wouldn't rise
and numbify me before I could get with Laura.

You gave our girl three years hell, Mar accused me in a low scream.
Where's this getting us, Mum? Laura asked her from the door,
putting her open-mouthed poor dad to one side. *Fred didn't know.*
I told him nothing. You knew that. I let on nothing.—
Bloody right there, shouts her father. *I'd've come and found yer,*
you Dutch consignment! I looked him up and down:
useless as buttons on a sock. Would marriage turn me that way?
But, those days, they had a child, no argument. You stuck.

Don't steel yourself to marry me. Even on account of them,
Laura grinned, as we said goodbye at the gate.
That week I saw two nuns come down the street
with stiff stuff framed around the faces, like photos
of dead women, and one of them said *Hello Freddy.*
I always liked the Sisters. I saw an elephant, too, chained
on top of a brewer's cart, being drawn by six horses,
and I saw Captain de Saint-Adroit, spruce with a whangee cane,

pacing up Scott Street. *Morning Captain.*—*Morning Boettcher.—*
Then Laura and me wed at the Registry and set up down the East End.
The numb nothing didn't get me and didn't get me,
night after night. I walked insulated from the ground
each day, but it came no higher.
It was like living with a tigersnake no one can see
attached to you. They'll call you mad if you mention it
but you know it can bite. And you'll die, and be in Hell,

working away at your job, still pretending to live.
What a honeymoon! But—what a honeymoon we did have, really.
A secret stops you from becoming one flesh, but I reckon
the one flesh that couples become is their children, anyway.
That must be what Christ meant. There it's exactly right.
We were two fleshes and enjoyed both them, and cracked jokes.
I got work on a dredge, filling swamp with the river's bed
that I might have lain in; I greatly rathered our one.

BOOK 2 *Barking at the Thunder*   [85]

But sex talk is boasting, so my time thought.
Also, our one flesh avoided me and had nightmares,
and we'd been so proud of giving him a room of his own,
a third of a balcony glassed in and walled off, facing
the same sea that we enjoyed through French windows and our toes.
At work, they'd nail the dredge to the bottom with long spuds
and scoop away, bringing up old half-digested things,
kettles and cable, bottles, shells, once the frame of this big monkey,

and the mud ladled up like lobscouse out of a drowned galley.
It was more like being at sea than on the drogher:
that was bush navigation; here were salt breezes and flags
and sirens pooping, and buoys. It glittered and flowed—but we stayed,
going on board every morning with a sandwich in our pockets.
I was too newlywed to get pally with the blokes much
except lame Charlie Bourke, who'd been away four years and one.
The one was for shooting the horse his wife's main suitor was on.

He used the bank revolver. *The missus was innocent. Just too pretty.*
By gophers but that corn porridge scours you! But I gave him scours first.
When work got hard *Let a banker have a go!* and he'd fix it
and *Freedom my arse! Our jail fought the German jail. No difference,*
was his slant on the Great War. *Murder. With screws to keep us at it.*
My mother and her Herr Sietz came round to the flat for tea
and we went to them. Sietz would preach on and on
against the Jews. Queer, because where he came from barred them.

Para-Germany was set up for that. Jews had betrayed the Fatherland,
he reckoned. And on and on. I didn't listen. I was grateful
how Mama and him were always on hand to care
for Joe, if we went out. Our sad little boy would light up
when Oma and Mr Seeds appeared. And we were mad for the Charleston,
the Black Bottom, the foxtrot. I danced well on my secret cork feet.
There were pumps beside our bed and jazz garters on it, my hair
was teak varnished in oil, there were tassels on the lampshades and Laura.

This greedy riot of Negroid Jazz and flivvers
comes, Sietz said, *of profiteers gorging on our Fatherland's*
reparation payments. It will poison them.—How?—It will overheat
the economic engine, make it seize. Our lifeblood
will yet prove to be the Jews' poison. They will wheel worthless francs
and pounds and dollars in pushcarts to buy a sausage!
As I have done with Reichsmarks. The Reds then will kill them in the street.
This curse goes with our gold.—I dunno. I haven't got a car

and my fatherland is here.—Here, where they call you Hun?—
They have renamed everything except the Pomeranian dog:
why not it? Mama asked. For once I was quick enough: *They probably*
thought Pomerania was England's nickname, I said.
Mama didn't laugh. He was making her earnest, this Sietz fellow.
Still, they were teaching Joey German. Good, I thought. It's handy,
a second language. I'd always had the two. And he wouldn't
learn anything off me. But Laura, she was dead set against it.

Wanted to give up going out, over it. I couldn't work out why
and she wouldn't say. *Not in my house, not near me, not a word!*
Blow them with their Yosef! But then she'd cool down
and she and Mama got on well, I think: I didn't
understand a quarter of what they told each other.
Onetime there, it was night in the flat but still day downstairs,
somebody was knocking. Cos Morrison, there with a black woman:
Fred, meet Dulcie Morris.—Dulcie. I shook hands. *Mrs Morris, I mean.*

She had a nice brown face and a redhaired white toddler,
and the most awful haunted look. *Dulcie works for me.*
Little Henry isn't mine. Some say it of course but he isn't.
Anyhow the government's rounding up black kids that look white,
putting them in orphanages so they'll forget they was black,
and breed out to white, in time.
Could you put them up for a couple of weeks? Coppers call,
you might say Henry's yours and Dulcie's just the maid.

Cos looked at me. *Yes well. Coppers know me, like. They owe me one.*
So that's how my later career started, casting against type,
as they call it in show business. But if you don't notice kids
you only have to save them from trouble they really get in,
and anyway Laura had agreed and fussed them inside
and sent me for boards and nails to screen in more balcony
for their room, all before I could ask questions.
One I didn't was, would Cos pay Dulcie's wages? Hah. What wages?

as it turned out later. Shelter and keep were what he paid,
and minding the Welfare off them. *But we get real tucker,*
Mrs Morris told us later, when she was out of her shock.
Cod Morasdan don't give us that moolingmah, that sheep guts.
None of his meat got holes down it. And I got on with Henry,
gurgling at each other, him dot-dotting round on his feet
in Joe's socks on the lino, me catching him just launching off
downstairs in his flying shirt. *Pity I missed that age with Joe,*

I told Laura. She didn't pass any comment.
That's when I had the accident. I had my back to the bucket
as it rose from the water, and a snag offcut of copper sheeting
went in above my ankle and of course only switched on the agony
when it reached above my knee. Green water, green metal, green blood—
that was me fainting, and the red-hot ploughshare of pain
still splitting upwards, ripping trouserleg. Bourke and the boys
tore me off, into the boat, over to Cohen's wharf, Cohen himself

raced his car round their warehouse and we off scattering bikes,
horses and cars, straight up Watt Street, with fellows tying rags
over the sop and squirt of blood, me burbling this Latin *agonis
flexuosa, agonis flexuosa*: God knows what it means, it was churchlike
and you have to grip on to something. At the hospital
they plonked me on a table and started. As I went out
I heard the doctor say *Nurse, why is this man not bleeding
below the knee?* As if accusing her or me of something.

When I came sensible I prayed to God properly, with the pain,
and the stitches felt like bootlaces pulled tight, knee to bum.
I wore a high legging: I was one. Laura came, morning and evening,
Dulcie Morris came, Charlie Bourke and the dredger crew came,
and the doctor raised his question again: *It's amazing:
below the knee your gash has almost healed. It never bled.*
I pondered what to tell him, but knew to say nothing in the end.
One of the boys ate a Cornish pastie on a visit—

and so I told the doctor I kept the dessert in my calf
and the meat above my knee. He got red-faced and snapped
There's more to this! So I asked him hadn't he seen
weird things in his work? I had. A shifted cargo
that re-trimmed itself, on my second trip out of Melbourne.
I mean, it can't happen. The mate said it was the good Swede hull
shape that did it. It had before. The designer had been a genius.
I skun out of hospital that night, still leaking in my bandages,

and went to earth with Cos. *Mister Morrison, can I be your white baby?*
Pouring straight metho on bandages is savage nursing
but hobbling on a pole to the ferry had been worse. I was finally
in pain college, learning stuff I'd forgot or never learned.
God knows what you're running from, Laura said. *It's real to you.
Will there be police?*—No, it's not law trouble, I told her.
Dulcie Morris made a poultice of hot stewed leaves: *My brother,
my father, uncles, all girl-mad. All been speared in the leg,*

she laughed. *This cure 'em every time*, as Laura held me:
God, missus, they spear your bloke with a crosscut saw, eh?
When I could stop yowling and think again, I thought:
This isn't my real punishment. And my real punishment isn't
for womanising, I don't think. Or none that I did. I didn't say this.
Queer, how you lose points, denying to women that you womanise.
Herr Sietz came to see me, told me about the Fatherland's winter
that seemed to go on for years, from late in the war—

Graf Bobby, he snorted, *in his apartment, shivering*
he asks Alfons How many degrees is it in here?
Six, your High Wellborn.—How many outside? Three, your High Wellborn.
Then in God's name open the window and let those three in!
All ruined, you see, the great families; closed, the princely courts.
The Reds in Braunschweig installed the scourings of the slums
in the best apartments. Fishwives rolling out dough
on the polish of a grand piano! About me in the war

he kept a stiff silence. I learned not to mention it.
About himself in the war, he was more like vague:
I think he'd made substitutes for butter and nutrition,
or maybe it was clothing. I know he kept a paper shirt.
In a way, I'd been torpedoed for it. I didn't tell him that,
nor how when I was a leper in Germany there had still
been plenty of pork and potatoes and leek soup
for those who had hands, their own or somebody's, and mouths.

When I'd gone from aching to itching along my seam
Cos took me home. I happened to ask him about
the Silly Man, the Pindimar Warden—how was he?
Ar he committed suicide, Cos said. *Poor bugger. With his lies*
about Billy Hughes and all. He got brooding back on the war
and all he'd seen. You're guilty of what you've seen
he used to reckon. Anyhow he hung himself in the finish.
Last time I saw him, he'd run out of talk and big world plans.

I felt icy. It was spring, but I lay there wrapped up in blankets,
hearing the baker's cart pass in the sun, and the butcher's cart
and the rabbit man sing out Rabby-oh! anytime of day.
Our couple of weeks' savings were gone, and so was my job:
we weren't in a lodge. One of us would have to get work.
Laura tried some big stores, but I beat her to employment.
How was as quietly stark weird as any of it: I saw
Joey climb the stairs in big straddles like mounting a horse

over and over, coming up. Love rose in me: my little boy.
I reached down. His mother was coming up right behind him. She smiled.
I reached down and lifted him up in something he always
squirmed out of, from me, a cuddle. I spose I took advantage
of his tiredness. Well he flew up, light in my arms
and let a scream like a whistle splitting the pea.
He hadn't seen me. He had been looking down,
but something in me turned over, and I knew it was considering me.

I peglegged downstairs. Inside me, I walked like a man holding
a hide with the very last of the water on it
or a man with mumps afraid to think one randy thought
for fear it burns him sterile. I ran into Cos in the street.
He seldom came to visit us, I think because Laura made fun of him
for things he said, like When I was on my honeymoon—
Anyway he was with young Oyster Harris, who was done up
like a pox doctor's clerk: *Yeah she caught me. I work in town now.*

What happened you?—Blackfellers cut a canoe out of me.—
Yer not in fighting trim?—I'm savage as a cornered apple.—
We had a few beers. Cos reckoned he'd see me right for work
when I was ready. Somehow we got round to what causes war.
Cos' reason was new to me. It was because men aren't gelded.
Most big animals you see around, the males are cut to calm them
but here's the most dangerous cleverest equipped beast of all
and we're all let go round proud. Stands to reason you get fighting.—

You're a raving ratbag, Oyster Harris said after a while.
I just shuddered, feeling even more considered. If the null
came back, I'd go to sea, and send Laura and Joe their living.
Every night, I'd wake up three or four times
frightened each time I'd find my body gone. Long rubber branches
with just a glow of dim life down the cores.
Like being my own padded cell. Like being inside out.
Entire but not proud, most of us, I heard inside my head.

I bargained with it. If I go and be nice to Sietz,
make peace with Laura's people, write to Shahira—write what?
Laugh, if you haven't wrestled panic. The tram went singing
and banging to Waratah. *Volkmar goes to his work,* said Mama
and of course he isn't here with me! I nearly didn't get coffee.
I was spared the Paraguay *monte,* which I gather is the bush there,
I was spared the Jews (and so were they) or Elizabeth Foerster-Nietzsche
the widow he really worshipped, back in his bloody Fatherland:

She's the one he ought to marry! I flashed at Mama when she told me.
You haven't been lonely or fifty years old in exile
snapped Mama. Then after a big glower by us both:
With your father it wasn't exile, she shyly admitted,
but they killed him. So I said *When will you marry Sietz?—*
Soon.—And go back with him?—Where he goes I must go.—
Not if you don't want! Would you go to Paraguay? I grinned sourly.
If he wanted, yes. But our eyes are on the Fatherland now.

He'd made a proper case of her. I tried to get back to our old talk
full of stories and noticing. *Remember the willy wagtails*
who bumped the house wall picking spiders off it? I asked.
Of course she remembered. *And I told you they lived,*
and perched, and often even flew, with their hands on their hips?
Then we talked of who'd been hard on Mrs Khan for marrying the hawker,
and how the eagle was an innocent, and hadn't heard of Tsars or Kaisers.
I know you always liked that baby-talk, she smiled.

On the tram back, a couple of men in wide flat hats
were looking classic and half-ignoring a miner
who was boosting his union. *I reckon we could bring the country*
to its knees, he cried. *And you'd be with us, eh?*
Yeah well we joined ours, one of the two men said.
Like, no ticket no start.
The miner, as I reckon he must have been by his crib tin,
went on, and they stared out the tram windows, as it jerked.

Musta served in the work-force. They go on like that, one man said
and the miner pulled up short.
After a mile or so, he tried again, and the other man
said *I think he's at least a sergeant in the work-force,*
don't you reckon, Tom? There was more silence, then:
Old Monash is looking for miners, ain't he? For brown coal.
This feller'd be right in his glory, with that brown coal.
The miner stormed off the tram. *Think you're fuckin smart!*

but the two went on looking classical right into town
where a wave of dockworkers coming off shift jerked the windows
and rocked the gleams about.
Men feeling like factory seconds, like less than men, if they hadn't
gone to the war was common still. You saw it everywhere,
a mention of cartridge brass or bully beef would put
a dozen in their place. At home, the smell of pipe tobacco
told me Dulcie Morris was back with us, and Henry.

That night, Laura giggled asking me how we got on
at sea, all men together? I sang a song I'd learned
and she gasped and laughed and commented: *In the rigging?*
The galley table? and *Poor dog!* and *Those wouldn't be delighted squeals*
and *Broken glass? You horror!* She hummed but wouldn't sing the words.
I was cheering up, I was thinking it had stopped considering me
when I had this big bad sudden row with Sietz
over the savages he said we were harbouring, their threat to Joe.

That got us to red faces. Then my primitive father,
the peasant—that brought chairs pushed over on the floor:
then of course to the Jews. *Monash? Pah! A sheeny Menashe—*
Yeah well his people were Prussian, and I love the way
a Prussian Jew from Melbourne thrashed the Prussians!
Bugger him, he'd made me, for the first time ever,
take sides in that war. Bayer, anyway, against Preusser.
Laura wasn't nearly as sorry as I was about it. *Good on you!*

Next morning my arms were gone. No hands, nothing, to the shoulders.
I felt this in the dark. I crept out of bed. You tell no one:
I'd proved that. I went to the kitchen and looked:
my seeming hands and arms, they moved as always and were there—
but I was a trunk too, and helpless without arms or hands.
I cried, I shook. I swayed side to side: hands flapped me:
I hit myself with them: only what they hit felt the pain.
After a long time I looked at my leg. Healed to the knee, scarless,

and a sewn mouth above the knee, itching at every pucker.
I was coming home, to where I hated, to the book I hated
but which educated me. Coming home where was no 'us',
no 'we', no sharing. Or none that wasn't careful where to stop
and so was all stops. I was coming home to my suspicion
that the null had more strength in it, greatly more than I'd get
just by not hurting. That it was the disguise of huge strength.
I touched the world for now with just my head and middle limb,

and that was a frenzy, before it would be gone.
Laura was dazed, dazzled: *Who am I to argue? Holy sailor!*
she sang as she peeled our last potatoes for supper, and hummed
with a little smile over the final tomatoes.
But the woman in the flat under ours came out on their landing
to meet me this day: *Listen we don't want a blacks' camp*
in the house you keep your nigger slut in the bush!
It comes like that, no warning. *O you slimy bitch!*

and that night I woke and wasn't there. Touch blind,
head and trunk and all, again. I crept up and cried
in the galley kitchen again. Then I shut my mouth:
Next day I met Norm Bunt and he put me on
to an auntie of his who'd inherited a removal business.
Lift that wardrobe, she ordered. *God love us! Lift that piano.*
Here, use the sling. You know how, eh? Christ, and you can.
Righto, Sailor, you're on. Take the dray to this address look.

So I went from the foxtrot with Laura to the jazz waltz on stairs
and the slow waltz through doors with partners who mustn't touch wood.
And what did I learn? That's Ronnie Robilliard, his question:
What do we learn from this, customers? Ron was a contortionist.
He'd reach in his pocket with one hand and bring out two,
scratch his ear with his shoe. *What do we learn from this?*
To tell you the unvarnished, since you're a mate of Norm's,
I'm having a layover till a wife and her husband leave our shores—

What do we learn from this furniture-wrestling lark?
Lighter colour, lighter carry, mostly. Poor folk rarely have bookshelves.
Norm has a friend who can't feel. This after just two weeks,
but it's his business. Any friend of Norm's.
He left me bobbing in his wake, regularly. *Er, I, ah, um—*
Just do the impossible and end-for-end that chiffonier,
he'd say after a dazzler, or *click!* he'd say to the dray-horses.
Ron worshipped Norm Bunt. *Any friend of Norm's, anytime!*

At home, I wolfed boiled beef and collie and talked millions,
light-headed as a fowl. Don't ask me why. The condition
took its own slants. Joe watched me carefully
but whatever he hoped for, it was never anything I offered.
I'd tramp up the stairs, he'd watch me all the way up, and
turn away as I reached him. *Gooday, Joe!—Hello*, in a flat voice *Daddy*.
Odd times my mother came, without Sietz, for a visit
and they, she and Joe, would go off speaking Oma's language.

Laura looked at me sideways and got weary on the stairs,
up and down all day. Cos, who came over now and then,
said it was all from sleeping with our feet to the East:
The way the dead man lies. Never get a proper sleep doing that!
Then I tipped it might be a baby. But it wasn't.
I wouldn't mind moving, she said. And some days later:
That you heard from downstairs. That wasn't the first time. Poor Dulcie.
I wanted to storm down. *You could only hit the man*, said Laura.

Those first weeks back in the nothing, I strained, I struggled
hammer and tongs to feel. I burned willpower by the cord,
I recited Sietz' slogan *The World as Will and Exhibition*,
which I think is a book. I swore, I jabbed at my skin.
Nothing. Just the puncture-noise, the blood oozing, the burn-stinks.
We'd be out on the dray, we'd crest a hill, I'd see the ocean
and think Why stay? That's the place, that out there, for freaks,
misfits and cripples. The big blue don't-give-a-bugger.

Ron asked me one day, *How long have you been like it?*
but I snarled him quiet, and went on brooding about
being useless, to Laura, to Joe who smelled a rat in me.
Why not just slip off? Leave a note on the mirror
and hi-ho for the big ports and the orange nights.
I'd be an outer mongrel. Back then, there were no excuses.
There still aren't, in sport, in factories, but then it was absolute.
No excuses. So I'd put the horses' nosebags on

while we loaded people's sticks, and Ron he would cheer up
little kids crying or struck dumb, leaving home.
He'd do a headstand, then a handstand and walk on it, boots up;
he'd look rightways up between his knees, he'd lie flat in the air
stemming up on just one hand. *You could do that one, Fred:
no cramp or strain, for you. What do we learn from this?—
We learn to mind our business*. Then we'd go where they said
and make the new picture of how they wanted their lives.

I wanted mine ordinary. All us, no secret I anywhere.
I could hardly bear myself, or stand to be strong.
On Melbourne Cup day I was in this pub up Lambton
listening to Spearfelt win it, thinking how when I'd first
heard wireless descriptions I thought they were directing
the sport, not reporting it, and this big bloke, king of the bar,
straight after the race and all the cheers and swearing, he
got talking arm wrestles. That's how the king got made there,

and he had forearms the size of fighting sharks
and hands that chewed at you. He wouldn't have noticed
me but for Ron. *They reckon you got a fair wrist on you—
Not me*, I said. *No.—They said yer did.—No mate. Mistake.—
You ain't squibbing it?—*Yes, I had decided to squib it.
I grinned at him kindly, and went over to the table and chairs
that were in the bar, pulled out a chair and sat on it
as I thought. Ron was behind me.

I thought their king of the bar would chip me some more
but he didn't. He turned a bit green and stepped back
and fellows got craning to look where he was looking:
He's squatting He's leaning back though You try it You'd swear he was sitting.
they all talked at once, then *Hey mate how do you keep*
doing that? I didn't drop down that they were talking to me.
What are you sitting on? snapped this authority-voiced fellow:
My arse, I snapped back, and touched it in my irritation

and even then for seconds I didn't wake up that
there was no chair under me. I wasn't squatting, but sitting
perfectly easy on the lock of my hips, knees and ankles,
all sprung angles, like the steel chairs that came out later.
I shot up, like someone caught at his business, whirled on Robilliard
and looked at the chair he'd shifted and let me miss
so I'd sit in mid-air on my muscles. *Bloody bastard!*
I punched the swing doors open, out, spoke to the horses

and never looked back. I was clear of there, and him, for good!
I heard Ron running and jump on.
Get away from me, I said.—*But Fred, I knew you'd do it.*
I'd seen you do nearly as much, sit not on the chair
that was there, but the one you believed was.
You don't belong in donkey-work. Show business is your place
with the rest of us freaks and misfits.—Get away from me!—
I know your secret, Fred. I know what can be made of it.

That night I was hungry, and tore the tucker into me.
Joe whinged and I swore at him, Laura flashed and sulked
and it was all getting very ordinary.
I asked the boss for a different offsider, and got one.
I was so upset that to this day I can't remember
his name, and I worked with him, making furniture into cargo,
lashing it tight till there was no air between it.
I remember he asked what I wore for socks. I said *Sweat.*

A lot still did, then. But he was coming down in the world.
I took to wearing pyjamas so Laura wouldn't see
the bruises I didn't notice getting, but she knew.
She didn't know exactly, or believe the truth I'd told
and taken back. She wouldn't allow herself that.
But whatever she was not allowing and yet still knowing
ate into her. And I didn't admit. I only had the little
that I did still have by never ever admitting.

My mother reckoned I was developing a real
twenty-to-eight expression. The wind blew that way for over
a year, and we nearly lost Joe to whooping cough.
The Welfare got Dulcie's Henry while Cos was outside-fishing
and Dulcie went mad and cut her head about with a chisel
in the scrub, and the flies blew it. She finished up with a sort
of a brown bob all made of scar, with whiskers out of it.
The court said this proved she was primitive. Not a fit mother.

Primitiv was also a word Mama had started using
where she never used to. That summer she chucked the piano job
and married Sietz. *I'm not going to watch*, I said, and didn't.
You should give me away.—You just be glad I don't! I snapped.
Volkmar says—I don't like that Paregorian arserag—
Friedrich!—taking my father's place, and I won't watch it.
I was so mad I told her this last bit in English;
I think that made her face fall worse than all I said. .

We often got storage jobs to do. Deceased estates,
people sailing overseas, all that. This day, and I don't know why,
the boss accepted a foreclosure job, where we had to
go with the police to take away some people's effects.
I jibbed at it, hard. But it was go or take the sack,
straight away, or a few weeks after the union ban.
The bulls joined us at the place, this little yellow slum house
up Tighe's Hill with cardboard and dead towels in the windows.

The place stank. Little things ran ahead as you walked in.
The bloke looked just like the prisoner in the Military Police van
I went back to Cairo in. Face whiskery like mould on a loaf.
The women were milling round all talking at once and crying
but one, maybe the wife, was different. Still-faced,
breathing, in the half-dark there. *You'd help the coppers then*
against a working family? Who'll help when they come for you?—
No one, I said. *Sorry, missus.*

Start with the table here, I said to Sweat-for-socks.
The woman grabbed it, and the copper elbowed me aside:
Release the table, missus! She was a strong big woman
and didn't budge. They started to pull her, the pair of them.
Quick, help us, snapped one. *Bugger that*, I told him.
I order you to help us!—Against one woman? Not me.
Her fingers were clamped on that crusty pine table like as if
it was worth something. Like it was her limit.

Then one of the coppers, ginger-faced, with big pus pimples,
hit her fingers with his stick. Bang! They went straight,
she went white, she screamed a terrible scream
no one could forget, with her teeth and dark gums all showing,
and I hit the copper, square in the face, so full-on
that he bammed arse-first out the door like the breech of a cannon
and the husband came alive in the same second, flew at the other
copper *Wooargh!* and bit his face *narrgh!* with spittle everywhere.

I had to knock the man out to unfasten him. *Hot water!*
I said to the others: *bathe this face!* My one was out to it,
breathing, with his boots still in their kitchen. The hubbub
of other women and little kids would jam your brains. I told
the offsider to drive straight back to the depot, and I left,
walking fast, caught a tram at Throsby's Creek bridge,
packed a bag at home, explaining—and Laura looked like death.
You're just so delighted to be leaving us, aren't you, sailor?

Thump. Right in the guts. *They'll be here for me in an hour,*
I said. *I'm off back up the Myall first. I'll send for you.*
She didn't believe it and clung to it. *You'll send for us.*
Did I get ugly, this last twelve months, Fred? Did I?
I held her and hoped I was warm. *I'll go to Cos.* She flashed:
That old bugger, renting live women to be ghosts.
Yes, go to Cos! You make a good queer pair!
But then I nearly dropped. Joe said *Come back soon, Daddy.*

I walked to Stockton ferry, but there was a policeman on board;
hardly likely after me, but I sheered off, and walked towards the steelworks.
That's how I met Ron again, and sent my life spinning for years.
There's no more Freddy Bo'sher! Freddy Bo'sher's for the clink now!
he yabbered on, as the horses switched and stamped.
I'll take you to old Lule Golightly.—Tonight? I asked.—*No, now.*
He sent his offsider to deliver their load and get his wages
and we walked off together. *Choice, eh, Fred? Just to drop work cold!*

But I was seeing police everywhere, in their officer hats,
not like the Bobbies' helmets before the war. Now coppers
were Officer. They liked that. It got you more than Constable.
There were ones in leggings and leather officer caps
chauffeuring motor cars, there were similar on motor bikes
and walking ones in hot choker coats. But we weren't stopped.
Ron knew of my doings and fancy dress dodges in the East
and was thinking me up stage names: Bismarck? The Dungog Uhlan?

We came to a weatherboard house on a big block of scrub
just as a tall woman slung cold tea out off the verandah
like cracking a long gold whip. *Gooday Lula!—Gooday young Ron!—*
How are you?—Ar, just. I sleep in little squares
like pissy milk chocolate. Once, I'd snore off the whole black block.
Don't stand there on one leg like a chook that's cold. Come in!
(Ron did Charles Atlas exercises against himself). *Who's your friend?*
We were introduced. She said *Ar.*

The house was small-eyed, against heat, and the tread of Lula
rocked crowds of glazed photos on every wall. *Johnny Wirth,*
she said, as if introducing me. *Miltie Hayes: The Whitest Man I Knew:*
you know that song? Hughie McIntosh that built the Stadium:
you know, for the Burns-Johnson fight. See that yellow streak, Tommy?
Hit that yellow streak. I was there. There's Mo and Sadie with Nat.—
Stiffy? I asked.—*You'd know him as Stiffy. Here's Abo Con Colleano,*
first man in the world to do the forwards purler.—

Eh?—The forward somersault on the tightrope. You lose sight of the wire.
With the backflip you don't, so that's easy. Here's le Petomane,
he could fart the Marseillaise, or anything. Here's our Gladys.
All my dear showies. She left me among the signed acts
and the faces that were acts too. Was this to be my dart?
I wished I could look forward to it. I sat around some more
like ordered but not collected, as Germans say, till Ron
gave me the office, through the door, to follow him.

You want to be an artiste, eh? said Lula Golightly from her cane chair
on the cool back verandah. *I'm prepared to try it,* I said.
You haven't dreamt of it day and night, though? Burned for it?—
No, I admitted. *Ar,* she answered. *What's your talent?*
Didn't Ron say?—I'm asking you.—Oh, well, I can lift stuff.
Heavy stuff.—How heavy?—I lifted a motor car.—
Mm. You'd be better off busking. Betting in the pubs. There's no act much
in heaving weights about. The crowd think they're hollow anyway,

if you bring your own. You've got just one weight they trust.—
Which? I asked.—*Yourself. Your big sailor carcass. Will that lift?*
There was this short rope hanging off a bolt in the transom
of the verandah. *This firm?* I asked, and drew myself up one-handed.
Hung. She watched. *Slow, for an act,* she said. *Do something.*
I lifted myself, chin to fist. *More. Think now. They've stopped gasping.*
I put my chin over the transom, tried it, hung by it no hands.
What'd I tell you? cried Ron. *Shut up, Ronnie,* she said.

Thirty seconds, thirty-five. You need some more action now.
I folded my arms. *Right,* she said. I put my hands in my pockets.
Right, she said. I reached up, gripped, unhooked my head
which was swimming fit to burst, and swung up to hang by my feet.
Come on down, said Lule. *You don't need trapeze. It'd be
a letdown.—How he sat in the pub on a chair he only believed was there*
babbled Ron.—*Too subtle; you and I know that's rum, the crowd don't.
He can't hang in the air on a bar he only thinks is there. Can he?*

What do we learn from all this? Well, I got a job,
thirty bob a week and keep as a rouseabout and learner
in their tent show. I'd have to send it all to Laura
and it wasn't enough then. I'd have to buy us a caravan
but: how to get the money? We'd be on the road in a month,
north to Queensland, by way of New England and Toowoomba.
I wrote and explained, and explained. Also, I thanked Ron,
and he shook two right hands above his head like a boxer.

The word for what I needed was *routines.*
Lule told me dozens: they helped me think up my own.
We had one, the Jack of Suits: I'd hang by one foot in a loop
in singlet and working trousers: I'd unroll serge pants from my belt
downwards, my head up, between the shoes. I'd button a huge white shirt
over my ankles, tie its tie, put on its coat and weskit
and there we'd be, a giant gent and a working man,
one up, one down, and revolving slowly round.

Another, I'd hang by one hand from the swing
and draw my knees up and sit like on a chair
there in space, and drink tea, and write imaginary postcards.
Later, both would get real. And I'd change hands drinking or writing
which is impossible. At first, though, after much of this, my arms
wouldn't lift, and I'd spasm all over like a fool
and my hands would cramp to hooks like the Bugg girl's poor shot hand.
Even a miracle man needs to exercise his miracles, grinned Lula.

She'd done it all, Lule Golightly: read the cards, beat the drum,
danced, sung, been sawn in halves by Les Levante,
outlined in knife-punctures by a Russian drinker. Elephants,
unicycles. She loved to wheel the piano out
and gather people into a singsong. I'd sneak outside
where beautiful beautiful brown eyes didn't thrash
your ears like hailstones, and Clancy's boom stayed up.
Better tunes, she'd say next day, *than I get from the Jewish pianola!*

I gather that's a cash register, or was before people got ashamed.
As the time came closer for off, she made me learn to drive
and gave me a working name: *How about Freddy Neptune?*
You work below the line. The company were assembling
most of them family. It was like a ship gathering its crew
a few days before sailing. Except most of these were married couples
or anyway paired up, men and women.
Who was exactly who would distil out as we went, I reckoned.

Laura and Joey were in two rooms up Mayfield now
but we didn't meet there, for fear of police. We had picnics
in the bush. Even that stopped when the Great Golightly Family
got on the road, after layoff. I'd supervise the local fellows
who put up the tent, in each place. Rig the king-pole, set out seats
and the wire-walkers would rig their own trapeze, and Doddum
the big-jawed dwarf would waddle out with his ladders. Lionel Dodham,
he was the clown; there were him, and Ron, and Mandore the magician

and Betty Crowe who was Zazie the Highwire Queen
and belonged to Mandore; all the rest were Golightlys.
I was general hand, and worked on my routines and tried them.
Jack of Suits laid an egg, chinning the wire and clowning there
went all right, but chinning a noose horrified the audiences
and Lula dropped it. *Too many up here with ancestors*,
she reckoned. Walking upside down from the wire
by hooking my feet over it was all right but wanted something.

Mandore honked down his nose that I ought to do it
in Digger uniform, but Lula said that'd get me killed.
I never got stage fright. Ron taught me never to look
at an audience. Not clearly. Keep them just out of focus and they
will tell you everything, if you don't try to listen.
That's all Irish, he admitted.
We were playing cards in Bendemeer, that had nearly been
made federal capital once, then wasn't, and went back to sleep,

and Mandore pointed his big boiled-meat nose at me
and said *Your wife's not with you. Are you parted?*—
No. Or just for now, like, I said, thinking nothing.
Men who leave their wives can't satisfy them generally, he said.
Bang. You don't expect it. I opened my mouth three times
and closed it four. Ron joked *You'd better be careful
of Fred. He's so strong, he could do a Risley with a horse.*
Which, when I cooled down, gave me the idea for my finale:

Doddum would lead a horse on, I'd ungirth the saddle,
put it over my shoulders and carry the horse off. Bodily,
as Leila Golightly said. It used to slay the crowds:
they still knew the weight of horseflesh.
But I wasn't ever, much as I hate to admit it,
in the same paddock with Mandore. He called me a displaced Rube.
I know it's all sleight of hand, but some of his act, you'd swear
it had to be real magic. He'd performed for kings and such like,

Lule told me. *What a comedown to us, eh?*
I couldn't see that. Any audience is people, I reckoned.
He got this loathsome disease, she told me,
and it drove him out of Europe. Maybe. It looked like bottle poisoning
to this sailor. But then I'm prejudiced. He hated me,
I slowly realised. *Has your wife got children, Freddy?*
It was always sex. Or as Doddum said *Which sex?*
The lying one? Or the complaining one?

Both were over his head, Dod reckoned. He'd cold-cream his makeup off,
put on a civvy suit and sit drinking in the pub
of whatever little town it was till he fell down in a lump.
He didn't talk much, with it. That on sex was his longest speech,
spoken with such a longing disgusted look
you had to glance at your boots, as if you had made the rules.
Mandore's look agreed with that. And he'd see them kept.
Betty Crowe just wriggled, as if in a bath with herself.

Cos sent me on a letter from Sam. They had three daughters now
*and I'm finally a qualified chef de cuisine, which is
the platinum grade of slushy. I cook at the Pyramide in Paris.
Loads of bigwigs stay here.* He named a few, and one of them
was my father's cousin Hjalmar Schacht, who Mama
used to skite about. *Come and let me feed you.* And then:
*I do get homesick, and wish I had the right face
to show in Gympie.* He told me what that name meant, gympie.

To stretch my earnings, I used to slip off to the pubs
and back myself doing strong stuff. In Quirindi,
jolting, I stopped a truck with a chain; in Tamworth I lifted
two men and a girl, all perched like fowls along a board
and in Glen Innes a Vauxhall car was driven over me
on two planks. I spat blood for a week.
Tenterfield was a frost: I dropped an anvil and cracked it
and had to pay up three quarters of my winnings for it.

Lule warned me it'd be the sack if I overdid
the private stuff. *More routines, we want from you:*
broader, broader. You're too artistic. You depress the customers.—
They laugh, I said.—*Yeah but it's a worried laugh.*
Ron and I got to work with some souvenired steel pipe
and made two circles of it, with four struts joining them up.
I'd roll this on, telling the one about the swaggie sleeping
in a water tank that got blown away in a storm:

by this stage I'd be inside with my head braced on one rim
and my feet on the other, grabbing my imaginary blankets,
singing out as I rolled the thing over, sticking to the wall
that wasn't there, fighting off pretend stuff that was hitting me.
Then I'd stand the thing on end and be cocky in his cage, and a bat.
One day, rehearsing, I was braced upside down and Mandore, passing,
reached in and did something, and I crashed to the ground.
I bounced up and grabbed him, and I boxed his ears hard.

You witless impotent trash! he raved at me.
Impotent? No. I was just my own rubber, with a hole.
And who wanted that? Compared with what a man longs for?
Mandore, I had him frightened for some reason. He sniffed
something rum about me, but couldn't get it right.
Did you see what he did? I asked Ron.—*He knocked above your knee*
and the reflex spilt you. I had to ask about that reflex,
I'd never heard of them. And of course I hadn't felt it.

All the Golightlys stood round with their cigarettes pointing at us.
Even strange Leila, that I once saw pee standing like a man.
Later that day, I got round Lula for a layoff
and went home on the night train. I woke where a sign said Dungog
and spat, there in the moonlight, and felt a bit of a fool.
In Mayfield I convinced Laura her two rooms weren't that much
bigger than a van, and I had the money, from my pub bets
(Jesus no man can lift that!) to get us one. And she finally

agreed to try the road life. No more pearling wedding dresses
and waiting for postal notes. *No more lonely bed,*
she said above my head. *And, well, I've got over that other.*
You poor man. I don't at all mind. Threading the needle. You know.
So: we went back up on the train together with Joe
and in Warwick I bought this Panhard van all timbered over
except the cab: that was high and mainly open, with its steering wheel
on a long shaft, and big black levers and a bulb,

and it had a hopping, wheel-straddling gait on the dirt
wheeltracks we used to call roads in those times.
I'm trying to remember what Laura said after Thread-the-needle:
I do believe you. See: I talk to you like a man
so you'll understand me. If you weren't hurt, I wouldn't.—
It's thirteen years, I said, with three off for no behaviour.
That leaves ten years I've been in this celluloid dummy.
How I earned him, God knows. It's like as if I dream him, and dream him.

I used to pair with Ron Robilliard on stage,
roll him on as a big coloured ball that I'd toss up and catch
before it unravelled out into a small man
and then we'd upstage one another, turn about:
he'd be standing on one hand: I'd pick him up by the belt
and put him aside on a tub, still standing on that hand,
or I'd be gripping an upright, flying like a flag
and he'd block the wind, and I'd stop flapping and sag down.

If the audience were with us, we'd do it all in mime.
If they didn't laugh, Ron could do patter: I couldn't
for the life of me. I'd dry every time.
It worries you that you don't understand what you're doing,
Ron explained. *You die of wanting to apologise.*
Whereas I know being silly's what we're here for.
So shut up and be sillier. Ladeez and gentlemen, my mate
is really a public bar. I say 'police sergeant' and he shouts!—Hoy!

Round then, in Toowoomba, I'd just made some nice side money
heaving ironmongery, and Laura and Joey and I
were passing a bank, and two men in suits rushed up to us,
touched their boaters to Laura, pumped my hand. *He's a marvel*
Missus! We saw him Gawd lift? You knock that Atlas bloke for six, Fred!
They were having a joke on a mate. *Would you be a sport, Fred?*
Lift the rear end of his car up? Ease that block in under the diff?
We were gonna jack her. But you're a jack in a million, Fred!

I should have been ware of fellows who repeated my name so much.
Laura was icy, and asked them. *He'll jump in his car and rev*
and go nowhere, Missus. Thanks for the lend of your man.
This'll be a big laugh! They bustled us on, away, and Laura
was furious. *You aren't usually a complete fool:*
they buttered you up and rushed you. You only had to cry halt.
I tried; they talked all over me. You were mesmerised by their flap.
She begged me to go back and pull the block from under that car,

but I was ashamed, and stubborn because of it. I wouldn't,
and it cost lives. Be a sport: be a man: death's prize bunny-traps.
We didn't hear till later what happened. How the holdup men
ran out of the bank to drive off, couldn't, and the manager
ran out with his rusty Colt: *Hoy! Stop!* and they shot him
BOOM! with the engine howling, and the charge nearly chopped him in two
across the belly, the police yelling *Stand away!* fired running,
hit the one robber, a horse, the bank door, the other squealing *Not me!*

That's how we heard it from a woman who'd been there.
Every hour, we expected the police to turn up, at the show camp.
After the strong man. Every hour, then every day,
but they kept on not appearing. Had no one seen me lift that car?
Had no one noticed? It was a common joke, with the light
flivvers of those times. Peashooters, tailor-made smokes
and practical jokes, and every boof head with a hat on it,
but I'd caused two deaths.

That was new. I wasn't any more who I'd been,
no more harmless Fred who didn't deserve his punishment.
I stood offstage watching Mandore boil a man's fob watch
in another man's Borsalino, then send back both unharmed,
and didn't even bridle when he stalked off past me, whispering
Go on and do your filler. I must have improved, though. The crowd
yelled for more. A big curly man came up after, saying
You're the first that's made me laugh since the war, anyway.

I hadn't wanted to see Dad's grave, not there in Dungog.
In fact I found out later it wasn't at Dungog.
But this night I dreamt of doors laid on the ground
as if a door-making firm had laid out all its stock
just right on the grass, paddocks and countrysides of doors,
and I was told *These are the night addresses.* Each door had
an ordinary address, the house number or farm name,
painted on it. I found ours: Jabang, Clarencetown Road.

I understood this wasn't just brother Frank's home, or Dad's,
but all of ours. I opened our door and went in:
not down, but along a hall. I was on a balcony then
over miles-deep cuttings and teetering cliff roads
round the cheek of the world, or something as curved and high
but space wasn't stars, it was gravel, and tailings, and scarps,
and the millions of the dead were building this and digging it down
in a roar of dust, in enormous brown evening, pouring stones,

steep gangways, rotting lights. I was there to keep the dead working.
I came awake, shouting out, Laura told me,
and she held me, there in the black away from towns.
We were going well, in the van. It was good to be rescued
from day-old bread and the baker's sneer, and the post-office,
so she reckoned. Arthur Dodham, who was too short to drive,
often rode with us, in a legless chair slung above the galley.
More peaceful, he said, than the excitable Golightlys.

I never found out what Mandore had against me. Laura
simply said he was a bitch of a man.
He beat me, though. I still flinch, having to tell it.
It started when I backed into a fellow's bee-boxes
and knew it only when a whizzing fog gathered round me.
Luckily, Joe and Laura were inside the van. I screamed to them
to stay put, to secure every window and hole
and I jumped to block a grille that had no cover.

Well, the stings didn't hurt, but I blew up like the Michelin man.
My heart lurched; I breathed hard, and damn nearly drowned
and afterwards, when everyone was joking and sorry, he,
my friend the magician, only sniggered about my Achilles
heel or tendon or something like, and his laugh wasn't friendly.
All right, squire, I thought. You'll bloody keep, my long cocky.
And when we were playing Beerburrum, in the Glasshouse Mountains,
I saw a stinging tree. And picked a leaf. They're fire:

don't ever do it. I cursed myself, that I did it.
I came where they were playing cards, next to the trapeze mechanic
that Tom Golightly and Beryl used to practise on.
I was vamping on the leaf, making out I could play tunes on it,
and Mandore bit. Mentioned how skill was more reliable,
civilised and even human than simply being a freak.
Then he took the gympie leaf, pinched it between his thumbs,
blew half a note, before agony lashed through him:

blaze on his forehead, seared nose, red flash across his lips,
wringing and pocketing his hands, he howled phlegm and curses at me,
tried to scoop up stones to throw at me.
Everyone, Ron too, rounded on me for a cruel unnatural
Hun bastard, except Doddum left 'Hun' out. And 'unnatural', when I think on it.
I was for the sack. Lule just paid me and said *Out!*
I've done some low acts and bastardries. You remember them
with a better class of shame, though, when they come off right,

and that leaf bit clean through to whatever Mandore's real name was.
The Golightly women looked at Laura with sympathy and scorn
as we turned the van out of the showground, driving away.
South? I asked.—*Might as well.*
Will you go back to sea now?—
Nono. There's other jobs, and I'm handy. We can keep moving.—
Laura smiled and looked down. *Well it's another way*
of going to sea. But nicer. You're taking us with you!

and she kissed me. I dropped down then, slow bugger,
that she lived in fear of my leaving them. I'd lost my vanity
when pleasure went from me; I'd got back into not thinking
my being around mattered, to anyone. Joey helped there,
behaving as if his dad was really dead Joss Cope.
Now I'm whingeing. One result was, I never boxed his ears
or took a stick to him. Never felt I quite had a right to.
Clever Joe. And he was clever. On that trip, the air

was full of Kingsford Smith, him flying the Pacific,
him flying to Maoriland, and back. We happened to arrive
in Brisbane by way of Archerfield, the aerodrome.
Two bowsers and a paddock were about all we saw there, and some slow
coffee-grinder of a biplane exercising up above. We stopped
because Joe was wild to see where Smithy had touched down
and we got hot water from a woman in a house down the way.
Like one sea of hats, she said, *last winter when they landed*

in from America. All tipped up, faces showing like bottled peaches
as they circled, and closed jars again when they were down.
No: me go? I hate crowds. Only the crew had faces
looking from here. Them, and the bigwigs welcoming them.
She smoked and yarned with us. *Me? I read the tarot cards, love.*
I do people's futures. That way I can work at home.
Do you know this road, she asked later, *in to town*
was built by women? A road gang of all female convicts?

Hard old days. I know it was a good road.
I was speeding on it, and Laura asked where Joe was.
In the back?—*He isn't now.*—*Oh Jesus!* I slewed, braking,
firing gravel. He screamed, dropped in front of me: only
saved himself by grabbing a roof-strut. He'd been flying
on the roof, lying up, or kneeling, with his arms out.
This was in Breakfast Creek. We were still shaking
as we motored on in, past the sign saying Fortitude Valley.

I did no more hoisting for bets, in case the police were looking
for that strong car-lifter. It could wait till we crossed the border.
We ran out of cash short of that, in sandy country like the Myall,
a place called Elston. A couple were friendly enough
to take me on building their beach-house, and they fed us,
mostly on muttonbird: seagull boiled in hair-oil
is being kind to it. Ungrateful too: some like it,
and they tanned with the oil. It had darkened them like old furniture.

I did a good job for the Colemans, while they sold that oil
to the surfers down the beach. At night I'd have a long-sleever
in the Surfers Paradise, Jim Cavill's pub up the road.
Laura would drink shandies. It was fair contentment, quite good,
what we had then. Not big joy or passion:
I don't mean only love-passion, that I could give but not get.
I understood if I lobbed on some passion I could enjoy
it might become Laura's enemy. But she wouldn't hold me from it,

and that's love. I couldn't do that. I couldn't love.
My idea of love was like landmarks staying in place,
people being like places. That you checked, stayed a while with, drew on
without needing to ask anything. All settled before you started.
I was mulling this over, and the boy was making bubbles with a straw
in his sarsparilla so he wouldn't have to drink it,
when *Freddy Neptune*, said a voice behind me. *The Strongman!*
Two men in linen suits and rings and brilliantine

were grinning at us. *That's not my name*, I said.
*Not Freddy Neptune? That had the joke with the car
up in Toowoomba? How about Fred Boaticher then?
Is he the same fulla?—Who wants to know*, I said.
*Well, there's the rozzers. But we ain't them. We're ahead of them, eh?
and we're nicer to deal with.—What are you dealing in?—
Messages, mostly. For our boss. He wants to see you.—
Here?—No mate: Brissy.—What if I don't want to go?—*

Well then the rozzers'll catch up with you quick, eh?
They stood there, not expecting to be offered chairs, while I thought,
then Laura said *Wherever my husband goes,
whoever he sees, the boy and I will go with him.—
No need, Missus. No need. He'll be safe as a bank with us!—
Are banks safe with you?* she asked in this freezing voice.
*Missus, you've took us wrong. We're practically public servants.
Our boss is a Minister. Not of the Gospel, like: the Crown.*

I was surprised. We were let drive ourselves back to Brisbane
in the van. We camped in it, out at Mount Gravatt
then we were driven to a house like a station homestead
above the city. Women in tennis clothes met us, smiling,
and turned Laura with footwork, and stock-drafted her away
hesitating, till I nodded: I wouldn't get shot outright here,
the layout seemed to promise. Flower trellises, tennis, a peacock.
Then the man who showed me in said the boss was Queensland's head sniper,

whatever that meant. It didn't greatly soothe me. Sir Peter
had rosy polished skin and wore a suit as good
as my Cairo ones. A fine gold chain snibbed his waistcoat.
He didn't waste manners by answering my nervous *Good day,*
but nodded to a big detective-looking fellow
overdressed in cheaper stuff. *You're Boettcher?* asks this fellow.
*Can you describe the men who asked you to lift that car
in Toowoomba?—You pronounced my name right!—*

I marvelled at him. *I'm from Marburg,* he said, pronouncing that right.
*But: those men in Toowoomba?—Die Kraftwagenhebejuxveranstalter
von Toowoomba?—Don't imagine you can play with us, Boettcher.
People died of that car-lifting joke, as you so cleverly call it.*
I knew: the picture of that banker chopped in halves
with the shotgun had been haunting me. The awful mince-edged damage
inside the sopping clothes. Death, when you'd only expected dinnertime.
The high rump of that car, roof sloped forrard like a Pommy cloth cap.

*I didn't really study them.—That's a pity. You'll have the opportunity
when you're tried with them. Accessory before the fact of murder.*
I panicked and must have looked pale. Not such a joke, eh?
But then I thought, why bring me to this bigwig's house,
the first authentic Australian bigwig I'd ever seen,
but it seemed we had them, just to arrest me. No,
there's more coming, I realised. There's trade here, I'll be bound.
Will I go to jail?—Of course. The question is, for how long?—

*But weren't they police? I mean, they ruined that bank
robbery,* I said, not *job.* The big policeman looked furious
and growled *If you're tried without them you'll take their punishment!
You need them caught! Now, describe them, brother!—*
I didn't study them. They didn't give me time.
I looked at Sir Peter. He was watching me, and had been.
So they weren't police? I said. Sir Peter waved the detective shut.
Thank you, Chief Inspector. D'you mind if I call you Fred? to me.

I didn't mind, nor trust it. *Fact is, the blokes who worked that slanter*
on you aren't our main business. Though if you did a smice
from here, they'd think you'd spilled your guts to us. And then
you'd need to look behind you, a lot. They're in with very tough mutton.
It was weird, to hear that swell talk like a two-bob villain
in his expensive accent. *How would they know I'd been here?*
He smiled, and answered *They'd have been sent to jack up that car;*
you came along: they went the bounce on you. Forties hate common labour.

I could see it amused him to play the common crook
in front of his police. I knew not to try and hurry him.
They say you're very strong, Fred. He opened the French windows
and showed me out onto a porch. *Can you bend this crowbar?*
It was good steel, but I felt showing off might help me.
I had to wrestle, and use my foot, but I tied it
in a knot. A loose open bowline, but it stumped them;
after a while, Sir Peter said *I've got this associate*

living in America. He's mad on freaks and strongmen.
I want him to come home, but he won't, and he owes me money.
Will you fetch him for me?—He'd stopped the thieves' talk now,
realising I wasn't one. *It might be possible then,*
if you did, for you to live in Australia again.
That hit home to me. He let it, and then explained some more.
This man was holding money, a lot of money, for me
and some businessmen. (No, Chief Inspector, Fred needs

a complete briefing.) He decamped, took off with that money,
bought a mansion in Kentucky, had it declared an asylum
then got himself certified, as its one inmate. So he couldn't
be extradited. A lunatic can't be. The law's curious.—
I cut in and asked *Aren't there men you could get in America*
to haul him out for you?—*Ah, Fred, you do have a criminal mind!*
But no. If he came back alive then at all
it'd be without our money. It has to be from here.

As I said: best of all natural human miracles
he loves strongmen. He even has some, as nurses.—
I cut in again. *Even if I got him away from them,*
and all the way home, your money wouldn't be, like, on him!
Do you just want revenge?—*If I get him, the money will follow,*
Fred, never doubt it. And some of it will be yours.
I thought, and shook my head. *I won't want that money*, I said.
Just my fare'll do.—*We envisaged you working your passage.*

Less conspicuous. You are a sailor. We'll pay expenses and a fee,
if you'll accept those, but strictly on results, afterward.—
What'll my family live on?—They will live, Fred. Be content.
How would they live if you died for fizzing to us?
Or if you were doing a kathy in jail? He grinned
and sang '*Kathleen mavourneen, it may be for years*
and it may be for ever.' Tell us your decision, Freddy.
Dear God, I'd been right to hide my cursèd gift. I should never

have rescued anyone, or let anyone bet on me. I should
never have survived my first bashing, by the Provosts.
It wasn't worth asking whether the Chief Inspector or Sir Peter
could call on the Toowoomba jokers, or call them off,
nor who the bank robbers had belonged to. *What's your man's name*
over there in America? I asked, with my shoulders drooping.
O wise move, Freddy. Stout man! You'll get all the details,
not in writing, of course. Are you good at memorising? Excellent!—

It's a big country.—I don't care how far we go.—Me neither.
We drove the van south-west, camped the night in Cunningham's Gap
and I was tormented with dreams, worst I'd had in many years.
I was on this good road, with Laura and Joe. We were walking
and we met a gang of women road workers, with picks and shovels.
They wanted to dance; they spun and grabbed at our clothes.
Theirs were blackened, their skins were like crackling. They were
the Trabzon women. Joe and Laura were gone then, and the road

was away out at sea. The women splashed its edges, to cool it.
I woke up yelling out, and had to drink some milk we had,
then no sooner I dropped off, I was deep inside the world again
in that enormous place of work and ladders. I had a corn-bag
of coloured paper money. I was handing it out, marks and roubles
and Argentine pesos, every currency I'd ever handled
but in funny amounts: six-peso notes, fourteen-rouble ones
with animal heads on them. The dead people hated that money,

but I had to make them work. The whole space was creaking and groaning.
This time when I woke, I had to go outside and stop shaking.
Bad words were in my head, still from the dream: he's dying
of peace and contentment. I felt quite sick and faint
and stared at the stars up above the scarp of the mountain:
the milk-way, the big kite of the Southern Cross, and his two wives
as old Ridgeway had taught me, in his story. At last I slept some more.
When we came out next morning, there were the two Toowoomba jokers

in cardigans. It was April and chilly. One had an axe in his hand:
Fred, Missus, I'm sorry, but I'll have to chop your tyres now.
The other man was doing pistol-shaped hand exercises.
Fred, you know that ships go from Brisbane, not inland.
I measured my distance looking down, jumped, and disarmed him
of the axe, and sprawled him under their Franklin tourer.
Then I heard a report, like a bass string twanged all through me
and there was a bolt-sized hole halfway up my thigh,

but then there was a shriek and scrambling. Laura'd jumped the gunman
and had him down among the steering wheel and levers
with her nails in his face and eyes, growling and screaming,
her growling, him screaming. I opened the far side door,
drew him out and punched him quiet. We found his gun and hoyed it
into the brush. The axeman scrambled up and ran
west down the Gap. I let their car's brakes off and it chased him
and made him Whee! Whee! like a pig till it veered away and crashed.

I was getting faint and wobbly. We had some cotton wool
and plugged the wound. We drove on down to Warwick.
Laura was a new hand at driving, but going well, and Joe
was right out of his shell, making a moving-picture out of
all that had happened. *Then Mum got him down grrarrgh!*
Laura didn't appreciate being cast as the guard dog, but Joe
had to deal with it, she knew. *Now Mum is driving rirr-rirr.*
The doctor in Warwick tweezed the bullet out, click! *My word,*

you're a stoic, Mr Beecher! We were just finishing
our dinner when a police trooper stamped into the pub dining-room:
Frederick Adolph Boocher? I arrest you on charges of being
an accessory to the murder of Walter Henry Colefax—
That sure stopped the spoons in their trifle and apple cobbler.
Soon I was back in Brisbane. Jail food wasn't half as tasty.
They let me sit and cool, to get me frightened, and then
the same men who drove us to see Sir Peter collected me.

As we clanged out through the doors, a little black shearer, Alf
Ferrier, that I'd yarned to, asked *Where are you off, Fred?—*
America, I think, Alf.—I'll see you on the pictures then.
Well he was right, as it turned out. He was the one
who told me he liked jail: it was better than how his people lived,
in the camps, and had a lot more privacy.
They drove me to the docks, and took me to a café
to say goodbye to Laura and Joe. First thing Laura did

was check my bullethole. It had healed already.
Only a week, she whispered, and looked almost afraid.
You know it's not my choice, I said, *this going to America.*
I'll be about three months. She nodded, not believing it.
You're his hero, she whispered, nodding at Joe. *Did you know?*
We said our goodbyes, arranged about letters and money, then:
Let him start on his adventure, Missus. He's had enough Daily Telegraph,
and I was escorted to the ship I'd been signed on.

BOOK 3

Prop Sabres

At Auckland, and all the way to Suva
I thought of jumping ship and sending for Laura
and Joe to join me. But how would they have liked
to live away from their home country forever?
And I was wild that government and like criminals
could run me out of where I'd settled back to living.
I was going to beat that.
After a bit, too, I enjoyed the deepsea work again.

We had a decent crossing. Storms in the Tasman, then calm
right to Hawaii. Off Diamond Head, waiting to sail in,
we sighted this swollen skyscraper lying down in the sky,
shining like foil, getting huge, coming on over us.
The crew ran to look. It had engine-houses out on sponsons.
Diesels beating away. It had the Yankee red spot
on a white star, and sailors in gob caps waved to us
from the bridgework underneath. *That's the Los Angeles,*

our skipper said. *Like a windjammer with its sails inside it.*
They have these gas bags, and men inside rigging them.—
Is the hull made of tin? I asked. *No. Sailcloth, metal-painted*
over an aluminium frame. A German idea they are. Zeppelins.
So this was an airship, like flew to East Africa. I'd heard of them,
and I stared after this one a long time as it shrank
among the landward cloudbanks. I imagined men belaying down
on lines like spiders in great skeleton rooms.

Liners upside down. Did they make the gas they rode on?
The skipper explained it all, laughed, said I should sign on one
and never knew he was a prophet.
The other thing I remember from that angry trip
was Sengupta the ship's carpenter, a Fiji Indian,
gassing about what he called the Wheel of Karma.
You rolled it, and it always rolled back round on you.
I thought: Why on you? Mightn't the others it mashed clog it?

And couldn't another person's push send it down on you?
It'd have to be a highly spiritual, different wheel
always to squash the right pusher.
Still, Senny was honest, with his coconut hair oil
and his elephant holy medal, eating just vegies and milk.
He taught me to slap a chapatti hand-to-hand
till it was thin as paper, and cook it over shavings.
He never let his tiffin tins near the galley.

We sailed on to Dago, then through the Panama
to New Orleans, where the black people laugh and agree with you
if you're white. Senny moved straight in among them
and invited me, but they tangled me up in offers
of good times and women, and fenced me out *Ohh yassuh!*
to everything I said. I wandered off down those streets
of knotty iron lace, like the Australian slums,
and couldn't find a drink, and remembered about Prohibition,

but it didn't matter. I had business to do and go home.
I went up the big river, working on tugs and barge tows
and the fellows taught me how to spot a speakeasy
or a honky tonk and get let in, when we tied up in the towns.
I'd never been deep inside America before.
It was like our east coast country, but with darker light.
It went on and on being fertile, with rivers and lagoons
coming into the main stream, and palms, and vines on trees.

Coppers dressed like workingmen or pilots. Hotels were called a House.
They had separate cafés for white and Coloured people,
as they sometimes called them. I left the boats and took a train
for Versayles Kentucky, as the dead-looking trees put on leaves,
then rode with a mailman past black and white horse fences
and farms with big red sheds, till we came to the mansion
called Saint John. *This here's the main gate. You won't get in.*
That's a crazy house, and you don't look like a crazy.

A bell said Ring, and rang. Big stiff black dogs came bouncing
and barking inside the wriggly iron gates there.
A man like a butcher's block came waddling side to side
like as if from sore privates. *Yes?* he asked.
I'm to see a Mr Thoroblood, I told him. He stared out.
Git, he said. *This is a prite clinic.—I heard*
he wanted strong men for an act, I said.
No Strains, said the block man, and *GNARR!* to the dogs, who cringed.

I waited, he smouldered. *I told ya, no one from Stray*,
he finally said. I noticed how the gates were swung
on their hinges: they'd lift off. *I'm pretty strong*, I told him,
so you take me to your boss or I'll go on in anyway.
Cunt on you! he screamed, and started jerking door bolts,
so I lifted off one gate—it was a job to balance—
and when he charged me, I tippled it towards him.
He caught it, strained to hold it, and couldn't tip it back

and the dogs sat when I said *GNARR!* to them. A madhouse,
as the mailman and Sir Peter had both said. Next man I met
in the huge starry garden, had a pitchfork. *You Mr Thoroblood?*
I asked, tipping he wasn't. Another muscle man in an undershirt
he was, American, sweating through a blond hogged haircut:
You cain't see him, he said. *Show me your pitchfork*, I answered
in a friendly voice. And bugger me he handed it over.
You'd be a dopey mug, I told him, because I was in a fury

but it wasn't a weapon. He'd been going to spread manure with it.
I follow the Lord Jesus and I never do violence, he told me
and I found he spoke the truth, in the time I was there and after.
I went up the gravel to the main front steps of this palace
and peacocks opened and shut there. I had no plan:
too wild, I suppose I was, to waste cunning or devious on a man
who was keeping me from my family.
I knocked, the door swung open, a woman was on the stairs.

This blue-black strongman came hurrying with a stiff whip,
got the nod from this lady and told me *You leaving, boy,*
or you gonna be whupped. The whip was all in one, no handle,
just braided thick at his end. I grinned at him. He lashed
me one across the shoulders, of course no pain at all.
I reached up, caught the whip and snapped it off him
and chucked it out the door. He goggled, and found a razor
but a voice from upstairs said *Put it away, Adelphus.*

Dressed in a puffed green what you call smoking jacket
our Mister Thoroblood posed like a Hollywood heavy
up on the landing. I knew him by the Australian accent,
it had to be him. *If you're Basil Thoroblood*, I told him
pack your port: you're coming back to Australia.
He tapped a cigarette on a gold case, smiled and nodded
not at me: the black man came at me again:
I picked up a big blue vase *Not the Ming!* screamed his woman.

I forward passed it to Adelphus, and he staggered, changing gears
out of his fighting set, to catch and hold it, and couldn't.
When he dropped it, it sounded more like Mulligan! than Ming.
You clumsy nigger bastard! the woman raved at him.
When I moved towards the matching vase she cried out *Basil no O no*
don't let him don't make him!—*So my value is less*
than a Ming vase? Basil asked. Poor Adelphus just stood
but managed to despise me: a trickster runs out of tricks.

I went up the stairs. The white man asked *Who sent you? Sir Peter?*
and backpedalled along the gallery, but I rushed and had him
and took a little ivory poker-player's gun from his hand.
Where's your room? I asked. *You're so masterful!* he marvelled
but I twisted his arm up behind him and he dropped that scoffing
and croaked *In here* like someone bargaining for air.
Five minutes, and I had him in a sweater with a carpet bag
then I took out the dogchain I'd brought and looped it through his belt.

You're certified, remember. That's how I'll explain you if you fight.
He was starting to worry. *You have got a plan, then?—*
We'll go downstairs now and you'll call for your car.—
What if I don't?—You'll hurt very bad and want to.—
What's your name, he burst out, *what's your bloody name?*
I winked at him. *I'm Mr Brisbane to you.*
The black was still there. *Adelphus, get your boss's car,*
I said to him. He looked at his boss, who gave a sign.

My plan, if you call it that, was to get us driven
to the nearest port, take him aboard a British ship
and get the captain to arrest him, outside the three mile.
Any British court would return him then, to Brisbane.
You haven't even checked our advantages here, he babbled.
This could be your paradise: it is to the other fellows.
This could be your Oxford, your harem, your Olympia!
As we came down the stairs, I saw there were people gathered

inside the house and out, talking, and their voices rising,
women and men. Who is this guy? Has he got a gun?
Where's he taking Mr T? Look, he's got him on a chain—
The Ming vase woman and a couple more came at me
Where are you taking Mr Thoroblood? Let him loose!
White women and black. *I'm parted from my family*
over this bugger, I shouted. *I can't go home without him!—*
I'll fetch them here to live on the estate with you, cries Thoroblood.

Let our boss go We love it here We love him!
all the women were yelling. The Ming vase one slapped me
with a whipcrack noise, and again, and stepped back puzzled.
I started to be hit with dusters and umbrella handles
and than, just as a mob of musclemen raced in,
I felt deadly sick. I let the chain go, and sat down.
The strong men hauled me up and went a few biffs
as I faded out. I woke up on a stretcher below ground.

I could tell by the damp coal smell and brown-paper light
that I was underground. I checked myself over.
Whatever it was had passed. But queer. I'd never been fainty.
I was down there with the furnace and garden tools
I'd guess a fair few hours before the door lifted up
and Thoroblood came down. I couldn't understand it:
he looked almost windy of me, and more than that, almost horrified.
You're alive? he asked, hardly joking. *You're alive.*

Can you sit up?—Of course. You think I'm crippled?—
He stared at me. *Well, you widen the definition,* he said.
*You're a different species of strongman, if you're genuine.
And I think you are.* He shuddered.
Are you going to starve me down here? I snapped at him.
No. Ah no. I'll have a meal sent down.—
I daresay you won't be sending the coppers? I asked,
thinking he might carry out a sentence of his own,

but he didn't seem to want even to mention the chain.
Next time he came down, after Adelphus had fed me
coffee and sandwiches and a dirty mutter of *You
are a phoney, man,* the boss seemed more himself.
He stood behind me. *What are we to do with you?
Chuck you out? Send you back to Sir Peter?*
So I told him about that. *Your family are hostages?*
Yes, he said, *that tedious cruel scheming of theirs bored me.*

*Tiresome as satire, their mean victories. I'm a romantic
to their eighteenth century. That's why I came over here.—*
With their money, I said. *That was your win, was it?*
He looked me up and down.
You aren't a coward, he said finally. *Yes, I admit it was
a gesture they could understand. For purposes they couldn't.*
Next time Adelphus came down, he looked at me straight at last:
Ain't your mouth hot, man?—No.—You kidding me?—

*What about?—We put so much chili pickle in your sandwiches
you should be breathing fire. You telling me you didn't notice?—*
No, I didn't.—Jesus you something else, man.
Shortly after this, I was let come upstairs and wash
and change my clothes. There was a blood spot
the size of a crown piece on the back of my shirt. I looked
at it, and wondered where I got it. I looked
at my back in the mirror, but there wasn't any wound.

In the next days, I started to meet his strongmen,
and their womenfolk. Of the nine bright shiners,
as he called them, two, Adelphus and Peyrefitte
were black, and so were both their wives.
I'm allowed most freedoms in our paradise here
but even in a madhouse, a nerve clinic, what you will,
if I allowed race mixing, we'd be finished,
driven out with a fiery sword.

So there was the butcher's block man, the only Australian;
his name was Tiny Calser, which I found out was McAlister.
There was Jesus' true servant, that worked in the gardens on his own
and was called just Iowa. There was Hortensius O Morahan
known as Hort: he was a circus trouper.
There was a fat man who slept a lot and never worked
but put the front gate back on where Tiny couldn't; he
had been hung and lived, they said; he gave his name as Sibling.

Another circus veteran was Tommy Dynamic, who never
stopped skipping and pumping and slapping on powder by the fistful.
Peyrefitte was a quicksilver smiling fellow built like scaffolding,
thin and jointy: I couldn't see how he'd be strong.
Adelphus was a burning quiet angry man,
one of only a few that ever put the wind up me
and I've never quite grasped why. That leaves Iron Rees
who was frightened of something; he said *Strength will never save you,*

and trained like a demon, and last was Bulba Domeyko. He was truly
what Thoroblood called him, the Short Giant. When the rest
did their stack-up, nine men in a diamond pattern,
one on two on three on two, he was
the one at the bottom, supporting them all, and saying
Buh! at odd times, well apart and thoughtful. Buh!
He hardly spoke English. His hobby was mathematics,
pages of peculiar reckoning with letters mixed in the numbers;

he'd smile, reading journals of this, and write it to send to them.
They all looked me over, took me to the gym,
which had all the rings and bars and exercise gadgets
you could imagine; more red leather than a flu patient's throat,
and they tested me out, sort of sidelong, with conversation.
I could support three of them in a stack-up: that put me
about their middle rank, counting points for not showing effort.
What they really wanted, though, was a line on my peculiar stuff.

Are you a natural? Or did you work out?—
I must have worked out without noticing, I said
humping cargo on ships.—You humped the cargo?—
Hey that true you can't be wounded? I shivered
at the danger in that one. *Course I can,* I answered.
My flesh is exactly like other people's, I added.
I didn't say 'even to me', or that strength wasn't
the point, with me. They were still laughing at something.

The boss, Thoroblood, seemed to be keeping me on
even though his wife or lady—her name was Azores—
seemed to get the creeps just looking at me: she would shiver
and pretty soon sweep off, whenever he and I got talking.
Write to your wife, he urged me, *get her to come and live here.*
When Sir Peter falls, as they all do, he'll go skidding
right into the abyss. And then it'll be safe to go home.
For you, if not for me.—Hah?—You only crossed one Sir Peter.

The house had this great library, walled and lagged with books.
Read, he urged me. *This is the gymnasium of mind,*
far the best thing I inherited when I bought Saint John.
It was a headache to look at whole, so I would lever
out one book at a time, and read news of grandfather's day
in la-di-da wording, sometimes with drawings called figs,
and fome went back to the days of fcrapping with fwords,
books packed with reading, but most of it was courting or principles.

He noticed, and one day burst out
I'm truly sorry. I beg your pardon. I'm ashamed.
I looked at him. *You are a genius, in a sphere*
the arrogance of mind has disdained and tyrannised. Even I
have been urging that Renaissance snobbery, pushing at you
its paper vaulting-horses. Corrupting a somatic master.
You were right to resist. Sitting Bull versus the missionary.
He went on, and meant it, as I held a big green book

a blind man had written about conquering Mexico.
You can trust a green book, Cos Morrison had told me,
never the black or red ones. Keeping a straight face.
I never could understand how Thoroblood had been
a crook, or trusted by them. Which only shows that I
didn't know crims, or have much imagination.
He would talk, to me or any of us, about
bodies and corporals, embodiment and incarnation;

about never being the body that an evil poem
uses for its vehicle; about how a true poem could arise
from the body, as well as from consciousness or dream,
and might well be the wisest of them. Too many of the other sorts
were around, he reckoned. The dream was the intellect's pet
tiger, in America then, paraded up Broadway on a leash chain.
All beyond me, but I thought how the Turk Colonel said the world
was made of poems; Basil was telling us how that worked.

The other cleverest person round Saint John
was Racine, Adelphus' eldest. A green-chestnut girl,
she read all the time, while her mother slanged her for laziness.
I am lazy too, she told me. *I guess I'll just live with it.*
You're not like the others. Are you a boojum? She asked.
A what? I stuttered. *A spirit living in a dead body.*
Hort touched you with the lit end of his cigar
and you didn't flinch, she said. *Held it hard down*, she said,

on the back of your neck. There's no sign of a scar there.
I looked around, and ran my hand round my neck
and passed it off. *Do you get a lot of these—boojums*
in America?—I'm just a bitty girl,
Racine replied, *but women do meet a slew of them,*
my mama says. She went on with her sandwich and book.
It took me a while to steady my pen hand
and write to Laura, sending her the last of my wages.

I wasn't sure whether we were all Thoroblood's guests,
servants or bodyguards. Meals were in a posh panelled hall
at tables for each family, or in their quarters if they liked.
The Thorobloods had their table in among us
or sometimes the tables were rucked together into one
for like a banquet. Some of them called him the Aussie screwball
and played poker all day, and drank what they called white mule
out of preserving jars. There didn't seem to be wages,

and I wondered if he was keeping me where he could watch me.
Send for your wife, Fred, he urged. *I can't have an unattached man*
stirring up trouble.—What trouble have I stirred?—
He shook his head. *Hort killed a rival once*
for Arlene his former lady. Hugged the man's ribs in—
Here? I asked.—*It was here, yes.—No police work?—*
This is an asylum, Fred. The victim was certified
after the event. How I wish you'd smuggled some Cointreau.

I thought of the Irishman's enormous back and shoulders
with the tattoos like fermented banknotes under his skin.
It sounds like a feudal retinue that you're in,
Sam replied in a letter. *Look up Feudal System in his library.*
It's what Mafias were called for the sixteen or so hundred
years they ruled the roost. When your robber baron
asks you to rob for him, or kill for him, will be decision day.
He went on to write that it had been fifteen years

since he had been home. *All my wiry sweating*
Gabi Gabi country. Bopple nuts, wind in the cypress pines.
Our part was where the rainbow was brought down
with a shied boomerang, and lay all up the coast as sand.
I enlisted in Childers; our photos are in the Town Hall. But
I'd be far too cheeky to live as a blackfellow there now.
If you can't take your quarry home—to be murdered, remember—
move your household to Paris. Talk Australia to me and be regaled!

It was tempting, but: no money to move anybody.
I was a child at Saint John. All my needs were met
that needed meeting. We'd drive to Lexington or Louisville
and mooch around, go dancing, or a few of us would crowd a car
and go to the Cumberland Mountains, off cement roads
onto dirt roads like at home, that you could taste.
Down them were farm trucks and old wheezing cars
and fast closed trucks that'd drive clean over you, with loads

of corn schnapps for some city. The corn paddocks ran up slopes
above log houses adze-squared and gone silver with age
like slab houses at home. Poor people who ate syrup
with bacon lived in them. Sibling knew heaps of those.
They'd invite us in and feed us on the best they had
and we'd play cards with them and tell yarns.
I told seafaring ones: the Marie Celeste, the Waratah,
the one about the fat dog alone in the lifeboat, that sailors

wouldn't have on board, though there were no guilty signs.
When things got tuned just right, by their white whisky,
by getting past jokes about honey-holes and revenue,
the fiddle would come out, and a sweet stringed instrument
with a waist in its hull, and whangy, would get unwrapped from rag.
I don't know why, but the notes of it fairly rang in me.
One song, of the tiny wee man: *His legs were scarce six inches long*
Yet massy was his thew (I think was the word mmm hmm)

Between his brows there was a span,
between his shoulders two...
He took and flung a mighty stone
as far as I could see.
I could not, had I been Wallace Knight
have heist it to my knee...
The girl went with him to this hall: *The roof was of the beaten gold*
        the floor of crystal shone

        but in the twinkling of an eye
        the sainted dance was gone...
The women of the house sang this, then one of them
played on the dulcimore, as they called the peanut-pod instrument,
and they sang other songs, about women killed by love,
of couples both killed; their love was a dangerous business.
Sibling got sick of it, this mood, and he snorted
That wee tiny guy would be powerful handy cutting coal

and it all went to men's talk, about falling coal prices and wages
at the mines a lot worked in, and a fellow called John L.
that some were all for and others were savage against,
saying he'd destroy farmers. *Bosses say a union comes round*
spoiling for more wages they'd just close down the mines.
Coal's down near plumb worthless anyhow.—Well, we lived before it,
didn't we? With no rheumatiz or black spit. Nor no company store
boosting up prices. The arguing went back and forwards

till one old lady said *I remember what stopped when the coal come.*
And everyone was quiet.
Thoroblood didn't seem to mind when we were off gallivanting
and it started to nark me. I was a bird in a collection—
or if I wasn't, what was I? Also, I started not sensing
even my connection with the ground. I had to keep looking
at my boots, that I wasn't simply rowing in the air.
I'd think about hitting and bang! the hammer would arrive

on the peg I was driving for Iowa in the vegie patch
he called his truck garden. I was losing the sense of where
the parts of me were. My nights were overflowing into day
that insecty late summer going into their Fall season.
It came to me this was from being and living
in an asylum. It was making me worse, to fit in,
because I'd gone from seeing it as Thoroblood's bolt hole
to thinking yes, it was a madhouse. With no treatments.

One time inspectors did come, a doctor and men in suits.
The women dealt with them, kept them talking till Azores and Rees' Fay
slipped into nursing uniform. The doc examined Boss Basil
and a couple of the boys. Sibling made a little fuss
asking for his death certificate. Then they left us, carrying real
tan Canadian whisky. Just a day or two after,
the boss's narrow face was blue and maroon, and he limped.
Iron Rees had bashed him. *When you study power, then naturally*

it will sometimes discharge, was all he said. *Poor Ieuan.*
Rees didn't get hunted. He'd been another one the doctor swabbed
but he went on all the outings and picnics, Day Release like Basil.
One evening away fishing in a river down a gorge
Sibling told a mob of us about the time he got hung.
He knew the Governor had turned him down when the deputies
brought him a steak dinner and sent in Irma from the cat house.
After she'd cried, and held him the longest time, and gone,

the preacher came and churched him up good, and at daybreak
they led him to the room with the beam and the little stage
he had to perform on, and he choked out a few dopey words
to the sheriff and reporters. He wasn't heavy then, and resolved
to stiffen his neck hard. But the drop was like a sledgehammer
and he found himself on a timber bridge going teetery out
over a ravine above the green trees, with people
and horse-riders hurrying past him, most hiding their faces

as if ashamed. The bridge was long long, and took a turn
out over a dark lake. It seemed to be more of a pier
stepping out and on out, over shallow greeny-brown water
and then deep blue water. He sat down, and got afraid
because of that deep water, and the pier had no more rails
for a long while, then did again. He looked back, but the land
had disappeared in haze. But it was okay. The pier had
started floating. It was a big raft going on

no longer out on piles but sitting sweet on the water.
Then he and all on board came to the steep of the sea
where it went down over the world, and there was country
just over beyond, break of daylight country, and crowds
with people he'd known but were dead now standing over there
showing no sign of death. They and others like them
were rushing out across on just a green in the air
and leading the rest from the raft home to that country,

but someone beside him, who made his heart turn over
just to be near, and that he never quite looked at,
told him he would come by a different road another time
to that same shore. He was too early now
and would have to be fat first.
That's what it put in my head. That I'd have to be fat
and lean again, before I crossed over into safety.
Now I understand life and I got no fear in the world.

When he crept back to life in his grandfolks' house
up a hollow in West Virginia
he reeked of camphor and rubbing alcohol, and his neck
hurt so bad he carried his head under his arm
for weeks, it felt like.
Back at Saint John I made the mistake of yarning with
Fay Rees the Englishwoman, Iron Rees's wife,
tall blue musical woman, who talked in her posh accent

with a sort of mouth-full relish, as if words were chocolates.
Nice woman. But I paid for it. One day in an upstairs corridor
I must have heard something underneath my hearing
and spun round in time to dodge a long-handled fighting axe
Rees had unwired off the wall in the suits of armour room.
It buried in a newel post, and he laughed this laugh,
I only wanted to see if you'd re-join
if I split you, like. And we were into it.

I was fighting in my own division now, for my life,
but his holts on me didn't hurt and mine on him did
and my punches did. I got the upper hand gradually,
pictures and ornaments going smithereens in all directions.
Then women came running yelling and one of them hoyed
water all over us, that must have been hot. Rees screamed
whopping it off himself. We both had blister-skin hanging
like wreckage of wings. I decided to get out of Saint John.

Money would find itself. I'd got too far inland
and yet, in my head, I was still just come on shore
and staring about. Deciding to go calmed me, each time,
for a few days. I'd go, but where? Land of too much opportunity.
And it was harder to step back into a young larrikin's
knack of jumping fast sideways, after steady years.
One thing I did decide. I dodged aside in Louisville
one Saturday, and joined the confession queue in church.

That was really rare. Like a lot of men, I felt
beneath church. As well as sore that it wasn't magic.
Well I got half an hour. The queuing ladies must have thought
I was Jack the Ripper in there. I got pulled up on
believing I'd killed no one, in the War. *You helped to fire*
guns at cities? You sent horses for fighting men to ride?
It's important not to fool ourselves, my son. One model
of how this Sacrament alters the soul is how

it first clears the mind. What other tales are you telling yourself?
On my numbness, I got nothing. See a doctor,
and Get your marriage regularised. They were red hot on that then.
We don't see all of blessing and absolution,
I know—but where I felt them was in being treated
as just another person, among the Saturday confessors.
It put gravity back under me, I noticed hours later.
I went to tell Thoroblood that I was off

and in the corridors I passed two women in a huddle.
One was Tommy Dynamic's wife Ernestine. She turned on me:
You stalking like a Goddam heron. You're one of them too:
You don't even pretend to want women! I opened my mouth
and Ocelle Peyrefitte sang *All that meat and no-o-o*
potaters with a wicked friendly wink
that told me to shut up. I shrugged and went my way
along the corridors. Mister Thoroblood was occupied

with a visitor, but signed me to come and listen.
The visitor, in an expensive suit, was cranking up
the gramophone and laying a record on,
black and combed like the oily hair of both them.
It crackled and talked: *How is everything at home, Rastus?—*
Everythin's jest fine, suh. Except your house done burnt down.—
But Rastus, that's serious! How did that happen?—Well suh
it might have been from the candles round the coffin.—

I was introduced to the visitor. Congressman something:
I've lost his name. He cackled over his record
and offered to lend it. *I concluded as a young man*
that the black is a sub-species, on his way to a separate form,
call it Homo servus. They lust to draw back from that
by stealing the blood of Homo sapiens, while the two
can still interbreed. But we true sapient humans
gain nothing by engendering an intermediate sub-race

of criminal degenerates, polluting our cities, our Republic.
I want to make congress between the black and the white
illegal. A Federal offence!—Thoroblood gave me a look
and blandly asked *And you'd like a donation to your*
campaign? The Congress man glanced at me too,
irritatedly. *You have enjoyed a considerable welcome*
in our country, Mr Thoroblood. Then his poem gripped him again:
Have you seen the drug-sodden mestizo lands to our south?

He went off, finally, with rhubarb and promise-noises.
I will in the end donate to his Canute-project, said Thoroblood,
or I know there'll be trouble over my visa, or worse.
I said about leaving, but he passed over it.
We're the opposite, of course: we're breeding old Jacky out
as fast as possible. Smooth the dying pillow
for nocturnal visits. Excuse me! He wrote inside a folder
and handed me a cheque. *For your family. No no, please,* he said.

I stared: enough dollars to keep them in style, or fetch them over.
You never scratch, he said. *You surreptitiously check*
where your hands and feet are. Hot water didn't cause you pain.
You don't dress for heat or cold. You jump and land stiff-legged
as if you had tubular shock absorbers. You're strong
but you're stranger than a strongman. You terrify Azores.
He waved his hand. *No offence. Just letting you know.*
I don't think you'll leave here soon. You're afraid of America.

When you're ready to tell me your story, I'll be happy
to put you beyond all financial care, for a long time.
Do you know they call you the Phantom?
And the Spook? I knew the mob were wary of me.
Then he moved to a lie, but a good guess too: *Do you know*
they call you the Leper? I looked at the panelling walls
and considered. *I thought that for a little while years ago.*
But if it was true, I'd have all dropped off by now, wouldn't I?

Down in the gardens, where I used to knock round with Iowa
because he was the only calm man on the place, and calmed me,
I found him sitting with Bulba Domeyko, helping the big man
to squall and cry. *What*—? I asked. It was terrible, hard crying
like you have to forget you're a man or a person to do it.
Iowa gestured me away, to one side. *He*
got another letter. They get smuggled out of his country, Ukraine.
It seems the Bolsheviks are starving all his people to death.

They just drop, in the pasture, anywhere. Some haggle bits off to eat.
Seems the Bolsheviks come and take every morsel of food,
or the farmers destroy it so they can't. Either way it's death.—
This is the ordinary people dying? I asked—*It does seem so.—*
Many?—Millions. I shook my head. It was no better, but worse
that this wasn't the first time I was hearing such a story
and knowing it was true. It was in the rules, as Heimann would say,
chained to his machine gun as a drive at British fairytales.

I forced my mind back to the poor man whose big strength
couldn't save any of his people. Or had saved just the one,
if it was strength got him out of there.
No, Iowa said. *It was the math. He was a steelworker and*
Lenin sent him abroad to a fancy math wizards' meet
to show what a Soviet worker could do, just in his free time.
I can't follow his English, what happened then. An elephant,
he lifted an elephant in a circus, that is certain sure.

He was lifting worse weight now, and we were squatted down
either side of him, muttering.
I knew, but you can't help longing for the angel hosts,
so I did ask: *Where's God in this? Where's his mercy?*
Iowa didn't hurry an answer like a salesman.
After a while he said *We stop, when someone gets to hurting.*
You and me, we stop. Don't we? Most folks respect true distress.
We, and most, don't know better.

I made a friend before this who I couldn't help either.
It started at a speak in Frankfort, where I went some weekdays
to brood and drink weak beer.
There was this woman: my eyes ran over her like tongues.
Men do that. Our brains are set to do it
even if it mostly stops there. And might as well then, with me.
She sat down at my table in the corner, opened her paper
and asked me something about the first at Lex.

The first what where? By the time I'd fumbled with that
she was asking my accent, and next thing we were talking
properly, both in turn, not me gassing to batted eyelids.
I told a few seagoing yarns and drew snorts
then suddenly found it natural and good
to tell her why I was marooned in Kentucky.
She leaped to a window they had there for laying bets,
gave instructions and cash over, came back and sang trumpet sounds:

Tarantara! Post time. It's how I make my living.—
Big wins?—Not many. Just by keeping the margin my way.
Forty fifty dollars, most weeks. You can live on that.
And your family are marooned too. Her conclusion, more than a question.
She looked at the table. *I've heard about your Mister Thoroblood.*
I'm sorry you're stuck there. Among those hoodlums.
When I started explaining Thoroblood's theories, and the strongmen
she waved her hand. *You're green, for a sailor. They're gangsters.*

Emily Monroe was peaceful to be with.
No challenging or managing a man
just for the power of it, none of that big mauve Mystery
some women go in for, to keep us off balance and belt high.
We could have big paragraphs of talk
then go back to our blatts. Weird, how German Yank talk is:
Hamburger and *fresh, all over* and *auto* and *dumb.*
They live half in translation.

What did you think to do among the mountain folks
up there in Wolfe County?—Just visiting—Well I guess you were.
You, not your buddies. The countryfolks are kind to a visitor.
They call it clever.—I thought they were a good bit like
small farmers at home. The cocky settlers. Us.—
Do your folks murder each other, in Australia?
I looked at her. She said *Bushwhack and shoot each other down?*
Lay for each other, knife-cut each other at dances?

I'd hit something iron in her here. *Well not much at all, no.—*
Then you'd better have your hill folks send over a big bottling
of their peace medicine. This was all she said, the first week,
about the feuds. But it turned out one of our strongmen
was her cousin. Drew Sibling. *Did he tell you he got hung*
and saw the blessèd land?
She shook, in nice places, laughing.
Crazy thing is, he just might could believe it.

I noticed when she talked about the mountain people
she sounded more like them. Stately not citified wrong English,
with no German in it. *So next Wednesday then?—*
Next Wednesday, yep, if I'm spared.
Of course I saw Sibling in between. But I didn't mention
his cousin Emily. That week he and Iron Rees
almost killed one another, screaming as they laid in the boot.
Ty Calser set the dogs on them, and got a mastiff crippled.

[130]

I was back in the bar in Frankfort as the wall clock
struck one. There was Emily wearing a helmet hat
with netting over her nose. She sipped a cocktail
so slow she'd drunk half when the clock struck one again.
No betting today?—All laid. She asked me about the sea
as if she really wanted to know. So I tried her on real stuff
like what happens to engines when bunker oil cools down a trifle
and codgers who remembered the rope's end for grown men.

She never cried barley. I hadn't had real talk
with any woman for too long, and I edged into it,
letting my guard slip, a bit, and another bit.
You get to the place in your mind where the women of your life are;
if you're half smart you don't introduce them to one another
but I was longing and more lost than I knew
and I talked family. When I mentioned Laura's first
husband had died in the war, just as the clock was striking

one for the last time, Emily told me her man did too, same year.
But not in this German war. Mine was shot right at home.
He was the last in Breathitt County.
The coal mines were opening, money coming in, better times.
The feuds, we thought they'd finished. Then she told me,
the sniping from the woods, pistol play in the towns. Fifty years of it,
judges shot in their courtrooms, jurymen followed and cut down,
and the cruelty, to make each death cause most grief,

most get-you-killed madness. Drowning someone's idiot girl
and hanging her over their fence still in the bag.
My grandaddy was a Union lieutenant in the War;
after the service, he learnt locksmithing off of Eli Yale
and went out west, installing safes all over,
married a voting woman in Wyoming, had a family
then he got a hankering to see his mountain home.
He was back a week and Bose Tumbull shot him in the throat.

Twenty-five years after Appomattox. It killed his father.
Two for the price of one bullet. It trapped his wife and sons
back in that mountain land they didn't come from
and made them poor. And McHaigs and Tumbulls
went hunting each other like varmints. It's not romantic.
At the funerals they'd scream and rip and roll in the dirt
shrieking the name. I've seen that. I bust out in panic
just seeing my daddy with two men one morning, in the pasture,

I took out running straight uphill to him. I knew
they were going to kill him. They would do it when he
lost holt of the talk, of his power with them, and resigned to it.
I got there in time. He didn't look at me, but drew me
firm against his thigh with one hand. Then I saw
the men were just outsiders. From the railroad company.
When they were leaving, with their hammers and survey pegs
he said Ain't it pitiful, the notions our children do get?

She was staring at her knuckles. I scarcely remembered
that I'd have to ask her what Appomattocks were.
I remember Main Street in Jackson full of militia
in their belts and blue shirts. My daddy was always for peace.
He had cause for revenge, but he despised it. He faced down
old Hayes Tumbull in the street. I would be ashamed
to say or do anything a backshooter might understand,
he told him, with his fingers in his snuff can.

It seemed like she couldn't stop the telling.
My husband Tom Monroe he was a brakeman
on the Louisville and Nashville line, before we married
and a little after. He was a truly gentle man
but noways a pantywaist. He sang in a sweet tenor voice,
he called the squaredances with such tomfoolery and fun
even the poor bitter girl-shy drunks would crowd in
from outside to listen.

The L&N line came up the North Fork right by us
and Tom would light off of it on his free days like runner
and come courting me. I never looked at any other man.
We had four years, but someone was idling and drinking
and studying on evil. To punish my daddy partly,
to make us grieve and never enjoy the modern day.
Tom was a foreigner to them: he didn't die for himself,
he died for me. I caused it. My name, my daddy's name.

I was going out to pick us a sallet of greens. After breakfast.
I heard a shot, echoing. A sharp loud shot, like a deer rifle.
Tom was by the smoke house. He walked towards me, he looked
horrified, he tottered like a little boy. Help me, and his chest
overflowed with blood. He was so feared to die, he gripped me dear hard.
That was the end of us. I'm cursed. I got my man killed.
When I could think, I got out. I can't live there: I go
back on visits, to care for my mama, see my sisters,

but I can't live up there, in the old grievance hollers.
I gave her hands back to her then, and we tried other subjects,
coming out of her story. To joking: *You like widow women?*
and later *Go home, to Australia, Fred. She's waiting.*
You're killing your life's time here.—Go home like your grandad?—
She nodded at that one, looking into her glass.
Only gangsters shoot people, in your country?—Pretty much, now,
I agreed. *The rest'd organise and declare you black.—*

Declare you coloured? I don't get it.—Sorry. A joke, I said.
But it kills some people. That Friday, Baz Thoroblood looked sick
and he wasn't at dinner. Young Racine served me pie:
I do suspicion we be going to Chicago soon, she said
in a low voice and her down-homest talk. She was keen to go there.
Why? but she'd moved on. Then I heard the stock market
had started collapsing. Millions would be lost. Panic.
No millions of mine, I thought. But that weekend was hushed,

whispering on the landings. It seemed Azores had gone
on the Friday afternoon. And on Monday the rest of it went smash.
Thoroblood was on the phone, and pounding its cradle,
then he was walking round, with all eyes on him.
At dinner he rose up, dinged a spoon: *Ladies and Gentlemen,*
our revels here are ended. I regret I can no longer
provide hospitality, when present supplies are exhausted.
That's when, Ocelle? The end of this week? Thank you.

Some severance pay, in money or goods, will be available
to help each of you on your way in this new world
we have suddenly entered. I have no fears for you. I
thank you for partaking in this experiment we have lived.
The contest for the body now seems to lie between
jazz-time and march time. But I am privileged
to have lived awhile in a world evolving beyond those, to which
beauty culture and sports alike had given me clues:

the super-human. As yet so unconscious, so scattered.
I'm proud to have concentrated that world to this brief clarity,
even if fixing it eluded us.
Well it's what he said. I'm good at remembering what was said.
Next day he told me Azores had emptied his accounts
in the Lex banks. And his investments had turned to dry leaves.
I'd be glad if you would stay. Between ourselves, means could be found
for one. At this moment, I'd prefer a fellow countryman.

In return, I'll keep you posted on Sir Peter's fall
so that you can rush home when the coast is clear for you.
He paced along, there in the gardens, and said *Azores*
was troubled by you. She stabbed you to the heart,
with a skewer, in the right spot and deep enough, from behind
do you recall? The day you tried to abduct me.
You swooned, but didn't die. Or ever mention feeling the pain.
You were her murder victim, and seemingly declined to notice.

That's hard on a killer. She's badly wanted you gone.
Exorcized, even. She was an uncomplicated person.
He went on to say how things would run down for a bit
till they stopped, and whatever was to happen started.
I went to the bank next morning, to transfer the last
of my money to Laura back home, and there was a growling multitude
in the street, and a man pleading with them through shutters.
So that was all over. I drank with Emily in the speak

and both of us talked and were both completely guessing.
When I got back, her cousin Sibling looked
from under his card sharp's fedora and asked me
Are you just a john or are you Emma's sweetback man?
There it was. Defend a lady's honour and the rest of it,
because I'd half understood him. But felt tired.
Why always be the man, for nothing? So I just replied
She says she bets on horses.—That's malarkey, Sibling spat.

You're a sucker if you believe that shit. Maybe
you ain't worth hustling, though, a faggot like you?
That way you wouldn't know diddley, like you let on.
He was desperate for fight, it seemed.
Your cousin reckons you were never hung, nor saw the blessèd land.
I said to overheat him. He swelled up like a turkey-cock
to go for me, I thought, but then he fell over sideways,
kicking and gargling. *Put a stick in his mouth!*

Don't let him bite his tongue! his lady screamed out, running.
I sat with her and him, through it. He hated like poison to admit
his condition. You don't show helpless. He knew too.
Whether it was mothering or sistering I'd needed
I never went back to Emily. I couldn't mention her
in my letters home, and that had to mean something.
If I'd gone that next Wednesday, I'd have missed out on
the big blow-up that finished off Saint John.

I was coming out of my room, with my duffel slung
over my shoulder, and heard this man-roar below.
Tommy Dynamic was in holts with Peyrefitte, both rolling
among the ornaments, punching like some weird animal,
crippled and kicking itself. I saw Ty Calser run
at Hort with a curtain-rod spear screaming *Kill you fun bast AAAR!*
as Hort throat-kicked him. Iron Rees scuttered round the edges,
squealing and jinking till Adelphus hair-caught and knee-smashed him

and Sibling jumped through a panelled timber wall
like a bomb of chips. He was fighting no one.
Basil Thoroblood tore up from the cellars shouting *Please!*
but no one bothered with him. He started to grin, and shake with joy
and Sibling had got a sunken great iron maul
and was smashing the doors and walls in. And Iowa was smiling,
leading the wives and children outside, from their quarters:
Don't cry, sisters. They're just taking this old tent down.

It seemed that Bulba Domeyko had hanged himself
down below. I saw Peyrefitte and Hort
carry him upstairs. They lay him on the library table
with his big tongue out, and heaped thousands of books on him.
Thoroblood wanted to go in there, but I stopped him.
Too late, too late, Basil, don't you see? I said to him.
Rees carried up a keg, I smelt it was mountain whisky,
real oily bust-head. He smashed it open. I pulled Basil out of there

with one valise in his hand. As we got to the garage
and backed the Duesenberg out, a long blue flash
showed in every window. The families said a great Oh!
and shrank together, as the big house shook all over
in window-blurts of fire, everywhere lighting up at once.
Then the women crowded round us, I thought we were for trouble
but it was to kiss us and hug us. *Goodbye, boojum man,*
says Racine Williams. Fay Rees said *Take me with you, Fred,*

in her rich relishing voice, smiling and desperate—
but I had to move, yelling out *I'm going home, Fay,*
knocked sideways by surprise and all as I was
at her. I'd had no notion. But then I put it down
to the day's big upsets, as we stopped some miles down the road.
It wasn't about me, but rescue. Blue cheekbones, that I'd half noticed.
There were red birds fluttering, scarlet, with pointy heads
and little greeny-grey squirrels racing up around trees.

I felt alive again, just being away from Saint John.
We were talking what to do. *New York for me*, I said
and get a ship.—*Duluth*, said Iowa. *My folks.*
And Thoroblood said nothing. *How much booze did you store?*
I asked, remembering the long blue flash. He shuddered.
Let's say I won't go to Nashville, he managed at last,
my backers there—Had he been greedy for more money? Or spent
all his stake on his muscle men? I never found that out.

Can we travel together, Fred? I would have rathered Iowa
but I agreed. His nice car, in chrome net panels, got us as far as Louisville.
There, men burst into the diner where we were eating just with forks
and Basil picking at his food. They pulled out guns, put them back away
and between them a blond man walked in, wearing jodhpurs
and tweeds, cravat and gold pin. *I'll take the Doozy, Thoroblood.*
I'm sure you have enough for trainfare and your sustenance
even after your fire. I see two of your specimens stayed loyal.

Then he nodded, and one of his hauled off and shied
a white ball at Basil. First time I saw a man catch
a baseball in his eye socket. Because it stuck there. He screamed
and flung, and we both helped him, remembering the guns.
At least we'd brought our bags inside with us.
When we had Basil bandaged and full of aspirin, I parted
from Iowa with handshakes and bought tickets on the B&O line
to New York City. The last time I paid train fare in America.

I kept thinking of poor Bulba Domeyko, his thin blond hair
over a monstrous black boxing glove and his tongue for the thumb,
jolting up to the library. He couldn't carry his whole people,
was it? His whole family? The whole world? Evilness?
Or what was it he swung choking for? Iowa had said Why guess?
Basil held ice to his split plum of an eye
and whimpered at times. And I didn't blame him.
They weren't even Nashville, he muttered. *Just Turf people.*

We raced through days of country. Big fast signboards:
Pillsbury's Franklin Auto Syrup. *You know I invited Jack Dempsey?*
said Thoroblood, recovering, through forests rusty and dead gold:
I hate that northern season. Miles wide of separate railroads
poured across New Jersey at last, tightening in on Manhattan
with ships moored in hundreds to her, like boots along a floor
with their names on their heels. Which one would I draw,
backing out under all the stacks of windows?

None, as it turned out. The ships were either idle
or had no jobs left. The docks and streets were crowded
with men fear had started rotting.
There were men in suits sitting round in the middle of the morning
with stunned faces. The cheap hotels, the sailors' flops
wanted to see your money first. And I still had Basil
in a topcoat that got us too many looks, where we hung out,
but there were plenty like him. *Must be millionaires*

who had parachutes, I said, to cheer him up,
but *I almost wish I hadn't had, myself*
he answered. Then *That moment when they let go of the illusion
and excuse of fighting each other, and turned on Saint John, ah
that was beautiful, Freddy. The logic of my research
and I was slow to grasp it. But I did. The shift from alibi to gesture
turns everything liquid. You saw how the fixtures splashed,
the men had a swimming motion, wrecking them. Grace shook off morals—*

He dabbed at his eye with a dirty silk handkerchief.
*So rare to see the body emerge pure, with its instinct-mind
openly in charge for more than instants.—I don't know,* I said.
*My body's mad. It's turned its back on me.
Won't tell me it hurts, won't tell me it's cold; tells me nothing,
obeys but don't answer. I'm alive in this celluloid ghost.—
So my guess was roughly right,* says Basil. Was ever
such madness talked, even in a bar on Houston Street New York?

A skyhook took Basil. We were still drinking the last
of his adventure, in another bar uptown.
I was hot for home and Laura: I was speculating Canada,
maybe out through Halifax—Men were beside us.
*You Basil Thoroblood? Okay. Then you ain't him, punk,
which is like your lucky day.* The talker had one of those
burny riddled faces from bad pimples when he was a kid.
He showed a flash of gun. *Scram.—This won't be rationalised,*

Basil gasped. I said *I wouldn't feed them junket from a shanghai.*
He was nearly crying as he cracked hardy: *Idiot swank! I need that!*
I wasn't sure enough my vitals would heal a bullethole, but.
I kept looking back, but soon was out the doors.
After that, it started to be trains
and learning to scale them, 'ride the rods' as they said,
chucked off and pistol-whipped by the cops of the New York Central line
and trying again. Seeing the wide Hudson out through cracks.

Once there was a destroyer sailing up that river
with a long banner saying SINK ARMY! Once were deer
on a street in the night. The freight I rode into Cleveland
had snow inside it and on it, the only snow there
because Cleveland was bare black. I'd meant to drop off at Buffalo
for Canada, but I was slipping into a dream.
Oh, please Mister come help him! A woman was crying
at my side. *This engine's tipped back on him!*

I ran with her, down the freight yards. Men were collecting
round a ship's diesel engine, half off a flatcar, with snapped chains
and awful agonised yells under it. I could hear the man would die:
no time for holding in. I got two good holts on big Otto
and heaved at him, against all his iron inclinations.
I'll bet you could have cut pump-washers off my ring
that morning, as the Digger said. No more give than Gibraltar—
The others had been hopeless, poking at him with planks.

And then he moved! I didn't feel but could see it.
A gap. Getting. Higher. Between his. Bolt-flange and the dirt.
The crushed. V-trench. The flange had made. Up. They slid the man out.
But I was mad as Basil. Maybe in memory of him, Basil,
I went on widening the gap under that big Siemens
till it was level, and ten men got under each skid
and it boarded the flatcar, snubbing me cold for beating it.
Well the crowd were all over me. I'm licking blood off my lips,

finding more in my ears and that first woman with her mittens
rubbing my hands, crying and kissing me.
That's all right, missus, okay!
I nearly got away
into the crowd when the ambulance roared up dingling,
but two young fellows took me by the sleeves:
Jerry Siegel, sir, and this is Joe, Joe Schuster.
We heard you lifted a flatcar off of a man?

They were nice keen boys in their diamondy sleeveless sweaters
and their ties, and I'm afraid I had them on a bit:
Yes, I'd lifted the flatcar. I was from Dungog. Which was a planet.
We were all strong there. I was under average, if anything.
We Goggans dressed like so: I showed them a photo from my wallet
of me from the Golightlys' show, trunks outside my tights.
They bought me breakfast, and I went a super bout
against a stack of eggs and sausages and pancakes.

They went away laughing. I'd brought two boys amusement
and forgot to ask how the man fared. I wrote to Laura
that I'd get a ship on the West Coast easier
and was heading there. At least the Depression, as
they'd started calling it, wouldn't be in Australia.
She and Joe would be all right. I'd have to chance Sir Peter.
Laura's letters that I'd got at Saint John I'd wrapped in oilskin
to re-read on the track. I couldn't get more now, till LA.

That year I met a lot of fellows named Slim
or Tex or similar, and heaps more who didn't give names.
I saw dogs walk the roofs of railway boxcars
pulling well-fed men who'd jump with them car to car
and handcuff hoboes, or shoot them running across tracks.
I slept in cover, or under tarpaulined machines
rocking west towards Chicago. I watched it be cold, and my carcase
told my mind to be hungry,

but there was mostly nothing when my dollars trickled out in dimes.
I was half awake and kept shallow, to get through it.
I would roll a half a thought between finger and thumb all day
like: here's a Christian country. I only have to go up
to any house and they'll nearly sure to feed me—
Why don't I? Why can't I? Me, terrified to ask,
them terrified to be asked. Because we both knew
we'd kill each other, over it. Need and help build such anger.

Where had I learned that? I would come fully conscious at feeds.
If you saw a fire down a scrub ravine, chances were
it'd be a hobo jungle, as we called our camps.
Bring some meat, not too green, or potatoes you'd bandicooted,
or a twist of salt, and you might score a black tin can
of mulligan stew. And when I crept off to sleep
without blankets, as I did, sometimes I'd find a blanket on me
before the morning. And once or twice a man loving up,

like in his sleep. *Sorry, shipmate. Shove off now!*
Then back to watching streets pass like chains paying out.
Round the big Chicago stockyards I rested for a week
in a derelict freight shed, listening to the cattle
mourn and break their hearts, and I fed on fatty trimmings
out the back of an abattoir, toasting them on jags of wire
and sharing them out. Then the packing firm got windy
of the buildup of men round our drum with the fire of scrap wood

and its boners' selvage went into bins. *For the hogs, buddy,*
or it's our ass. A dark white wind was blowing
and I set off for the port. Ships might be hiring.
Soldiers jogged by me in hats and straps, all singing:
> *Friday night the eagle shits:*
> *by Sunday I have saved two bits.*
> *She said dark meat and candied yam*
> *would see me hike for Uncle Sam.*

Sound off, three-four—they were getting farther away:
> *Preppy guys of gentle birth*
> *get well laid in Fort Leavenworth...*
Hey bindlestiff! A fellow in woman-proof grime
and riveted blue canvas clothes fell in beside me
and another in a slept-in watch coat, and two more.
When the first knife came out, I broke its arm
and the next one's nose, and put one in the Sanitary Canal.

The last one scuttered off sidelong, like a rooster.
Fish your mate out! I ordered him. *He'll freeze in that water.*
But roosters can't deal with water. I had to do it.
He came out chattering: *I'll die, man. I got nowheres to go,*
no dry clothes, man!—
Shit on you! I cursed him
but I got him a shirt out of my duffel bag, and peeled my
foul-weather jersey off and gave him, and found him a fire in a drum.

As I went on north into their iced high city
people stared at me in shirtsleeves, not rugged up and smoky like them.
You gone die like that! a woman roused on me.
She was right. I was silver, but I started to rock
like an ornament, and then dropped, as if I'd snapped off at the knees.
I was kneeling and stopped. People's waists poured past me.
There I am, in that purest white dirt, longing to be cold,
I realise now, with so many who were cold that year.

I was home in Newcastle, kneeling in my woolly trunks
where the surf wash spread and gathered back. Laura and Joe
were just away, but I couldn't get up and go to them,
and then I was in the night out on barren country
with the soldiers miles below killing stragglers, but thousands
had got onto the plateau and were lying out in knots of rag
everywhere, held down by their bodies and their tiredness.
Some still muttered, or sat up, others everywhere were turning

impossible. Forever more, to the waking world.
I was impossible, but I went on being left in the world.
I knelt on, among the stilled
and the huddling, with their wee mouse voices and mouse smell
and it seemed a wireless was sending a play in German
above me somewhere; *Mensch Meier, dieser da erfriert doch!*
as the moon made frost on that high gravel country
and I was thinking: Mensch Meier, in English that'd be Great Scott—

This had a nice ending, for a day or two, in a lolly shop
up by Humboldt Park, they told me it was. Foggy, with frames of trees.
Eat, eat! said the lady of the place. *All, chocolates, marzipan,*
fondant, pralines, bonbons. She was speaking German, between
all these words I'd never heard before. *Because soon our shop dies,*
like one in three—you see them?—already on this street.
Little ashamed dead shops. One day the rent could not be met.
This day will come for us. So many have no longer even bread.

I didn't ask your plans, since there is no future,
her husband boomed at me, humorous. *We have retreated*
into luxury; it is after all our trade. She is grande luxe,
my wife, isn't she? Her warmth saved you, in the taxi.
Say nicely Thank You, Elfriede:—I do thank you truly, Elfriede—
So, eat, eat!—What brought you to America? I asked them
Perhaps we died! Here was the heaven of Germans
till the days of Victory sausage. You had such days too in—Panama?

Perhaps you knew my cousin, he had a shoe store in Hawaii.
I'm ashamed how keen I was to escape such generous people,
but soon I was sharing out marvels wrapped in silver and gold
to blokes in a boxcar on the Burlington and Quincey line,
Glad you grabbed this stuff when they kicked you outa heaven, bud!
Among the blokes was one who opened his crib tin up at noon
and stared into it for a long time with such bewildered sorrow:
He's done that since Detroit, his mate said. *First day they was grub in that pail.*

Then, just before the railway cops came,
we were passing a high school, the oldest of the fellows
in the cleanest work clothes was saying patiently
John L. Lewis is a bosses' stooge, to a man called Doughboy
in an Army tunic stuffed with newspaper, *because his way*
would improve conditions but leave the bosses in place,
and Doughboy was busting to argue, but not, as if this was instruction
he'd signed up for. You're back to a child, as Norm Bunt would say.

Then rollick! went both sliding doors and in stormed the bulls
whacking us and screaming *Let's go let's go move!*
and on with the cuffs, and belting us with these wicket-sized clubs:
A bum is an Animal and this train ain't for Livestock!
What harm? This Company Sells transportation: you are Stealing it!
and soon we were in jail, my first time in America,
I'd dodged well, to then. *You, Limey sailor, you jump ship?*
You jump ship in Chicago? Answer me, fuckhole! What ship?

I kept very mum, hoping they might try me on all
the ships in port, and one be short-handed and take me.
After some while, they fed us stewed mince on toast. *Shit on shingle,*
one of us crowed. *Power!* said the clean twill man,
we force authority to feed us. Capital has collapsed. Three years!
Three years to the Revolution, tops. Doughboy nodded uneasily
The rest of us stared around. You can't win arguments.
I been in Kentucky: I seen them hoe-bread mow-rons,

the Detroit fellow next to me said. *Was you there long? Hey,*
I guess not, you ain't been shot.—Where I was had white fences
and thoroughbred horses.—We had this big nigger at the plant
used to work breeding horses: he had to guide the stud horse
into the mare. I'd like a job just like that, hey,
with a big nigger guiding me in: call that the dignity of labour,
hey Cuskelly? The Communist bloke only had to come back
with some comeback. But you saw him decide to go prim.

Suddenly the doors clanged open. We were off to court
in a black maria, but I was the last in line
and one too many to fit. Put back inside
but not locked up yet, I sidestepped into a room
full of desks and paper but no one working just that minute,
and out the other side. And into alleyways at last.
My duffel was gone, that I'd carried since Brisbane, but
so was I gone. Off on the Rock Island line

to look at silos and ploughed snowy levels all day long.
When we seemed to be on a long run, no local stopping,
I sneaked up on a brake van. Empty, and warmer-looking than out
in the hungry open, on the buffers. Easier not to fall from.
I slept, and when I woke up a man
without a head was sprawled against the far wall.
Howdy.—How do? He had a Negro voice,
so the nerves could calm down. Not much more talk for hours.

The Mississippi?—That's her. His coverall read Socony Vacuum.
Later, voices were talking in a low white daylight leaking in:
Bastards promised me! My job was safe. Bastards promised me!
We seemed to cross on a long high trestle over
a city of all women. What few looked up at us
growled and shook fists. *It is not desired any more*
was being said. *Keep going. Desire is finished,*
and we went on into like a huge hall in the air.

We made a long night stop in the middle of Iowa
and were still there at spiderwebby sun-up
and into the day, as the white farms yellowed a bit
and some of their houses that hadn't smoked at dawn
went on not smoking. There was a soft knock, and scratching,
then two more fellows dirty-faced with stubble like us
slipped into the boxcar. Looked round, and at the Negro.
Hey, it's like that, says one. *It does seem it's like that, Nathan,*

says the other one. They let it lie for a while, then
spoke to me and the blond white man: *You boys
want to hear a song?—Maybe they heard it already, Cole.—
Reckon they heard a lot of Ma-aa-mmy already on this train?—
Reckon that might be so, Cole:*
            How dey shine, glory shine,
            when I gets to Heaven
            an' dey meets me at de do'—

*You're better than that movie guy Jolson with the rings
around his eyes like a big old ra-coon, Nathan!*
I was starting to understand. The Negro man was tense
as over-strained wire, and had been since it started.
*Only thing, they ain't going to Heaven.—No they ain't.
Them old Bolsheviks say Darwin made the world,
don't they, Cole?—And they're the new preacher men.
Scientific.—So it don't matter nohow*

*if ra-coons wash their hominy and hog-guts in cold water
or not, they won't see the Jubilo?—Not even
if they wear brown shoes and keep their hands off pussy—*
The black man's voice came out like rope hauled through a sheave,
tight and furry: *Four to one be about your weight,
you white-sheet mother-fuckers.* First time I ever heard
that high blue prince of swearwords. *You got it for free?
I pay ten bucks an hour to be called a motherfucker!*

as Lasky said in Hollywood. The two white hoboes
rose up and clicked open great big pocket knives;
Coon hunting time, Nathan!—Time to hunt them coons, Cole.
The black man slipped out of his old cardigan and wrapped it
over his right hand, and I knelt up and squeezed
the knife out of Cole's hand. *Two onto one isn't fair,*
I told him, and let his arm know he wasn't to fight me.
I kept it bent while the Negro bamboozled the other one

and got his knife off him, and bashed him up, and ripped
the slide door open and booted him out *Waaa!* as we
were still just started up travelling. *Lemme go!*
Lemme out, he's my brother! screamed the fellow I had.
You're a poor judge of brothers, I told him. And so's he.
Better keep you apart.—*I kill you Limey sonofabitch*
*I'll—*he flew off into a snowdrift
about an hour later, like a dog-end into fluffed mash.

Logan Shirley was the black fellow. We didn't ask the promised bloke
what his name was, and if he said it, I forget.
Logan was a rough neck, but mostly a cow hand before that
on the ranches. It was better for coloured in the West.
He had worked cattle in snow, he had shot a painter.
That right I couldn't get into your country? he asked.
Oh I could slip you ashore, I answered, easy.—*I don't mean no wetback,*
he said, being haughty, *I mean respectable and legal.*

We came to Omaha in a snowy wind
and he said *I'm going to visit with my old lady.*
You should come too. It was thanks for saving him, I see now
but I was ashamed of my hobo clothes, and jibbed
at how I would have to be special and explained
all the time, on his side of the wire.
When I cried off, his face went distant again
but he gave me a sweater. *You must be freezing, man.*

Omaha on its hill, and that Canadian white wind:
I drifted to the Harvey House, that was a chain they had then
of railway hotels, and collected a greenish iced feed
out of the bins. Your pride can bear it, come the day.
I was breaking some jelly quietly on the brickwork,
I swear I was! when a man in a dinner suit
wrinkled and luxurious as a walrus hide leaned out smoking
without a cigar, said *Hey bum? Lady inside wants to see ya.*

I followed him past wrinkled noses, through the kitchen
out into a grand open dining-room, up to this table
all light and cane trims. A woman around her thirties
with a long face and headache expression and real diamonds
at her throat, my Shepheard's Hotel memories told me,
looked up and snapped *I saw you, all right? I've got
work for you.* Then I disappeared from her eyes.
Give him a room to wash up, fresh clothes. Charge it to me.—

Okay, Mrs Coyle, the flunkey bowed. *Come on buddy.*
It seemed that 'wash up' didn't mean the dishes.
The bathroom was porcelain, with yellow-metal soda taps
in behind black glass. The shave I had made a crystal sound,
the clothes were Western, classy suntans, not working blue.
And yet, I thought. The flunkey hadn't wanted
to tell me much. *Maybe she'll have you turn her barbecue
out on the ranch.—She a rancher?—Hey, I don't know nothing.*

She'll be back for you this afternoon, is all I know.
So, I thought, adventure. But: I'd a family to get to
on a ship I would find. Also, who was Mrs Coyle?
And who was I, to anyone in Omaha? Who'd miss me?
Fur and real diamonds meant she could pay me, and
pay to cover her tracks, after. After what? A sailor
mightn't know much of the ship he signs on, but he knows
it is a ship. And going to a place on the map. *Hey buddy,*

she say I could get a feed?—you want grub too? Okay
I guess it'll be okay. A New York steak, yams, fruit pie,
all the trimmings, while I thought and brooded.
And decided. I put on Logan's sweater underneath
the Western jacket, and edged out, down corridors of rooms
that murmured *Oh baby* for what might well happen, and the noise
they write with ZZZ in comics. And on, past the railroad depot.
Stories need adventures; I didn't. But one clue might have bought me.

The boxcar I rode up the Platte River wasn't snug wood
but steel, with long air slits, a cattle car with iced shit
and platings of glassy hose-water. The blown snow
blazed into it level at all north slits, a ladder of meal
from an ice sawmill going flat out. Hibernating along,
I walked down a concrete stairway, on and on down
past floors with big word numbers PING and PUNG
and ancient machines that stood out in shadow on these floors

and the train itself, it was the Yankee Pullman style,
open, not compartments, well even the divides
between carriages vanished: you could see a mile
along it, people sitting, people terrible to look at, swaying,
as the speeding tunnel bent and aligned, people in mirrors,
and the tube train was spiralling too, going evenly way down—
I suspect I was dying, and would have if cattle hadn't flooded
in on me in the night. I stood to Denver, braced between cows.

There we all poured off together, me bobbing among cattle
and cowboys fished me from among the horns. *Hey shoot!*
They wouldn't believe, from my clothes, that I was a hobo:
I say he's a Omaha high roller been caught with marked cards!
Nah, he's a state legislator tried to close the Governor's cat house!
When I spoke, and had to say what country I was from,
it was sodomy with kangaroos. They took my clothes on a stick
for their cook to stew clean, and fitted me out in their rig

and got me crawling drunk, on an empty stomach, because food
is charity and an insult, but booze can be lavished on a man.
I was on a life's career as a cowhand up north of Cheyenne
before the night was over, but next day I got the Western suit back
and they rode out yipping with their drove mob, and I returned
to dodging round the railway yards. Spong! went a bullet on steel
right beside me. Cops, rugged up, wearing gloves,
which could have spoiled their shooting and saved me, they were banging

wheels and peering under. It was true: men would kill you
for being broke and trying to scale a free ride.
Like Adelphus Williams' father, dropped with a.45 slug
up a nostril, for slanging a line gang foreman
one hung-over Monday morning. *Goddam sassy nigra!*
His little boy had watched. Baz Thoroblood told me about it.
I dodged them, gradually working further off and off from them
in among a repair gang *Give me a break fellows!*

carried a rail, then dropped it and ran off again:
Come back we'll hire ya! the big stage whisper behind me.
I could see the cold, how it would kill me dead
whether I felt it or not. I'd found tarpaper in a line shed
and wrapped myself round and round and got through the night
but it wouldn't be enough in the real high country.
I marked a hay depot, and got in there at dark
and stuffed my clothes, a foot thick. Not as if it would tickle!

I waddled to an open gondola car and rolled up in
to lie in a sort of hammock of sagged tarpaulin
over a clinky load. I adjusted my beanie cap
and as the loco stamped and climbed America's high gorges
I was lost in thoughts that might still thicken my voice
to tell about. My father's poor death, my distance
from being able to help my family. The insult called 'rights'.
I rode under stars like the glints on a surgeon's cutlery.

After a long while, though, Iowa sat there beside me.
I'm in Duluth, he said.—*I'm in the sky*, I answered.
you've come to lead me to the blessèd world
well I'm glad that it's you.—
No, that angel will be according to your soul;
I ain't an angel nohow. I came to keep you company
because there's worse company round, when you don't eat regular.
You're the one Thoroblood was waiting for: the body's word.*

Did he tell you?—*All I know, I half disappeared years ago*
but have to pretend I'm still there, by memory or guessing.—
You're stuck in the door, maybe, that poor Domeyko dived through
when he got the letter you got.—Bulba got it much harder.
Among men, it's not so bad; there's no touch to keeping in touch.
Women's company, though, reminds me I can't reach anything.
I can get life and not touch it.—But your word is keeping you alive:
without it, you'd be plumb dead, riding outside through these mountains.

You say Bulba got a harder letter?—It was about his own.—
Those burning women weren't your own fellow people? asked Iowa.
But women, I said, horrified.—*Men would have been okay?*
They were burning then anyway, everywhere, as they always done?—
Germans and Australians. I guess and then every tribe.
I wouldn't kill any. A working man doesn't get much choice.—
God's noticed that, says Iowa.—But I said: *beggars sometimes*
have to be choosers.—And the women burned to test that? asks Iowa

I sheered and whistled on through fast rock cuttings and sky,
then: *Yes. I'd have killed for them. And it made no difference.*
Somewhere, in the day, we slowed past a tall church built
like as if between skyscrapers, but there weren't any. An angel
of gold was blowing a long thin trumpet on the top.
People say you can't see this from lying in a railroad wagon;
I can't have seen it, but I did. The angel's name is Moroni.
At speed after there I asked Iowa: *What about it? God saving us?—*

It's a promise, he grinned, sitting up with his hair not blowing.
Buy it, and nobody's a failure. No one's book is closed.
Refuse it, and there's high mucks and drudges forever, even dead.
And the death gets shared round just as much, or more
It's kind of the compass.—*And we choose?* I asked him.—
It's what you say yourself: beggars got to choose.
He sat on the steel rim, smiling like the day he told me
Jesus came to lose. Then I looked again, he'd vanished,

and when I sat up, to see if he'd tipped and crashed down
we were in yellow desert and stone-heap hills. That day, stopped,
I climbed off the train, forgot my stuffings and went looking
for water, water: my tongue was like a buggy strap's end.
I saw men come out and step back, and one run yelling
but I walked on, all rustling, and drank at a tap over rainbows
of tar and oil. *If you're Bigfoot I reckon you're moulting*
said a voice above me, a coppery-faced man, an Indian,

with that faint re-balancing blur, like stokers when the ship's guns shoot,
that tells you here's one who's never ever sober.
Smart of you to get among the gasoline cars. They won't shoot here,
the deputies, but they're still coming. Hesitating, and getting cursed.
I ran tiptoe to the outside edge of the tank park.
The fence of the railroad land was hundreds of yards away,
bare snow, with tracks to trip you. Back through cops to the station
was no big distance, though. I kicked my boots off, I unbuttoned

pants and all everything, I flung it all off in a cloud
of ginger hay and plunged head first splinter-nude
through the middle of them, the cops and depot screamers
and cheering cowhands under the sign LAS VEGAS NEV.
How long can a man stay naked in a modern city?
As long as he keeps running, and ahead.
Not that Vegas was modern or a city, back then.
I ducked between horses' rumps getting off the street

and out among paling fences. A man my size was standing
on his back porch and I begged him for any old clothes.
He looked up, and I stepped back. His face was so miserably sad
it darkened the air around him. *Come in then*, he said at last,
my wife is poorly. Their house was what's called a shotgun,
rooms one behind the other. This poor woman, in a bed of tangled patches
was gripping a thick hawser rope hooked to the rafters, and pulling
on it with grunts and squalls. Pitiful. As if she had to haul her agony

up from somewhere, through her. The bed was moist with agony
as the rope was with dark slick. From two rooms away, I saw her
and smelt her disease, like nails, or locusts rotting in a drum.
He handed me clothes and I hurried them on, to get out
but I asked *Has she got long?*—*Years mebbe*, was his answer.
I had some old bottles of laudaynum but it's finished.
Times she bites on herself I have to gag her then.
I felt ears-boxed; I'd been skylarking. I felt unable and ashamed.

Somehow I got him thanked without making silly promises.
I can't pay: this is purely good of you. He half listened.
Back at the depot no one had been looking at my face.
I searched in the washroom for a chucked-away razor blade
to shave myself, but no. The Indian fellow came and yarned
and shared his bottle. White hoboes, I saw, were just visiting
where he lived full time. *I am a Las Vegas Ute.* He taught me
to tweeze out my whiskers, Injun style, and admired how I did on one drink.

I panhandled then till I was fed, and I won the Monopoly:
I didn't go directly to jail, but to San Diego.
There were ships. All idle too. Like plates in a rack.
Not even a watchman's job on them, watching condensation drip.
The city was shirtsleeve warm, though, with chimney-sweeper palm trees
and Marines everywhere, strolling or in cadence:
>   *Legation guard and Shanghai dick,*
>   *them Berlin gals dance chick to chick.*

Sound off, three four—I got so down I nearly joined them,
but what if there were mail or a ship in LA? Then, on a Sunday,
a black panther squirmed out of a smashed truck and came snaking
up a tunnel of screamers and shouts and fruit barrows, leaped
at a woman who reared back—I grabbed its scruff and jammed it
to the pavement, all its weapons faced the one way, I kept that
the face-down way, I rode it astride, this muscle man near my weight,
this yowling twisty python, furry pressure cooker of joints—

I couldn't wheelbarrow it, like a dog on a farm, it would have
doubled under itself like any cat and got me.
I was screaming for a net, like for me in Berlin, or a tarp.
If I was to kill the thing, break its neck, I'd have to
change my grip, I heard a woman yelling
to police with their guns out *Don't shoot him! Oleshka!*
Olesha moi! and level-sounding stuff then in some language
like soothing commands. But then a slug punched through its head.

That's how I got back to LA, gratefully employed
in the circus of Madame Maria Rasputina, lion tamer
or dompteuse as she called it. *You would have saved poor Oleg:*
the rest can only think Kill the Wild Beast! Kill! I shivered,
remembering the black muscles in its stubby arms, the great talons
on that shock-haired butcher lizard writhing under me.
But: for ten dollars a week all found I tore phone books and chain,
heaved donkeys up with people on. And General Delivery had letters

from Laura and Joe. *Life together isn't really very long*
and we've missed a year of ours almost, now, and
Don't think the Depression isn't in Australia. We will manage
for a few months yet on what you sent, but then... and
They have emergency rations called Sustenance, run by the police.
The sergeant here caught one woman's little boy with ninepence
outside the pictures, sent him home and cut off their supplies
on the grounds if they had money for luxuries... Do you sleep wild again?

I do dread that. And Joe asked to come to America.
I sat on the Post Office steps and felt despair
till a cop moved me on. *Let's get the ass in gear, buddy!*
I went back to the circus and talked to Maria. And stepped back
because she flared at me: *You have family there?*
And you are in America? Why? I explained fast, hearing
the echo of the sack in her tone. It seemed runaway fathers
weren't her favourite men. *When you save fare, go home!*

I found her story out then. How her father's name meant Reprobate
and the worried Empress, blonde like a hundred before her, who couldn't
resist inside-out eyes and God-talk. Maria cried at his bad death,
poisoned and shot and bashed and drowned. The body's tough Word
and he helped bring the Revolution. So had I, but I kept stumm.
Boredom is sin. Peasants are forbidden to be bored
yet my father was bored. Our family's little peace depressed him
so he ran away. Does your family perhaps bore you?

She flung back to her big cats, who soothed her with snarls.
We were coming out of layover, playing the near towns
out in the orange groves there, and into the hills.
Maria had been at me to work in the cage for triple money,
supporting lions on a plank harness. I was Nervous Nellie
but I tried it, in rehearsal. This day some big trainer-colleague
was visiting, they were smoking cardboard cigarettes,
he was to have a guest-star spot, she offered something special

and I was it. In the big cage with lion-yoke and Boris.
There was the crowd, there was Boris in leopard-skin and pockmarks
snapping *Davai!* and other Russian, there were two massive maned toms
making underground noises, as he deceived them who was boss.
He kidded one up, onto my rig, and then the other one,
which leaned at me, and I swung away, and both
clutched to stay on. By something in Boris's face
I knew if I stopped they'd be on me, but while I swung them

they had to hang on. But too fast and I'd spill them
and be done for pronto. So I rotated, I waltzed, with them
showing me their tonsils, I gave them a gripping go-round
with the idiot crowd loving it, the plank strapped on to me
so I couldn't drop it. Madame Rasputina swanned in
to the rescue, letting on it was part of the act, hand-kissing
to the audience *Slow down!* she snarls at me,
Durak! Slow down I will calm them, but I was too busy

unbuckling the rig; as I jettisoned it and they bounced
straight out of the dust I was so giddy I couldn't
climb the cage yet—and they were so giddy they charged
into each other. They wouldn't do that twice. I came right
enough to crab up the bars, out of swish and claw,
them tottering after me on hind legs, jumping, the crowd
in stitches, me spider-fashion on the cage ceiling, Maria
lashing and commanding, so mad I'll swear she lashed me too.

I was fired, and Boris blew out of the same cannon,
but I landed in the arms of a scout in co-respondent shoes
waving his cigar *Do I have a spot for you!*
You wanna be in movies? Everyone wants to be in movies!
Hollywood needs you, fella. Be at the studio, here, my card,
Monday at nine. Hey, the timing, where'd you learn the timing?
In Australia? Felix the Cat is from Australia!
Annette Kellerman's from Australia, standing on her head in the sea.

Well, this got me a retainer and a screen test
for a circus movie that didn't come off, but by then
I was set up in a boarding house in North Hollywood,
a bit ahead on rent even after sending a wad home.
When the dishes and table-bottles tingled during a meal
and there was a general feeling of lurch in the air,
that was an earth tremor. *Five a day: it's good form not to notice,*
said old George Flers, specialist in heavy-father roles

in the slapstick days: *Pop a collar stud, I could, with one swell of me neck!*
The girls in the house had jobs, or tried the herd auditions
while their money from home held.
After a while, I had to hang round studio gates too
with thousands of men. It was that or the orange picking,
and soon enough it'd be the oranges anyway.
Then at Paramount a fellow yelled *Kraut parts! Anyone here
was in the Kaiser's army?* Five of us stuck our hands up quickest.

A navy man in German is also a Soldat,
and we were to be the model for the other extras
on this picture called All Quiet on the Western Front.
Brace yourself for spit and polish here, Kumpel,
muttered one of us who'd served with the Hessian Guards,
*I've seen von Falkenhayn and I've worked for von Stroheim
and the real thing ain't a patch on a Hollywood field-marshal!*
but Milestone, our director, turned out not a ranter at all,

he was just gliding and polite and quick
even when he worked day and night and slept in his car.
When Major von Morhart the consultant had squared us and tucked us
from long boots to lightning spike, from collar to Gott mit uns,
we had to show the rest, tough guys from the American Legion,
the little fine points. A lot of them didn't just like it:
Keep your stinkin hands offa me you Heinie bastard!—
Hey Doughboy, I belief in the brotherhood of all workers,

says Gunst the Hessian. Of course I thought he was just needling.
I'm only working on this pacifist shit, says the Yank
*because I got kids to feed. I used to bayonet guys like you,
so keep downwind of me.* We got five dollars a day
and meals from the caterers van that we Heinies called
the goulash-cannon. We'd stay in costume some days
from dawn to near midnight. One lunchtime we came out
to eat and stood nailed to the ground. The most beautiful woman

we had ever seen stood in a white sharkskin man's suit
talking to Freund the boss cameraman. She'd dim to normal and laugh,
making Berlin wisecracks, then she'd look. And a man's
heart would turn end on. Hot coffee would run from his cup.
He'd see every blemish in his hands, every fault in him would cure,
he'd feel blue sea under flying fish—then she would be just
a very good-looking woman again. It was a gleam that came and went.
Marlene Dietrich, new to the studio, checking out our movie.

Boy do I wish I could bark your schnauzer-lingo now!—
Ohh get me a knockdown to that!—Walk on me, Pussy-in-boots!—
She bleached the colour from every marriage on the set,
I reckon, and meant to, then walked her force of life away slung.
Another time we were batting the breeze with some crew
and the brotherhood of man came up again. Oh I'd heard of it
and wished about it, for all the good that does:
I mean, what language would it be held in, for a start?

I'd noticed working men in Hollywood didn't always
treat big ideas as bullshit, nor shut up when the boys winked.
Bolsheviks never gave up, but they'd take a pull, elsewhere:
not on the Coast. *But it's great that small bosses and experts*
are on the bum too: we want the widest shock and hatred,
all possible classes to be the workers and smash privilege.
Every stiff who's still comfortable is your enemy!
It's the great opportunity. Russia's there as our arsenal and citadel.—

Some would say as our double crosser.—Those 'some' would be Trotskyites!
It livened up our breaks between being bombed and shot running
and pitifully wasted. Which I didn't know well and got the Turk front
a bad name for lack of serious manly horror.
One day a cameraman I forget the name of told the yarn of Eisenstein's
Ten Days That Shook The World, how the Red Guards were playing
the Tsar's Guards in the scene where the people storm the Winter Palace.
A lot of extras playing the people had been the actual stormers

eleven years before. So: Lights. Camera and—Action.
The guards fire, the people reel back. Cut!
A lot of the extras are kicking their last, there's blood everywhere,
dozens don't get up. No one had thought to provide
the guards with blank cartridges.
It was very political whether you laughed or didn't
at that story. Gunst was savage. *Will that get you a ticket*
to the World Nationalist Congress? he spat at the camera jock.

After that classy picture, I got a bit of work
on some ripe old rubbish, Kraut parts in Saturday serials,
clicking the heels in monkey-screaming kookaburra jungle,
Donnerwetter under the sea in U-boat sets that wobbled
like water themselves, firing squads for madmen in corsets
and brushed real wartime uniforms. *Belgian nuns!*
Since 1918 have I had no more Belgian nuns!
yelled one of us. All the Yanks in Wehrmacht rig cursed him.

Some months I'd send home fifty or sixty dollars, though,
living bare to the bone, no parties, no drinks, nothing.
Hey get some fun, man! You're missing your life, baby!
I'd walk the streets, they were circus enough: Thai dancers
with pagodas on their heads, real Ruritanian hussars, blanket Injuns,
cowboys in suits decorated like a Mexican church
and once a girl dressed all in fruit, injecting in a Cadillac.
Weekends, I'd go out in this or that friend's car

into the range country, the canyons and slip-sided hills
and maybe explore the ghost towns. That's how I
first met ranch hands. My mate Istvan Hegedus and I, his star name
was Steve Hegarty, but it never rose, his star,
were finding silver change, ripping up the floors of dead saloons
when we heard fellows ride up arguing. *I still say old rattler plays fair,*
always warns you afore he kills you, like a Mex gunslinger.—
They is an enmity set between that sonovabitch reptile's

seed and the seed of woman, replied a voice called, yes, Tex
and we came out. Introductions and politenesses, but then Tex
went off stalking his great enemy. *Come out and be et,*
you sidewinding asshole!—Don't mind him, he gets ornery
when he ain't had his prairie salmon. Crack goes Tex's revolver
behind a caved-in barber's shop. He carries out the headless bunch
of muscles all flexing hard, and skins it in plain sight.
I'll fry him tonight with onions. You boys work in the movies?

He wanted to himself. He was posing for it, making himself up
as a story, like most of them. Not much harm in it.
Most folk preen and watch themselves sidelong,
playing themselves, the Farmer, the sacrificing Mother.
It's just I was jealous. I had to live mum, with my story,
and never let it show. When they asked did we know Tom Mix
and Pola Negri and the rest, I told them those were just
characters. Different actors played them, different times.

There's a part of us, a self that doesn't really live
but is out to live forever, that watches and wrong-foots us.
It made me ask Tex his real name. He got his feathers up
and it gave him a smile. Another Sunday
there were these starving-faced people packed in a tin Lizzie
on its last wheels in Pasadena. They'd been trying
to cadge petrol from the resort people outside Tanner's Auto Livery.
Their real trouble, apart from losing their farm and no money,

was the husband had got lockjaw off some wire in Nevada.
He lay stallion-eyed and shivering in the back seat
among their rags and bundles. *How'd you get to here?*—
I learnt myself to drive, said the wife. *He needs a doctor*,
I said, and felt silly. That wasn't worth an answer.
*He cain't eat, nor drink now. I been trying to trickle water
between his teeth. I wisht he had gap teeth like most folks!*
I'd heard if you could get a lockjaw patient through four days

they mostly lived. His kiddies were too frightened to cry.
Well Hegedus and I towed their car to my boarding house, then his
and got told at both we couldn't bring Okies around
with their eyesore jalopies. So we broke into this derelict studio,
and found a spiderwebby Roman set, from the silent times.
I got the man lying down nearly straight on this couch
beside a gold table. Then I felt his face and jaws:
You'll die like this, shipmate. The muscles were wire rope

but I started gently working them. *Be careful oh be careful,
you'll break his face!* It was like the Tarzan's Grip label
just to get his mouth open an inch without cracking his teeth
in, or breaking his jawbone; you couldn't massage him open,
yet it was just nerves telling his muscles to stay tight.
It struck me, hard, how it was just nerves telling me
to be a live rubber man. His wife and I finally worked out
to stick rubber bungs cut out of a tyre in his cheeks.

They must have tasted horrible! But she could trickle soup in,
and water, and soft ice cream, without him choking,
and she started to. I wondered at the savage looks he gave,
even as he like absorbed the stuff; he wasn't swallowing yet.
I left them to it and went back to the boarding house.
Why not? Why get shirty? Appearances win out over mercy
a lot of the time. There was a trying-to-be-actress
lived there called Phyllis Gates and she gave two dollars

out of nearly nothing a week, to help that family.
She used to say, Phyllis, that I looked different in the face
when I'd been speaking English or speaking German:
You've been with your German friends today. And she'd be right.
*That language moves the muscles in your face differently
it makes you purse-lipped. You'll look English-speaking again
after supper.* Smooth very fuzzless faces remind me of her.
She used to say *I'm not beautiful as a presence*

so *I have to work by entrainment. The second rate way.*
Any actor who can be still and draw the light to them
as Gable does, or Dietrich, makes me seem busy. Too eager.
Vivacity is surrender, Freddie. Those times were the ones
I looked at her face, to remember it,
Green-eyed, melancholy. *I'm not going to make it.—*
Not make what? I asked her.
The family planted in Ancient Rome, with their washing

over all the Latin placards and Caesars' heads and sconces
they mustn't light at night, they were recovering
on the food I could bring them. The man was too sick to speak yet.
His wife sat holding his hand. *The bank that held our title,*
it died itself before it could put us off our farm,
but our bit money was in it and died too. The neighbours gave us
what groceries they could—keep still, Ira, they done it!—We et
the last of their sorghum syrup on the high desert.

I liked yarning with her better than with like showbiz people who don't
say what they feel—they don't know that—but talk to make themselves feel.
Next time I saw Ira and Bethelle I was seeing double
from a bout with electricity, right in my boarding-house backyard.
There was this young widow that some of the women, not Phyllis,
suspected wasn't widowed, and she had a little boy
she used to leave at home and pay extra to get him looked after
while she worked part time and haunted studios like us all.

I was home with a cut face from an exploding saloon
in an oater I'd been on, and Jayne the maid-girl she
was in the backyard with little Charlie; he was watering things
with a dribbling hose, but he'd made a fair circle of soak
when whing! down comes a wire from a knot of them on a pole
above the fence, and the wet ground jitters and sparks
all round the baby. Jayne grabs for him, steps on the wet
and howls and backpedals; I'm straight down the stairs

and run and grab the wire. Well it feels like nothing
of course, but ten times my nothing: I freeze
and it won't let go my hand: my head is full of like
newspaper print all the way back across the country
and I topple sideways bang! over orange boxes that splinter
but it stretches the wire away from the kiddie and he's rescued.
I know if I can roll one more turn and pull the wire
out of my hand, I'll live, but nothing's obeying,

or not obeying me: I'm blacking out and in
and the power stands me up on my feet again
and walks me towards it, step by step—then I trip
and it leaves my hand like the cracker end of a whip.
I was groggy all day, the women falling over me
till the lemony old piece who owned the house clouted on them
Back to your work! Do you require the doctor,
Mr Boucher? Then sit here: I will have a restorative sent.

I think she learnt ladying on stage, the way she overplayed it.
The restorative was like scent, too, some sweet Southern whiskey
I admit she wasn't mean with. *In your bare hands*, says Jayne.
The utility man say you should be dead for sure!
I looked at both of her and supped another double with bits
of diamond light off it everywhere. I knew how it would spread:
the whole house walking on eggs round me, the landlady
starting to find my story too big for the peace of her place—

So I went to Ira and Bethelle and he was up,
Ira and Ira, with this maroon and gold
emperor's robe round him, and the children in scrubbing-brush helmets
bashing shields with each other, and he thanks me right kindly
for all I done but he couldn't tolerate to stay
among Godless lying movie abominations. None of his
had ever been in a movie house, no more than the burleyque.
He was drinking buttermilk from a gilt bowl knotty with gods

as he told me this, and Bethelle looking at the ground
but I daresay when you've got nothing, your principles
are your only place and home,
for as long as they last.
The family didn't, I know, take a solitary thing off the set
though I heard the boys pleading *It's a helment, Pa: it's keen!*—
It's also not yourn, snaps Ira. *Come now, thank the Lord*
for Daddy's deliverance, says their mother, *through this kind man,*

and we stand in a circle under eagles and suckling wolves,
me hand in hand in hand with a farmer and his soul,
with his wife and hers, in a wobbly world, their doubled children,
all of us giving thanks. *Thou hast opened my mouth to give praise,*
and loosed my tongue to thine exaltation, O God.
I saw them again when we were old.
Back at the Stewart house, little Charlie's mother
kissed me and cried, but a couple of the men

who'd been red hot for her to kiss and cry and trail
her sweet blonde ringlets over their ugly dials got pretending
to be wary of me *Put that cruet down, Fred: I dassen't touch it*
while you're a-holding it!—Our heero the Electrical Heinie!
Lights his way with his hand.—Can't you get yours to spark,
buddy? I snapped. Heave up, slam back go the chairs
for a round of welterweight outside, the women upset and yelling:
I duck and sniff Tabasco, the bugger's shied the bottle at me.

Well of course after that I'm on a week's sorrowful notice.
Charlie's mother would have come with me, but I guessed
it would be for protection and gratitude, not my manly charms.
I got her off her own-made hook with talk about my family.
Now half the women, Laura wrote, *are grass widows like me.*
With their husbands away chasing work, they can get an allowance.
If hubby's home, they can't. So the men go, or get put, on the track.
No relief, on relief. I must think you trust me, to write this!

I was on the track myself then, for some months,
the track of the LA River, mostly, a bare chute of odd floods.
Phyll cared for my clothes. I'd sneak to the riverbed at night
and sleep raw on gravel where other bums couldn't. Lots more
money to send home, lots of holiday from nodding and agreeing,
but the torch-beams flogged our sleep like gold batons, up and round
as the cops searched us out. It was no sin and all punishment
being poor then. An address is mainly shelter from police minds.

Steve Hegedus had been at me to share a big walk-up apartment
behind Pantages Hotel near the corner of Vine Street
where they reckon Lon Chaney's ghost waits for the bus.
It wouldn't cost more if I ate mostly commissary food.
Only when I was in, with Steve and Artur Gunst and a man
I remember best by his star-name: Tad Buckingham
and the squinny bloke who told the bad joke about Lupe Velez,
did I find out it was party time there near every night

and me in for the cost of bootleg grog I hardly touched.
The fire escape was the swing-up kind, against burglars,
which never stops them. I would sit out there
as the whoopee went on. Inside would be ripe with sweet booze,
different smokes and that laundry smell. Odd surplus women might
come out and yarn; some would leave me in a flash of disgust:
What's wrong with you? Jim Cagney came, the surefootedest neat man.
Fellows offered me cocaine but I reckoned I'd take vanilla,

as the saying then was. Gunst told me how a German mob, the Nazis,
who were war-mad, had stopped All Quiet being shown
over in Berlin, by letting mice go in the theatres,
and he praised the Red leaders, Edgar André, Erich Mühsam, Max Hölz,
thousands on the streets right into the Nazis' hard thug army.
This is where I first heard all that, after I finished on Dirigible,
the flick I caused a near strike on, helping gaffers when I was Cast,
not Crew as they thought. Cast, with not a line to speak.

Tad Bajkowski-Buckingham would have it the Reds were losers;
they'd shoot everybody better-looking or smarter than themselves.
This was half to get Artur's feathers up. But I rathered listen to
this old saddle tramp tell how Running Bear and Pancho Villa
were better movie actors than Wyatt Earp. *He's buried here in Hollywood:*
I hept carry his coffin, or Alma the stripper tell Chief Rabbit Tails
about fan work and inside-leg work. You think a sober Indian
can't rock and hee-haw? Chief honey, *I speak with a tongued fork!*

Wesley Rabbit Tails and I were on a Poverty Row Western
another time, sitting round, as you do a great lot of,
and he asked me *You notice how horses whinny in the movies*
with their mouths shut?—Or whinny as blokes ride them into town?
I asked him back. *And murmur 'Feed me' at full gallop?—*
I like how they whicker 'Here I am in brush' or 'I am getting spooked'
without lifting their head, or stopping even. You think they do that?
Wesley asked me. *And in battles they're never gut-shot, here.*

I hate Hollywood, I replied, but he didn't hear me.
You know Tully Marshall? He was doing this scene with young John
Wayne on The Big Trail, *and he didn't know why we was all busting*
and looking away. He got to fidgeting
and drawled all the louder.
Next take went fine, right into the can. But the editors
kept the one with him and Wayne laconicking spots off each other
and their horses asleep under them.

One night, Ross Arbuckle came along
to the House of Shivering Springs. *He's a producer now,*
poor bastard, they said. He had these awful trapped eyes
and I noticed the women circle him, always keeping just clear.
Men brace on their knees, baby, don't you even know that?
Even great big men. Canoodling don't make you a canoe, I overheard.
Not Guilty three times sure had convicted him. We didn't talk.
That night I dreamed a cock bottle in the Roscoe Mountains.

I was an extra just then for the famous Prussian director
who I thought sounded Austrian, when he wasn't talking English.
It was some drama making out sex was all a con
and everything on it had him sneering snubbing mad.
I thought he wanted poisoning,
prancing around, whipping his leggings, snarling insults:
Were you taught acting by a KABINETTMAKER?
and his little bumboy co-directors having fits by rank.

Crowds of us sitting round in costume
in that great hangar of a set like half Vienna
with brutes and arc blinding through windows and a world
of toy overhead railways to get cameras above the violin work.
Suddenly a boy says *You Mr Bircher? Come with me*
and adds *I tapped you. Didn't you feel it?*—*I'm too tough,*
I said, like always thinking Sack. *Who wants me?*
tripping over wires, him trotting. *Miss Dietrich,* he said, awed.

She gave me the Dietrich face from a table set with coffee
as if at Kranzler, seated me and waved away men
edging and posing round her. *I've made you some enemies:
you could go far with that.* And then she smiled more like
between fellow workers. I babbled *I didn't know
you were in this movie.*—*I'm not,* she said
Do you know Rilke? His poem of the panther in the zoo?—
Bit of a luxury, the poetry, I said. *I'm a stranded sailor*—

Rot, she said. 'Bars pacing by have so worn out his sight
    that nothing's left to which it will respond.
    To him it seems steel bars are infinite,
    a thousand bars, and no more world beyond.
    His gentle tread, each muscular strong joint
    circling in the very narrowest space
    is like a dance of force around a point
    where a mighty will stands hypnotised in place.

    'At times his pupil, after a long recess
    will lift its curtain. There will enter a scene
    that traverses the body's silent readiness,
    reaches the heart, and fades from having been.'
It sat me up. This wasn't the Turk's or Thoroblood's 'poems',
big, dangerous, baggy. This was the grain distilled.
This was the sort that might not get men killed.—
I shook myself and we talked childhoods and homes.

Her near-starvation, my sailor years.
So why did you call me over? I asked her at last. She said
Most men would assume they knew!
Why are you different? I was at a loss for a cover-up.
I noticed you last year, on All Quiet. Sitting as if
the world ended before it reached you.
You bewildered and brave, not agreeing to this, though it
had been so a long time. One alone in the bathhouse not sweating.

How do you read all this? I strangled out.
Theatre, she said. *Even Hollywood is theatre. Everything*
in theatre is understood to be performance. Gesture, pose:
all get judged, expertly and sidelong. You know this.
You still do extra's work, though you could play major roles.
So: are you hiding out, among the performers? Are you
perhaps a murderer? A strange Yes was in my mouth
but it was madness. *No!* She gave me a Dazzling look:

> '*Let me be, World, let me be!*
> *Don't tempt me with gifts of love,*
> *let my lone heart brood above*
>   *its heap of joy and misery* (*Eduard Mörike,* she said,
> then went on) *I do not know what I mourn for,*
>   *it is for some unknown woe;*
>   *only through tears does the lovely glow*
>   *of sunlight reach me any more.—*'

I asked her *Stop.* And told her, in takes and out-takes,
stumbling over my story. She watched me closely for lies
as it tumbled out. Then she touched the back of my hand
which we don't know really. *Your skin is deaf, then?* she asked.
I gulped *Yes. Deaf all over?* I agreed there too.
Sie sind aber einmalig. You are but once. You're unique.
Now I do see. A boss cocky steamed along in his cravat,
wriggled with excuses to Miss Dietrich, and told me

You missed an Extras call, Boettcher. Once more and So long.
Very naughty of you to enchant our crowd-swellers, Miss D.
She gave him a woman's look that is worse than wit
and we talked on. *I think it's the Inner Man*
keeps me from some strife. Maybe he feels, and just won't tell me.—
Your Unconscious, said Marlene. *The Dreamer. That's high fashion now.*
Your It. That's how they now call Your Inner Man.—
I'm sure It, I thought bitterly. *I think I'm the unconscious one, not him.*

If I was so easy to spot, I thought,
Hollywood was too hot for me. I'd get called again.
I started to plan my getaway from then on.
In the New Year of '32, the Direktor, as they pronounced him
started work on his orgy scene. We were all to rub
ourselves up to just short of climax, to give us
the right charge and hot glisten of desire. Well, I thought,
I draw the line. A beggar must be a chooser.

Steve Hegedus, who had a speaking part,
told me this trick was an old one of von Stroheim's
from the silent days, not used since. Then he said a word
in Hungarian that I gather means sex with your mother between
the candles round her bier, reached inside his red-striped
K.u.K. uniform trousers and started, singing along
this rocking-horse rhythm *A grof a grof a vizbe fullt.* I knew it
as *Der Graf der Graf ins Wasser fällt.* The Radetzky-March!

Work dried right up for me. I found myself out one week
in the orange groves burning off frost in the night
with big fixed oil flares, lucky to get Mexicans' wages.
Funny how being broke makes a wind-vane of you,
switches you right round. Suddenly I'm offering my numb talents
to Aldo my agent. Look no pain! with a skewer:
Look at me break chain! He told me what Lula had told me:
The rubes believe its faking. I half believe its faking.

On the movies, they know it's fake. You was a freak that be different.
You're a freak you should look freaky. Freak without the look is geek.
So no dicerola. One day I'm lying round the flat
and a man in gloves comes to drive me out of town in a Bentley
way up past the Patton Ranch, to lunch in a piny country club.
Up there the sun's a pure place in the sky,
I'm in dungaree rig in times that wore at least cravat and jacket
but Marlene's my hostess and the times they know to lay off.

That day I first ate Tijuana salad, that got its name changed
to Caesar salad when people kept making cockroach jokes.
Another day I got found by the Australian colony
and taken to Snowy Baker's house. John Farrow was there, Frank Thring,
Annette Kellerman was there, but my eye lit on Ty Calser,
Thoroblood's gatekeeper. In the Bloke language, Baz reckoned,
every word could be shortened to one syllable: look at Tiny. *Watch self,*
was what Ty said to me. *Just watch fun self, Tiger.*

They were talking so much billy tea billycarts and barley Charlie
it was like they were making a big tent of Australia
to sit in out of their Yank lives. I was only homesick for my family,
not even able, now, to send them cheques to sleep with
before cashing, as Laura wrote in letters.
I'll take you back, said Thring with a soft nod into his neck.
Now go and talk to the Nobbies. Friends of your Lula. I went, dazzled.
The Nobbies turned out to be a retired vaudeville couple

so married they talked in tandem: *He likes the way—*
she puts the unexpected into my sentences—they come out near the mark.
Both as lean as old oyster sticks, signets and smokes growing on them.
We were in flickers—way before the War—did you know Australia
could have beaten the Yanks to Westerns?—we had them first: you recall
bushranger pictures?—Bobbies and Bushies?—sent up the troopers rotten
falling on their prats—the guns were smoke-squirts: the weapon
was ridicule—so the peelers got them banned—yes, in 1912

they had Parliament pass a law—and Hoot Gibson rode off with the genre.
But the Yank story, it's different—it's bringing things to a head
and settling them by killing.—Ours was the opposite, and new:
that violent death's pretentious, that only police natures need it.
Death'll silence both of you when it takes one of you, I thought,
and I was sorry in advance, because I loved them. Bang, straight off.
Comedy and consensus in place of government, they were saying,
but something in me was hungry. I hoed into mutton and lamington cakes

and when I woke, in a back room, Thring was gone.
I cursed and swore, but Snowy said *Thring is a card:*
he was just so funny about this Queensland big gun, Sir Peter
Something, a minister, before a Royal Commission.—
Did he go down, Sir Peter?—No, he ran the thing, from the dock!
Weird. You walk out of luxury you've been let have
and walk the miles home because you haven't got the fare,
and the party's on, as it was all through the Thirties:

you go upstairs into it. Charlie's mother is there with Tad
and winds round his leg with a purr and looks at you
with an eye that says You weren't willing: now cop this.
I knew she'd say something. She let me wait, and then
Too tired for fun, Freddy: not enough wattage for it?
Corny. The look had been enough. I went out on my grille
and sat in the air. And remembered when things had weight,
not just Float or Stick Fast. You don't know what I'm saying.

Last thing happened at the apartment, Marlene visited me.
On a cool afternoon with the new City Hall way in the distance
a long limousine drew up, an old fellow swathed in suitings helped her,
talking fast with all his hands. Kissing ends before telling.
She came up, and told the blokes finding excuses to crowd around
I have brought Fredy's lunch and will bake for you all if you scram.
They bubbled off like turkeys. Charlie's mother, she looked out
of Tad's room and died in the face, and I felt ashamed of that.

Food's a kind of love, Dietrich meant, one that didn't get played often
in black and white. But she had been through the blockade
the Allies had kept on Germany till the second year after the War.
I know poetry and starvation and cold cuts
said the most glamorous woman then in the world
as we stowed beef haunches and wurst in the Frigidaire.
I also know vamping. You don't want to be vamped.
I think you've seen where all that—her voice wobbled with dread—*ends.*

We talked, she floured and baked, but she once asked me
Will you sell our conversations? So I won't.
At one stage that afternoon Artur Gunst rolled into the kitchen
and asked me how often I'd been inside a house
in America that looked like the ones they showed in movies.
Once, I reckoned. *The first. But an Australian owned that one;*
he was a crook. I haven't been in Yankee houses.—
Marlene was up and bristling, I saw: this was aimed at her.

How often were you in a Metropolis? she purred at him.
I never even slept with the boss class of one, he snapped back
and they were into it hammer and sickle. Hammer und Säckel,
as they say in Switzerland. Bourgeois worker sow parasite—
You're a luxury toy: you haven't got a shred of working class
consciousness!—So how would you share me among the proletariat?—
I leave that to you!—I opened my mouth to defend
and got waved shut. *I can fill my fantasies*

and yours with blood and never spill a drop. Gunst really should
have brought the masses with him. Alone she had her army with her.
After Marlene left, they didn't lose much time
telling me I was a party pooper anyway
and should maybe go be lapdog to my consumer blonde,
or blonde consumer: they got that both ways round.
Besides, I was three weeks behind in my share of the rent.
That, that was right. And just saved Artur getting flattened,

which saved my life later. Weissmuller came that night
with his swimming mates, to celebrate his Tarzan contract
and popped some muscles for us, *like ten hard-ons at a time,
oh baby!* cried one party-goer. Don't you ever go to movies?
People used to ask me. I didn't in Hollywood, nor much after for years.
Phyllis Gates was there, and told me about the Zeppelin
that was coming round the world to demonstrate they were safe
after the English losing their overloaded R101.

I saw Phyllis put her hands and face on me, and do things
and I let her—but I only wanted to sleep.
It was as if Marlene had brought me a parcel of sleep
rather than groceries, which anyway got taken as my rent.
Next day I wandered off and walked the famous streets
I've never remembered the names of: was Rodeo Drive there then?
I know I walked past Ravenswood, Mae West's apartment palace
and clear up into Dobermann Pinscher land, Beverley Hills,

but I woke in the scrub below the HOLLYWOOD sign
naked with my clothes folded near, to keep them uncreased a bit longer.
I Indian-plucked my whiskers and found a set where shooting had ended,
a sort of Chicago with cap-marks from faked bullet hits
and started hibernating on a sofa behind flats. My tide
was fully out that winter.
It was probably no more than twice a week
I'd dress and come out, and line up with the crew

on some set at lunch call. They'd often cover for bums:
it's okay, to the studio cop, *he's my new best boy.*
One day, more in a dream of ships than hopes of a berth,
I hitched down to Long Beach. There on Terminal Island
I saw the Army breaking up a strike:
step, swing the butt, sprawl your half-starved striker,
step over him or on him, swing the butt, all silent, widening forward
into the beanie caps and rage-noise, with buckled badged rifle slings

raking faces open, the bayonets with scabbards still on
to show it's a civil action, the upswing of butts like the screw-boom
of a harvester made of sheriffs, in their suntans and level-brimmed hats,
mowing the losers. I found a man with his forehead skin
over his eyes, and walked him to San Pedro. That was where
I finally got inside an ordinary Yank house, of this kind woman
who bandaged Clay's head *My Lord, what terrible times!*
It was just a small bungalow with more gadgets and moderner photos

than at home. Nothing special. I'd have had more talk as she fed us
but Clay bit on his spoon and reared and smashed out, screaming
Aii bourgeois heejaw annunciar EEVEEE Chapel Chapel
which God knows what it meant: it must have been the bash to his head,
and he ran, prophesying and circle-dancing, with his arms spread:
every time I got near he'd speed on, I couldn't peg him,
up out onto gravel roads in the Palos Verdes hills
with their fat gum trees, different there because nothing ate them.

It was one of the awfullest deaths: he tore his bandage
off his head, ripped his red forehead back over his red eyes
and bled and rolled face-banging in the white dirt so a crust
kept drying and bleeding through again, and he desperately
shouted with no sense in it from the human bottom half his face
*Ar gyre gyreo illumezoho it's printer Franklin his his
reading we live tehew tehew! marry tobacco—*
No dignity in it, his eyes were horrified staring Save me,

shut me up! You couldn't hold him but at last
I got all his jolts pinned and went the dead man's carry
and people came at last; I'd been after him
all afternoon. So we got him, dead, to the sheriffs—
I'd felt him buck and loosen as he died. They laid him out
and questioned me. *So you're a indigent alien?*
is how that finished up. *Virgil, see if this here sailor's
jerkwater country got a consulate in Los Angeles.*

While I was still in shock from the printer's awful run
they took me to the British consul. *Ah Jack*, he said, *old lad,
much as I'd like to oblige I can't do you a free passage
to Sydney. Nor yet Liverpool. I'd have half the Empire queuing up.
I just might, might get you aboard a British bottom
in the captain's charge to work your passage to—who knows?
Perhaps vaguely homeward. There's worse than British bottom.*
I don't know, but he gave me my first legal drink in three years,

and he didn't have to. Their Empire wasn't all starch
and I had the run of it when it was draught Bass and long socks
from Kowloon to Durban, before the Bushido unstrung it.
He released me to go to the apartment for my duffel.
*Hey Freddy! The lady from Shanghai give you the air?
A long sighted man gets into the bed first,
a nearsighted man helps the lady undress. You should have
asked us about the protocol.*

I longed to be black and white in my shadowy Chicago
not out where nearly all I ever heard was lines.
And then I committed one. Steve came out with his pyjamas unbuttoned
and a blue stockwhip of a scar right across him above his navel.
I stared. He said *The War.*—*I'm glad they put you back on
facing forwards*, I said. The heavy tired closed on me
and I slept for hours. Phyllis sat beside me as I woke
and the soles of her shoes had dime-sized patches dark with sweat.

I reckoned she was down to cardboard linings, and said so.
Ah, Fred, she said, *don't be kind. Don't give me shoes.*
She lifted my elbow and linked her arm in mine:
I guess you're leaving soon. I don't know but I feel it.
I said her country was throwing me out, and then
that this might get me home, at last, to my wife and boy.
There were tears in her eyes. *I knock on every wrong door.
Why did you let me do those things?*

Well I knew not to ask what things; the penny drops
farthing by farthing with me, but I did know that.
Anything I said was going to sound like a promise
or else too cruel.
Like, how to tell Phyll I was sitting in the middle of the air
not supported, and touched only in my head.
I came up with *Will you come with me to see the Zeppelin?*—
Don't buy me Zeppelins. I need you, not a frame of hot air.

You're going to leave on that thing, aren't you? I know.
I thought I was leaving, for somewhere, on a British ship
but ears inside me pricked up. It was an idea.
Maybe they were going to as good a landfall as any
British one. I meant, for getting home.
I'd have to inveigle like a champion, or stow away—who better
for that than a trained stowing hand? Then noises banged below
and I went out on the balcony grille, Phyllis with me. Cops

were hoisting themselves up the fire escape. It was a raid. I swept
Phyllis off her feet and kicked out the linchpin
so the iron stair dropped GAJANG! and GAJANG! again
as we went down in crashes past them. *Hayes Office*, I yelled out,
*I just saved this innocent young thing in the nick of time!
Carry on, officer!* It should never have worked
and wouldn't nowadays. We walked for ages then
right to the Universal back lot where my Chicago was

because Phyll wouldn't go home to the boarding house.
Here's Phyllis then. She was still alive two years ago.
Next day being Sunday and no studio cops in sight
I edged out and got into the costume department. I don't know:
it was like as if a country had died out, or the world
and the clothes were left hanging, or on the shelves in bales.
I posed in a kimono, in an iced scarlet Grenadier coat,
in pinstripes and chaps, I snuffled miles of field grey,

getting drunk on the mothballs. Civil War dresses and Roman
armour hung over me in hoists. It was headless angels,
it was ranks of skyhook soldiers, it was every king's Colonel Blimps,
it was women laced like cream boots, or fattened with a bezel,
soupkitchen of helmets, breastplate cemetery, corpses of overcoat
and everything hollow, that you looked up into dreading feet—
I got a grip then, of good croc hide, and put in
just enough clothes to make up for my left-behind duffel,

and it still felt like thieving, and was.
Then I went and slept like a hero in his film can, till it
was time for Phyll and the airship. We managed bus fares to the field
where the tower-mast was, and half the Hollywood big guns
in ice-cream suits and chalk stripes and co-respondent shoes
and that queer American razor-edged look, steaming with lotions.
It was a sweet lilac sky, with air so clear the day moon
looked like a washed potato, up above the phone wires.

Then there was another moon, browner
with rays like umbrella struts, getting bigger, pointing at us.
Turning to port, to circle us, it lengthened to a breadroll
with glass in its chin, with a gallery of all windows
and its five big growlers beating and smoking. It sloped down
unsupported and enormous like a world. It swayed, crabbing
in the breeze, rigging hung from it, a huge honk voice came down
in a German accent *Able bodied men please help to steady*

the vessel by taking the rope nets—the big three-cornered lattices
of shrouds and ratlines called Spinnen, spiders, meant for ground crew
came sheaving down, and we nearest, just the men
if we cared to, hauled, to get its nose-ring down
in line with the mast toggle. *You can feel the sky pulling*, a man said
next to me. *Please keep clear of the propellors*
said the enormous voice and I heard a vast widespread Oh!
just as the nose linked. The props stopped and ran down

from shine to shatter as the motors cut. We let go
the shrouds and stepped back from her cliff of shadow
and the long tram of windows underneath. People up in those
were all yelling and pointing. I turned. It was Phyllis and a crowd
supporting and grabbing at her. Men with flashbulb cameras
running up to her, men with notebooks shouting.
I wedged through it all and she fell on me, having trouble
with her breathing and her face. *I walked clean through it,*

I was looking at you the engine just glided from behind me—
She walked through the propellor! Just goddam didn't look
she should be hamburger Sliced boloney Ist a richtiges Wunder.
Then the Germans swept us up a carpeted gangway and safe
from the Yank reporters, inside the ship in a saloon
with stylish fittings and big polished windows set aslant
as a glass keel, nearly, and a strip of more window underfoot.
We got coffee and schnapps and hushed voices, the disaster special:

Tell the reporters Miss (?) Gates is not for them yet ready,
and things I heard in German. They were desperately relieved
they hadn't killed her, and frantic to play down the incident.
Phyll bounced back pretty quick. Chillicothe Missouri
breeds as resourceful women as anywhere, it seems.
The young officer in charge of us was awestruck by the odds
she had beat, and babbled numbers *Fifty, sixty thousands to one*
but stiffened and shut tight when the second officer came back

from greetings and explaining. *Voss,* he clicked, *Leutnant, at orders.*
The Captain comes soon to offer the apologies of our ship
and our Luftreederei—airship line—and to congratulate you
your wonderful good fortune! And your companion is—?
Boettcher, Friedrich, I gave him with just the shadow of a snap
so he would know. *You are German?—Colonial. Kriegsmarine.—*
What ship?—Goeben, Constantinople and Odessa. Then wounded.—
If I wanted things from these folk, I had to look square from the off.

Well the Captain did come, after letting us cool off
and making sure the press hounds missed the early papers.
Phyll had her break, and played it. Dinner with the Captain
would be charming: she accepted. But she'd really love a flight, on
to say New York. With her fiancé Mr Boettcher.
Broadway, she said to me when we got on our own.
I know I can't have you. No one can. And this miracle, so called,
is going to lift me high and drop me Smash

if I stay here. It might as well take me to Broadway
and let me try my luck there. I thought she was wrong. They'd quite
likely make a movie of the Propellor Girl:
Starlet Spared from Fatherland's Blades, Airscrews Diverted by Love,
Grace Beats the Age of the Machine, Dance Step Evades Propellor—
I'm quoting papers. They'd have to do the movie in nine days.
The Captain thought my way too, so he didn't buck or rear
at getting her story a continent away, fast. Not when for two

days it kept his mission and the coming Olympics off page one.
Do you remember it? the prop? I asked as we promenaded round:
It was like the air was cloth, suddenly, and it took a gather,
she said. *That's as near. The engine passed ommm like a train—*
and we hugged and cried, as the shock caught up with me at last.
Being only engaged, as they thought, we had separate cabins
as was proper. The Zep sat like me in the air,
but for real, and it could rise. No other thing is like it,

no other ship, no plane; there's silence, talk's still going on
then the talk turns into shouts because you're hundreds of feet up
and when did it happen? You're drawing away like the moon
going back to Heaven. The only sound, sometimes, this catarrh
rush as the water ballast goes jettisoning down,
and then the engines catch their rhythm from one another.
I sat in the saloon, first night out, with pen and Zeppelin notepaper
writing to Joe, as I'd managed a lot of weeks to do:

This Sydney Bridge must be a marvel. Any luck I'll see it soon.
I'm on my way at last, via Germany. Might see Oma.
A toff told how in New Haven the streets of the cemetery
had the names and layout of the town streets. You were buried at your number.
It was the Night Addresses! I'd dreamed it long ago.
Suddenly I knew why I hadn't asked about the crushed fellow
in Cleveland. I doubted I, or Australia, or peace had
much effect in the adult world. The death and killing world.

BOOK 4

The Police Revolution

When we got to New York, that is not paved with gold
but with dollars of chewing gum, I did get a job
on the L.S. Das Rheingold. I had to climb a lot of notches
down the high noses of her officers, from being a travel-guest,
a passenger. And I'm not proud how the vacancy
I filled got vacant. There was a rigger in the crew
name of Peter Salomon, that three of the others smashed up
in a bar for saying the German fighter ace

Joseph Jacobs was as good or better a pilot
than Hermann Goering, and I didn't stand up for him.
It saved his life, maybe. He stayed on in America
and I took his watches over Far Rockaway,
over the Atlantic, over the pine-trees and fields
clear to Friedrichshafen, with its lake and church
and its hangars hundreds of yards long that we would tow
our switched-off ships into, a hundred marching men to a side.

Yes yes, Boettcher. We lift off for Singapore soon!
Meantime, I could eat, because airships didn't lay off
and pick up hands for each voyage. We stayed hired.
I thought of trying for a shift across to the Graf
but she plied to Brazil, not that much nearer home.
*Dear Love I'm boarding with a family Sievert. They build
sailing boats. Decent people, with three sons out of work.
The one at home, Jost, bled a towel full last week from a brawl.*

Far from my family, yet to the locals I was
the lucky pig himself, having a job in Germany.
Frau Sievert, knitting with her finger up, the Catholic way,
reckoned it was shameless, all the poor boys out of work
and blaming themselves, not the Bolsheviks.
Her Jost had taken his gold tooth to the pub
and a man laid hands on her—I got lost at this stage
and asked how big a tooth he had and did it

stick out of his mouth? The newer slang often stumped me.
Seems it meant his girl. *Where did you learn German then,
Herr Boettcher?—In our colonies, Ma,
that we'll get back from the English. Eh, Fredy, eh?*
Jost was teaching me how to bend planking
and treenail boats. We'd sail across to Rohrschach
or Romanshorn and listen to the Switzers
swallow beer and their language with never a doubt of themselves.

They're sort of Scotch to the Germans, so imagine:
Yon Hitler's a coof. He stravaigs aboot an aa
his buitlickers reach oot tae pat him wi their haunds
but he refuses them wi's ain haund cruickit back
like a bairnie fendin aff a guid skelp o the tawse.
It took Jost's father Klaus and I to hold Jost back
there in the beer garden. *November criminals Versailles—!*
Ye should hae focht hairder, says the Switzer, chewing wurst.

L.S. Hindenburg was building, Graf Zeppelin plied to South America
and Das Rheingold was to cover the East, Singapore, Shanghai
but the service hadn't started yet. We adjusted and tested,
filled in time, really. We went on training flights. On this one
over the Alps, we had a man out on a line
in his big felt slippers, patching a gas leak half way
down the curve of the hull, big white peaks pointy below him,
valleys and I spose cows. The young Navy sailor paying out

rope to him from the hatch slipped on the metal deck
and the rope jerked free, and ran.
He screamed and grabbed at it, couldn't hold it, it burned him
and leaped and whipped over the hatch-coaming. I was near
and came at the gallop and grabbed it. Bam! It jerked me
half out of the hatch, but I kept my holt on it
and started to haul it in, hand over elbow,
hand over elbow, till Zugbauer appeared and rose

white as the moon, and threw up soon as he was safe:
Urr Fredy urr! Sakrament! I thought I was a goner.
Straight down into the cuckoo clocks! Where's that sodding matlow,
that Navy breechloader? I'll pull his tongue out his navel—
Then he got sober: *But wait on Fred: I don't see anything*
you could have got a hitch around.—
There's me, I said.—*You're lighter than me, Fred.*
We'd have gone together. Something smells Spanish here.

The watch Leutnant came to my hammock and he said
Lift your shirt. As I thought: no rope burns there.
Show me your hands. Yes. I see, but I don't believe.
No one could do what you've done. Who are you, Boettcher?
I blessed the Golightlys as they pranced on stage in my head:
I was in a circus. Doing strongman work and trapeze—
He went, and I thought it was over, but
Miracles follow you, Boettcher, as the big Press cameras blazed;

that was the Captain, with his adam's apple at play
in and out of his wing collar. Tasting the sack he couldn't give me.
Or maybe not: perhaps I was the one shy of miracles,
over shy. Not everyone is Australian about talents
but a gift has to be within reason, in modern countries.
Here's me, the hero, Munich papers August '32,
here's me in Munich; the bandages were put on by the paper
to hide my healed palms. I'd been in the German Museum

studying the first Diesel engine and cetera. I came out
and the Communists were crossing the Isar bridge, red flags up
without swastika, and the khaki troops' red flags up with it,
yelling *Juda verrecke! Bolschewisten raus!* The mobs met
with this awful leap at each other, chains and iron bars swinging
in a big roar soon streaky with screams. The police were useless,
standing round in their flowerpot hats, terrified to move in.
When the fight drew apart, there were dead and crippled men

getting dragged away, and others like them being stood round.
The side that stayed were singing *Make way, make way
for our Brownshirt battalions/Clear every street for the
marching SA men!* to a wonderful tune, but I
was watching a Brownshirt with a stove-in collarbone
cough blood and cry till one of his mates leant down
and slapped his face. This woman next to me said
out of a hard jaw *That'll remind him he's an Aryan.*

Millions look up with hope to the swastika, the boys sang
and skuldragged him off. It gave you another picture
of Munich than huge king-post pubs and crockery churches,
but I was hanging round the Bahnhof, waiting for Sam
to come from Paris. Fourteen years had put condition
smoothly on him, and a first-class double-breasted suit
with gold tie pin. We sent his crocodile port
to his hotel in its own taxi, and sat down

to drinks in the English Gardens. *You have three grey hairs, Freddy.
I've got four, look.* We talked about being far from home
and how I supported my family that way, whereas
if I had their company, we'd starve together, with police insults
for our chorus music. *Depression makes Abos of us all,*
Sam nodded. *Yes. In my Githavul grandfather's country
Nguthumbuyn there is a mountain that stands
like David's city on a high place, a basalt palace*

four square on top of three thousand foot of steeps.
I've never seen it, but I've dreamt of it
with halls and corridors inside, like Mont St Michel
and the old men saying: See, we did build. Not just poetry
justifies us in the world. Stuff he couldn't tell
to anyone in Europe, and only just to me.
I quarter understood it. Just not to be a savage;
all that side of him craved a gallop in the sun.

In Germany one speaks German, I heard at my elbow.
It was a tight-arse teacher-looking fellow
with a red face and his collar in rolls of fat
with his mother, she looked like, all in grey with brooch.
I decided to sing dumb and spoke in English to him
but the woman said *Disgraceful. Blackamoors and riff-raff,*
and before I thought I'd called her a hag and a witch
and great big boys in khaki with collar tabs were coming

over to take an interest. I'd noticed the Litfass pillars
in the city, the tall like mail boxes for posters
had placards with this little kid in a singlet
chewing on a crust. *Capitalism steals even your last crust.*
Vote Communist. Vote Thälmann. These boys weren't Comm voters
any more than their town. *Where did you buy this nigger?—*
He's an Australian like me, I answered, getting up,
and I noticed they didn't try to sit me back down.

Do you always dress your niggers better than yourselves?
Or are you his white nigger? I noticed Sam was about
to speak. He did, and I translated it to them:
My friend asks what army are you?—Tell him the White army
that'll keep little schwartzers like him in their place.
Tell him take off his shoes. No need for shoes on Sambo.
I told Sam all of it, and told them from me I didn't
think Sam'd do it. And Sam did not, but asked

mildly *Is he out to restore the self-respect of Germany?—*
What's with this arsewipe anyway? shouts the SA man,
questioning me! Being puzzled sent him wild
and he leapt at Sam. I tripped him and head-kicked him,
took a broken litre-glass off his mate and floored him
and the third one who'd snatched out his dagger, I broke his arm.
A lot were leaving the beer hall, some giving me a cheer,
some looking death at me. *Why did they think*, Sam grinned

at the teacher and his mother, *that the Superman would be*
one of their kind? Or on their side in anything?
He had to nudge me to translate this, and I did;
Come with us, Comrades! Two fellows were urgent at the door,
help us smash these thugs from Cornelius Street. You can!
But Sam and I had years to catch up on.
The first truckload of Brownshirts pulled up outside the beer hall
as we watched. So we talked in a porcelain church.

Boots hammered past, searching for us. I made jittery plans
to escape from the city. *They'll have the railway stations covered—*
but Sam waved me quiet, and went on with old times.
When he was ready to move, coming on dusk, he said
Relief from starchy Virtue. Letting go the sphincter of Good.
Not Knowing Your Place any more. I could be a Brownshirt
thinking with my muscles. How tempting their corps must be!
with their Führer to supply rationale. They already rule this city.

We shared a taxi out to the first village railway station
and the stopping-train to Friedrichshafen.
I'll shout you a steamer ticket home to Sydney, Fred.
You know I mean it, and can afford it. Why not?—
Ah, Sam thanks a million, but I'm on wages to Singapore,
and I still believed it. He waved, and chuffed on west
to join the Paris express train. Something he wasn't telling me
and I felt it. Next morning at the Sieverts

there was this fellow in suit and tie and Nazi badge
sitting in the best room and the family tiptoeing around him.
He sprung up and Heiled Hitler when I hove into view:
I came to apologise for the rude mistake
one of our patrols made, annoying you yesterday in Munich.
A German hero one does not annoy!
You dealt with them in appropriate warrior fashion.
You're invited to the Brown House, to our German minorities office.

Welcome, folk-comrade! And he pumped my hand.
How did you know I lived here? I asked, bewildered,
then dropped down that this was Europe: every dog
and every man was registered. And the registration books
weren't barred to his lot. *When we start to turn*
this debt-slave republic back into a people, he crowed,
we will prove to know where everyone lives, you'll see that!
Your mother lives in Dresden. Frau Sietz. Have you visited her?

I tipped he knew I hadn't yet. I asked him:
The Volk are us Germans, aren't they?—Naturally.—But look
at this list of SA men in the paper, Baretzki, Kaduk,
Mulka, Breitwieser, Broad—Percy Broad!—Capesius, Dilewski:
they don't all sound German, to my ears. What are they?—
Those are the names of their estates and villages
in the East, conquered long ago by their heroic
Teuton forebears, in lands where we will make our Living Space.—

Old Klaus Sievert did laugh after the man went
and Jost told me *Father, he's still stuck on the Dear Departed,*
the Kaiser. That old ponce with his little chicken hand on his sword.
Fifty thousand a month we waste on that one, while the poor starve.
But his father didn't bite. When I got back to work
that Monday, the bosun told me *Get your duffel,*
Fredy my son. We're bound for the East and slit-eye mama.
I jumped to it with my heart singing Home Sweet Laura Home

and not a pang for rye bread with applesauce, not
a backward glance at Asbach Uralt. As we swelled up above
the Dornier works, a seaplane was splitting the blue
cobble of the Soil Sea, Lake Constance to you English.
Not seeing my mother, perhaps forever now, that did worry me
as I looked out for drier hills and the edge of deserts
but we never came to them. The land stayed green and green
and goose-ponds and beet-fields. Why had I let Sietz hinder me?

He was just a bullfrog. A hand-lifting belt-gripper now, I'd bet.
Don't we strike Turkey soon? I asked Balz Zugbauer that I'd hauled
up on the safety line. *We're over Russia, Fred,*
that's where we're going. East into the Workers' Paradise.
Don't you know our government keeps an air force
under wraps on airfields out there? We're carting supplies to them.—
No Singapore? Not at all? I was so knocked sideways
I croaked it out. Three years lost. God strike that bloody Sir Peter!

The aerodrome we winched down onto had
two long grass strips, some bell tents and squared-log cabins
and the Weimar flag over it. Our captain was received
by a snappy guard detachment and a colonel buttoned so tight
he looked like a scabbard and walked like dividers on a map.
Colonel von Passt. I'd played men like him in Hollywood
and I'd soon be ashamed I had. I'd got the walk
but not the character. That day and next we stood watch

or trooped ashore between times and watched the trainees jog
or roll in the Rhön wheel, a double steel circle joined with struts
like I'd thought up for the circus, or they might chin the bar.
I itched to show off, but held in, as the wheelers toppled round.
It was on the third day we heard a motor screaming
and saw a high old-fashioned lorry dragging dust
across the flats with two like it hell-for-leather after it.
The first never slowed at our pole barrier, it smashed

that barber-pole to splinters and made grooves to the HQ steps.
The driver leapt out and up those, stood as the other two too
ploughed to a stop. The Colonel came out and stood.
Red stars and blue patches were on the pursuers and they
were halfway to their man when the Colonel spoke and his
interpreter yelled STOI! The hunted fellow's face
told how near he was to fainting, but he wouldn't sway.
The rear flap of his truck was down, and all the length

of the steel tray was smeared with blood which big slack things
had been dragged through. I thought: a butcher's truck
for carrying carcases. The men in crumpled tunics were shouting
vrag naroda! and other Russian, but the Colonel's voice
never rose. I heard *Intergovernmental matter, higher instance*
and *the diplomatic channel*, then the Colonel's guards arrived.
I looked over the plains we were on, the slight swell and the odd
clump of whitewashed birch trees. A shiver came off it,

and I didn't know why. Something I felt through my null
like a louse ran over my liver. We got sent home
that very afternoon, with the hunted man as passenger.
He tells a bad tale, Balz said. *He'll hardly talk, and then
you wish he hadn't. He's German, from generations back
settled out here. Sounds old-fashioned Swabian. Seems
he's been carting dead people from NKVD posts in some
of the towns around, to a big grave-trench in the woods,*

*thousands of them each week, all shot in the back of the head.
Enemies of the people, they're called. The police have a quota,
a production norm to meet, so they pull in anyone,
men or boys, not many young women, them they fuck
as the price of their men's lives. Anyway our boy, he
gets sick of it, and of waiting to get a lead idea
in his own noggin, so he's done a bunk to us, for sanctuary
among fellow Germans. The Nazis'll have a feast on that.*

Bang bang, eh Fred?—Grandmother, teach 'em younger
they mustn't cry with hunger
but stand up for their right
with father and his brothers,
red flags above all others,
for freedom and the light,
for beef trucks wet with shite—
He gave me a wink and slapped off in his slippers.

We throbbed in over house lights where Germany was playing.
Headlights and torch parades, suburban slam-the-door sketches,
great miles of yellow footlights. Nothing of it seemed real:
it had all caught up with my unrealness.
No one down there would hurt if you hit or killed them,
no one would complain.
They were all in a movie. Shock caused a terrible calm
some men killed to jolt alive from, but often it left them more calm.

Having to write to Laura and say what went wrong
with my plans to get home was as hard a job as ever.
Talk about earn as you yearn. And the butcher's truck
part of it beat me. I couldn't write that. I tried.
That'd stay in me till it croaked out some desperate day.
It'd give me bad dreams. One was of a dead courtroom
with the usual picture of a fireplace and animals mounting it
up above the judge, and the floors all dragged with blood;

one was a happy dream of the poet Burns taking the poor
people to Australia on a cane ship so long it had
to bend around Africa; and one was a soda-bitten potstick
stirring in a cauldron; that one would wake me screaming out.
After the Russia trip we flew to Nuremberg
which I reckoned would be Nazi to the bone. In fact it hardly
gave him the smell of a vote. The mayor was mad for Stalin.
Adolf had his rallies there to nark the place and woo it.

Then we went to Dresden, and I got leave to stay
and see my mother. That was the most beautiful city
I ever saw in the world. You can only get there now by Zeppelin,
or else it's some netted building sites out on a great wide floor.
Back in '32, when Hitler was winning Lippe-Detmold,
it was narrow and high and carved in walnut stone,
shining with glass and money. I took the Falkenstrasse tram
past the big brewery to the Persian-rug apartment

Sietz had installed my mother in. Coffee and bee-sting cakes,
kisses and hugs and tears. *Will you settle now
in the Fatherland? Will your wife*—she'd forgotten Laura's name—
*feel at home in this country? How long have you been away?
Are you separated from her? Josef must be a big boy now.*
It wrung me, it shook me. And I dreaded when Sietz would come home
but who knew? Perhaps he'd mellowed. Perhaps being there was enough
Fatherland for him. It turned out it wasn't. After dinner,

when I'd been corrected, at thirty-seven years of age,
for calling him Volkmar: he was Herr Stepfather to me,
I got a lecture on the Jews in business, their interest rates,
their promoting each other, their profits from the War,
then selling out Germany. He had this Russian book,
but translated into German, that told their entire strategy
for capturing world power. *In countries known as progressive
and enlightened we have created a senseless filthy*

abominable literature, he read out, and: *The ill-guided acquaintance
of a large number of persons with questions of politics
creates utopian dreamers and bad subjects and
A tax increasing in percentage ratio to capital
will give a larger return than present individual
or property taxes, which are useful now only because they excite
discontent and strife among the goyim.* He even read *Think carefully
of the success we arranged for Darwinism, Marxism, Nietzscheism.*

*To us Jews at least it should be clear what disintegrative effect
these have had on the minds of the Gentiles.* Well well, I thought
and him so keen on Elizabeth Nietzsche once.
Then he quoted himself: *When we awaken Germany, and lead her,
we will cut this cancer from her dear flesh. We'll reclaim
all the wealth the Jew tapeworms have sucked, and drive them
out to starve in their flyblown Palestine.* My mother
wished us good night, and I saw I was in for hours

more of this, and drinking maté tea with it, since booze,
while folk-comradely enough, was abstained from by the Führer—
also, one is from Paraguay! Sometime after midnight
I was hearing about the ancient German lands
of Thule, far in the North. The cities, the civilisation,
the great warrior culture, all long lost beneath the ice
that drove our tribes southward. Someone called Josef Strzygowski
had written it all up. Like Sietz's Jew-hating manual,

it all started to sound like a half-smart man's excuse
for failure in life. The Bolsheviks, the Nazis, all the movements
had that same excuse-making, blaming-someone throb
in their speechifying voices. But also I thought,
in my bed at last, of a young fellow brought up on
a world he didn't live in. Germany in Paraguay.
At least I was raised unfussy and bush-casual
to fit where I was. I wondered if he spoke Paraguayan.

He was in real estate now. When he'd gone to the office
next morning, my mother took me round the sights
till my head was full of little gold plaster bums.
We ended up drinking coffee on Bruhl terrace
watching the Elbe unravel knots of light
away towards Hamburg. I asked did she miss home,
and she asked where that was. Not surely in that country
where she wasted thirty years going from foreign to the enemy.

We were alone among them.—But we had German friends,
German relations—You were not there for the worst.
We were alone, the relations were alone, each family.
The wives with British husbands were alone.
One should live among own people and own ways.—
My father did think that, and it gave way under him.—
He thought he belonged there. And he did belong to the hills
but not to the neighbours. That is what killed him.—

will it kill me if I don't give up speaking German?
I asked, and cold ran over my innards as I said it
at how much in me was already killed. For that reason?
She let me answer myself. *Split belonging's killed war, in me.*
Being on any two sides spoils you for all sides.—
For right against wrong? snapped my mother. *For decent against low?*
I was sad. That was Sietz talking. I looked over at
the towering Prot church with all its tiers of handholds,

and the cutwaters of the big stone bridge to fellows fishing
on the other side. *Are those the angler-Saxons?*
I asked Mama, but she let that go by. At last
she said to me *You wrote letters to us in German*
during the War. They were read. They didn't help us.
That was the last she said to me, except goodbye stuff.
We swapped odd letters, after, but that was the last of her voice.
She was fifty-eight then. It was thirteen years till she burned.

What passport do you carry, Boettcher? was the question
I got asked, back at work. British subject Australian citizen
it said on the little book I'd had to get
when a sailor's card didn't satisfy all countries any more.
I spent hours in head office with serious men in suits
and signet rings. It seemed I should never have been
allowed along on the Russian trip. My case would be considered.
It meant reporting to the police. It meant the sack.

I asked to be deported, but they informed me at best
I'd be sent to England *given yours is a British passport*
but that as one in possession of State secrets
I'd first have to be released, to depart. It might not be
in the national interest. I'd be advised in due course.
Meanwhile all I could pay the Sieverts in was work
which they didn't have enough of. *You're on the wrong coast here
to join the Jewish Navy!* Jost meant the merchant marine.

I sent my last wages to Laura for Christmas and gifts
and made up my mind to slip over to the Swiss side
and get packed off to England, via Paris I hoped.
I'd give way and accept Sam's offer. All of Germany
was humming with elections. Hitler had lost badly
and was fading away. A tough new general had come in
to replace the Hunger-Chancellor. The Sieverts wanted me
to have Christmas with them: pine-tree and bun-loaf and goose

like I hadn't fully had it since the summer I went to sea
twenty-two years before, after my one year's fulltime farming.
Stille Nacht heilige Nacht and snow on the fir-trees:
at least I saw that once. Then I went through to Bern
but they winkled my German address out of me and bounced
me not to London but right back to Friedrichshafen.
Er meint er isch Australier, isch aber en chaibe Schwab:
He says he's Australian but he's a bloody Kraut.

To make expenses, I put on my peajacket and went
hoisting things and bending things in the Bodensee pubs:
billiard tables, farm rollers, stone-boats, big draught horses,
it seemed I had everything floating off the ground
and pulling down Reichsmarks. Men shivering in the wind
in their thin old coats would bet on me or gravity
in Meersburg, in Immenstaad, in Kressbronn
and the little villages, Leimbach, Unterteuringen,

Ten marks on the sea-bear! And you could watch for nothing.
All the circuses were on winter lay-off. I had no competition.
The cops, when I reported to them, were distracted
and hardly interested. Bigger stuff was happening.
There were two nations in the country, normal and Brown,
and no normal authorities could lay a glove on the Brown.
Odd times I'd get work as a bit of a grunt act between
smarter stuff in a cabaret. I had cut loose from Sieverts

and was on the road by then. This night in Ravensburg
I had bent my bars and tied knots in my pokers
and the singer came on in a yellow-khaki shirt:
On the heath with girl or boy/I lose all my strength through joy—
He got that far and a block of fellows bounced up
at a shout of command and went for him
and no one opposed them. Everybody sat tight.
Where were the old Communists? Where were the Socialists now?

The boys with the Nazi badges looked me over. I had
a crumpled poker still in my hand, and I cracked it
straight like a whip. I never knew that could be done
and their mouths gaped like shop windows offering apes
for sale, as the German saying goes.
It became an act that I did from then on. But that night
was the first where everybody looked aside or down
when someone copped it. The Russian look was becoming the German look.

They took poor Bruno away, head-kicked and kidney-punched.
Ka-Tzet said somebody. *Prison camp, like England had for Boer
women and children. They'll re-educate him good there.*
I started noticing in every sizeable town
SA and SS were running things, and the green police
were taking their orders. Hadn't Hitler lost the election?
*Our Führer is Chancellor in Berlin now. The Day
of German rebirth is here. Show me your papers. Engländer?*

Australian, whatever, how come you speak German?
*So. Then you're Volksdeutsch. You should take German citizenship.
Go to the Volksdeutsche Affairs Office.* Amazing how quick
you learn to play on a new boss-man's fads and fancies.
I'd look crumpled and bleary from sleeping rough to save cash
and the SA would ask was I a tramp. *No German is a tramp:
maybe you need to learn this!—I a tramp, race-comrade?*
I learned to say. *Never! I'm an apprentice entertainer,*

these are my wander-years. Or: it's to harden me again:
too long since I was a soldier. Eh? Oh, the Kriegsmarine.
I was home in the Reich then. More than half the Nazis
believed their own bullshit. Dangerous, when a gang does that:
British justice, French culture, Yankee liberty—
but the Nazis would kill you in the open street
for their Blubo and race-purity, for calling Hitler a Slavenian.
They had their own church rules too. One day in Munich

I was walking along towards the Odeon Square
and a boy and girl fell in beside me, students.
If you go one more block towards the Feldherrnhalle
you'll be asked to give the German greeting. Local custom,
but perhaps you're unaware of it.—The Heil Hitler salute,
the girl said, not giving it. *Perhaps you give it all the time:*
it's very good exercise. I turned off by the Leuchtenberg palace
and surveyed the men in black nailed round the square.

What are the words above that arch down there?
I asked. They marvelled politely at my eyesight:
To my People as Thanks and Example, they recited,
grinned at me, and vanished.
The weeks went on. I still risked sleeping rough,
in spite of the Nazis' hate of tramps and all Bohemia,
because a bed meant registration and police
and leaving a paper-trail. I think it was in Würzburg

a voice in the street said *Freddy Neptune! Blow me,*
it's Freddy Neptune. I looked about, and a man
said *I'm Leila Golightly* in an Australian accent
I know: I was a girl last time we met. So Fred
what are you up to in Germany?
It ended with a job for me in Cirkus Kramer:
Whip that poker straight again: I never saw anything like that!
and Leila, now Leland, said *I am a true hermaphrodite.*

I'm the only AIF artilleryman who ever
got pregnant on active service. That daughter lives with Lula.
Are you horrified?—I was, till I recalled my own fix
but even the Nazis couldn't get me in the family way.
Kramers, the old man and his family, were getting ready
for the road again, testing ropes and patching costumes.
I'd be Fredy Neptune again, and do side bets for extra
but give old Otto a kickback. In Kassel I saw a man

tear down the street whimpering with SA at his heels;
he plunged into an alley. There was a shot, and they came out
glowering at me. *Go and look!* they snapped,
See how we treat trash. There was a cardboard placard
hung round his neck, as he sat there dead in his blood:
Congenital Criminal, it read. They must have been carrying it
from where they'd meant to shoot him. They'd had no time
to letter it there in the alley. I thought: he looks like Globke.

Globke the Berliner. From Turkey. But it couldn't be
or at least it wasn't. Crime hadn't paid, by this one's clothes.
I slipped his papers from the pocket of his worn-out blouse:
a spare identity card never goes amiss, and shame
on me to admit it, I inherited the cash he'd never spend.
Fanning a corpse: I never got lower than that.
Congenital Criminal. Eliminated for the Blood-health
of the Nordic Race. Heil Hitler!—*If the Führer only knew*

what his followers do. Not the first time I'd heard that.
Of course the bugger knew: I never gave him the benefit
of any doubt. There was none. He disgraced half my nature,
disgraced it forever. Someone starts a sentence with The Germans
and my heart still shrivels in me, at what's coming.
We got on the road and followed the springtime north. Drays
spreading manure on snow, pear and apple blossom, hot wurst stalls,
sharp bastards of Nazi cub-scouts out to dob you in,

slow crosses in the sky above the Wasserkuppe mountain. Nobody
now was game to talk politics with strangers. Even old warty Kramer
allowed how the dear Führer was Germany's rescuer.
Adoif Hüttler, he said in his thick Bavarian lingo
is a front-soldier. So was I. Fellowship of men, it was,
fellowship of men. He'll do away with all these repairments.
Leland shook his head, to stop me answering,
and went off to become Leila, for another night's card-reading.

You talk pretty fair German, I told her. *Where'd you learn?*
I mean she tangled up her Der Die Das a bit
more than a native might, but she had the tune.
It seemed she'd gone like me, by way of America,
got involved with a woman and turned into one to escape her.
The German? Oh, I picked that up during the War, was all
she'd say on that subject. And I shook
my head at the vanish she'd pulled on that poor woman.

I did see Minz. In Halle, or was it already Dessau?
Anyway I was walking with Leila and a carnie named Ansaug
who could lift iron weights with the vacuum of his lungs
or lick his lips, spring high and suck on to a wall,
no hands, no feet. He'd wriggle those to prove it. He offered
to show the girls his Fatal Kiss, and they walked wary of him.
It beat my one of standing on one fingertip.
Understand people? He was answering one of us. But we do.

What could you say about them that wouldn't be true?
I spied Minz at that moment, being complimented out
of a restaurant with officers, his civvy suit tight as a uniform,
head shorn, Party badge. No surprises from that human.
Rehearsing a ghost act, asks Leila, *with your head tucked under
your arm like that?—Some Memory Lane over there,* I mutter.
*Keep between me and that lot and be big.—Did you ever
hear me suck music out the big end of a clarinet?* asks Ansaug.

In May, we reached Berlin. We had a sheaf of dates
to play in Wedding, in Lichtenberg, in Pankow,
none of the snob suburbs. On our first free night
Leland and I went in spite of drizzle to the centre
of town to be impressed. *And when we get to Ber-lin,*
he muttered in tune, *The Kaiser he will sayy
Hoch hoch mein Gott, what a bloody woeful lot are the AIFHA—*
We were on the Spree-island, just passing the royal palace

and Leland was saying *I think I'll sit the next war out
as a little kept woman* when we heard yabber-yabber SIEG HEIL!
up ahead, over and over like surf, and saw a glow
brightening. We hurried over the Schloss-bridge
into Zeughausplatz, joined the edge of a great crowd there.
*What's on?—The students, they're burning all the Jew books
and German-hater books.* We worked through to the steps
of the Opera House, for a view. *We burn you, Sigmund Freud,*

*for your filthy incest-theories that demean mankind!
We burn you, Ernst Cassirer, for your corrosive Jew analysis
of noble poetic thought! We burn you, Heinrich Heine!*
they heaped the books in armfuls, to be shingles on a blazing house.
Second time I'd seen books burnt, and this time it was official.
What's that big place they're carrying the books out of?
I asked Leland. *Seems it was the university.—
Was?—Well it won't be now. Couldn't win its arguments.*

That's the public library next door, there where Goebbels is singing.—
He had a big bass voice, for a pipestem of a man.
A lot in the crowd were hesitant about their Sieg Heiling
but scared of those that weren't. And I listened to a woman:
Those sows of scholar books have weighed us plain folk down,
wrong-footed us, got us killed. I'm glad to see them burn.
Culture was always for Lord Muck, to sneer and pose with.
It don't work out in Koepenick. Burn, you fluttering shit-birds!

But I noticed her arm didn't lift. A bone in her shoulder,
perhaps, as old ladies used to say. And the crowd was dense.
As we were leaving, students fronted us: *You are English, yes?*
and we sang dumb: *No, mate, we're Australian.—*
You disapprove burning books in Australia? If you have books there?
I looked at Leland. *Auntie Lula had a book, didn't she?—*
She had three or four.—There was one she dipped in water
to give to sick cows.—What Sex is the Eagle? it was called—

By this stage they'd dismissed us for idiots and waltzed off.
There were hardly any words in my act, and I reckon
the customers were just happy to see heaviness get heaved
up where they might still walk out from under it.
To me, the weights that volunteers strained at, testing,
plus all the motorbikes, anvils, park seats with people on,
were just like Zeppelins: I laid hands on them, they took off
and floated overhead, as if I filled them with my breath.

You couldn't get round how quiet Germany had got
in three or four months, from big talk and whingeing and songs
and heart to heart midnight drinking that German men love,
that any men love, to bang! all eyes down, mum's the word,
the wowsers have the floor. When the police revolution comes
you find you can't guess who are police. Some come unstuck by that
and everything becomes police, the cups, the radio, the sideboard,
all that you'd better own, all that you belong to turns police—

If you're foreign, or half, you think of the strings that'll pull
you out of such country. Not many were foreign then,
or like loosely attached to places. Sailors, circus folk, toffs
of certain kinds, spies, adventurers on the pictures—
I remember one fellow, mousy and dark, who offered
me money to walk him to the station and see him aboard
the Paris train. I went, but only let him buy me
a stand-up beer. Then I twigged. He'd have rather paid a hundred marks

than stay out that long in the open. A hundred marks
is what he offered if I'd see him safe over the frontier.
I can't do the confidence, he said. *I bring suspicion on me.*
In the shack we had years later, I was sorry
I'd let those hundred marks go. But before those times
I nearly cashed in all my years, being a hero.
It was one afternoon, coming home to our hotel
which was the sort where the manager reminds men

not to use the curtains for like after they've pulled themselves.
There was a disturbance up the street, and people crossing
over to the other side to dodge it. SA men
had an old fellow down on the footpath, making him dip
his beard in a billy of milk and scrub the concrete.
Come on Isidore, put the rabbinical back into it!
How could you let the neighbourhood get so down-at-heel?
Don't interfere, Fred. You're mad. They'll flay you alive.

You'll never see Laura or Joe again. But a man, he can't
resist himself sometimes. I smashed them, one two three
and the fourth drew a gun on me, squealing as he did
and I crushed his hand over it. Where it would stay crushed:
a carrion like him, he didn't deserve two hands.
They crawled on the pavement, and the poor Jew said
You have killed me, young man.
It took till they staggered off for what he'd said to reach me.

You have got me my death. Run now or you will die too.—
Where do you live? I asked, as he put his little hat on
and his big hat over it. *Here, in number thirty*, he said.
Cut your hair and beard and make a bolt for the train,
I suggested to him. *Now.* But he looked an old man's look
like up through deep water. *That would expose my family*
and students to my punishment, he said.
and I stood there dumbstruck, holding my useless hands.

He nodded: *You are Shimshon*, wiped his beard and limped off home.
And so did I, towards the Crisp Curtains Hotel
but I hadn't gone far before a low tight whistle
came out of the courtyard of a grimy big block of flats
and a fellow signalled me in,
and on through more courtyards
and into a flat before he spoke. *Decent but not clever.*
You're a foreigner, right? Until your trail gets cold

you should occupy this room. No more heroic gestures.
Answering a knock at the door would be heroic:
don't be tempted. We'll work on getting you away
over the Reich border. Liverwurst, gherkins and black bread
were my diet. I thought of my savings and my clothes
back at the Crisp Curtain, and spent some time writing a cheerful
letter home: *Things may be moving at last.*
After you and Joe, it's white bread and gramma pie

that call me home. I've had my fill of Fatherland.
Now that Hitler's in, he is the fashion
like the War was, you remember. Millions are turning to him:
they call them the Fallen of March. That's March this year.
They've adored him for donkey's years since this March just gone.
What I hate about politics, it's not worth wasting time on
yet it fills up the mind. You aren't free not to give a toss
in these police times. It's like a tooth your tongue must go to.

You are the lucky piggy, my keeper said. *They haven't, squeeze thumbs,*
looked for you at the flophouse or the circus.
Maybe you shamed them too bad to report at all.
But stick around today. We're old unionists, we've got
connections on the waterfront.—Who are you lot? I asked
Franz's narrow cementy face made even more lines, smiling:
We're the dull lot. No romance, no Reich, no Working Class.
Just feed people, get them jobs. Have the State for that and public order.—

Why didn't that work, before?—Maybe the lack of poetry.
Certainly the depressions and defeat-rage. That whole opera
of the World War isn't sung out yet. But Hitler didn't win
the voters' mandate, not ever. He conned the snobs is the fact of it.
Now I think we're in for the opera again. And we'll all march
*because it's the Fatherland.—*I thought to ask him:
How's the old Jewish bloke?—They haven't come for him.
Not yet. Not the others. The ones you bashed will get him

when they've recovered. Unless he and all his mishpocheh
have emigrated by then. And he tapped the side of his nose.
Another time he came, with rye bread and rollmops and
an offer of work on the national Autobahns:
Adolf claims credit for them, but they started in the Twenties.
The pay's piss-poor but you get patriotic speeches.
Doesn't appeal? Only a ship? He sent me back to Kramer
with a promise of word when they had got me a berth.

Up went the junk again, often with people grinning on it.
Muscle-boys in uniform came to me *Join us! What have you
got against joining us? Come home into the Reich!
A wife? Divorce her! Forget her. Find a blond Berlin dolly.
Find dozens of them. A bloodline like yours should breed!*
By now, it was late summer. I was in shirtsleeves walking
down Manteuffel street towards the Spree, and a fellow
caught my attention. *From Franz*, he said. *Bremerhaven*

in a week's time. The Lausitz will have a job for you.
There it was, the key turned in my handcuffs!
Home to outwit Sir Peter. I would deal with him.
Tell my story to the papers—not the Brisbane papers.
It'd get believed. Or I wouldn't. Basil had gone bust
after all. And who in Newcastle would tell
who in Brisbane I was home?
That night after midnight men in leather coats scooped me up

with the frontways-opening door of a big black car
outside the hotel. *Where are we going?* Crack!
a fist in my chops. We whizzed through a black and white
movie of streets, then I was hustled through doors,
given a kicking in the lobby in front of other arrested ones
and thrown into an office. Artur Gunst from Hollywood
sat there in collar and tie and Party armband
in an all-black uniform with silver handles.

It's scarcely a year, Fred, he grinned. *I'd no idea
I'd be seeing you here.*—What is this place? I asked,
trying not to hear the awful sounds in the background.
*This is the Columbia-Haus. I speak English, so
I get to deal with the Anglosaxons. But you're German!*
Why do you hide it? A heel-clicker brought him a file
and he looked inside it. *Why did you leave the Communists?*
I blurted out. He shook his head. *Sex is a Nazi*, he said.

*Hollywood proves that and won't admit it. Nature's a Nazi.
It's such relief, coming home to a bullshit-free State-principle.
With Marx and old Jesus and the rest, you're always paddling
against the natural flow of blood and shit.
But Fredy, we're not here for one of those profound
movie dialogues. You've been spying, you've been a hero,
you've twice bashed Party-comrades, you've rescued a dirty Jew
and got him a trot round the boot-testing track at Sachsenhausen.*

I'd say the only thing that might save you from the same
might be to join us. Be the NS-superman
at the Berlin Olympics in three years.
A rat crawled inside me and I tasted it; I asked
What about my family?—Your widow and orphan son?
You abandoned them, Fredy. We didn't prompt you to that.
Hödeken'll care for them, the kobold who watches naughty wives.
Join us, Fred, or I can't save you. I beg you on the knees of my heart.

I was too clogged to answer. I thought my heart
was going to choke me, in fact. So I was dragged away
to cells that were, for most in them, the second last
thing in the world. Despair, and greasy fast talk
about connections, great dignity, and tears,
and unspeakable surprise—I crouched below it all
and gradually my head cleared. A year for Gunst to rise
to an officer in the Blackshirts: no, that wasn't on.

He must have been a Nazi already in Hollywood.
He should have stayed there; America was the New Germany.
But if he had, I'd have gone straight to hell
without this rotten rope I was tempted to grab. At least
the old Jew had only got jail exercise. I went to sleep at last
and dreamed that Hitler took off his riding pants. You saw
the black hair round what he had: a swastika,
sallow right-angles of flesh all knobby and stiff

that he wanted me to catch hold of. If I did,
I couldn't remember when I woke. There was the chug
of an air compressor, and door-crash noise, and cries
with words and not, pleading that sped up to screams;
there were shouts and heavy floor-draggings and long notes
too even for a voice to be making them. How many hours
or days I was in there I can't guess. A lot of sleeps,
but they could have been naps to calm the terror

that swells and seems it'll suffocate you unless
you can turn it round quick—and you've forgotten how.
My beard was past stubble to curly when they came
and led me out, and threw me into the street.
And went back inside. I was dumbstruck. I was
alive, and free in the street. They'd gone back inside.
I trailed back to the hotel and my goods were there
but Cirkus Kramer had moved on, to another part of Berlin,

and when I looked for Franz, no doors would open.
No one who walked out of the Columbia-Haus alive
was likely to be trusted again. I might be a V-Mann,
a trusty in the mighty jail of the New Germany.
When I caught up with the circus again, old Kramer
took me back on with a sick look like as if
he was under orders to. Was it still worth
going to Bremerhaven? Would the Lausitz take me now?

I nerved myself up to phone them, then when Long Distance
was truly Long Distance, with operators and message-runners.
They came to the phone and were nervous, they'd never heard of me, no,
no vacancy for me, please, thank you, goodbye, all right?
Leland was the only person in the circus who'd talk to me
with any enthusiasm. We spent the Lausitz's sailing day
getting blind together: *Cerebos, my old salt,
you are at last a many-headed hound. As I'd suspected—*

In Germany one speaks German was snapped at us in bars.
And well spoken too. Ought to be the universal language!
usually charmed them. They bitterly wanted that world-shine.
How Hans came to me, I was near the Stettiner Bahnhof
and he came up to me to ask his way.
Pardon please Sir, he started, like something learned by heart
and still shaky on it, and looked hopeful, ran out of words
and handed me a letter. He had a shock of hair and

a faint look of someone buttoned into his clothes by others.
The letter gave the address of a medical clinic
where he was to report that midday to be sterilized
by removal of both testicles in accordance with the Law
for the Safeguarding of Hereditary Health of 14 July that year.
Do you know what this means? I asked him. *I got lost*, he said.
He'd no more idea than a bull calf going to be cut
what was in store for him. I was up against partly why

I went to sea: all the gelding you have to do on farms,
sometimes it seems only one of any male thing there
is allowed its nackas. It used to make me sick
doing the job, and sad after, when they looked so bewildered
and broken hearted. Life didn't flow through them any more
but stopped at them and left them just muscle.
You knew they sensed it
and felt shamed by it. Stallions would kill geldings for it.

They're going to cut out your balls, I said to Hans
and he covered his ears with his hands. *That's rude*, he shouted.
Bloody rude, I agreed with him. *You don't want that, eh?* And
an idea hit me. *Let's go to the Zoo instead. Come on.*
Ding and brrr! says the tram and Hans agreeing with its noises,
we get to the Zoo and have ice cream and watch the monkeys
till they play with themselves and eat the spunk as it dries.
What will I do with him? I'm asking myself. Next week

he'll get another letter with maybe a cop to ensure
he keeps his appointment this time. I'd have to keep him,
kidnap him, get him out of Germany
to where? No country would want him, they'd send him back
to Germany and the doctors. Who were only doing what others
didn't do, but agreed with. I'd have to front Hans' parents
at the end of the day, but what could they do themselves?
for their poor big redhaired boy with his aimless hands.

His letter told me his address. *Frau Lenzing?*
I've brought your son.—Naughty boy, you didn't find the clinic?
I got invited in, as this kind gentleman
and had the feeling no one in the family, not
the father, not the mother, not the sister with
her eye sockets sticky with make-up, had wanted to take him
where they'd had to send him. I got coffee and cake
and on the radio, Hitler was announced, in big swells

of stormy music. When his hoarse voice came on
the family stood up, so I had to hoist my carcass too.
Herr Lenzing, who was a red-faced big blond fellow
unbuttoned his shirt and faced the barred cloth maw
of the wireless as the Corporal went on about Volkwerdung,
becoming a people. *That the words of our dear Führer*
should beat more immediately into my heart, he told me
when Hitler had signed off. *Even though he'd alter your son?*

That brought a shit-storm on my head. To hell with politeness:
why did I want the German race weakened with
sentimental claptrap? Cruel, as the mother put in,
so cruel, to want her poor boy burdened with desires
he could never fulfil unless in the disgrace
of some unfortunate girl forced to raise more imbeciles.
Like a lot of German houses they had these plaques on the wall
with sayings lettered on them. Green is the golden tree of life,

J.W.v. Goethe, went one. Make up your mind, I told it.
While they talked at me and the father got redder and redder
because the New Germany was costing his son's nuts and he was helpless,
I made out they were convincing me. I gave way bit by bit:
I'd have to agree. That works with cattle. I admit that.
Sex is a Nazi among animals, true. I just wanted
it not to be, fully, among people. So I'd get their trust
then volunteer to take young Hans to where they wouldn't

and whip him over the border instead. They'd thank me in their hearts.
Next morning Leland stayed Leila and we went
for drinks up the Ku'damm. *It seemed a femme day, Fred.*
I taught her my mother's song of the vain young man:
Was kann der Sigismund dafür, dass er so schön ist—
Poor Sigismund can't help it that he's gorgeous—
and a young Navy officer looked hard at us, but was
too pretty to risk his face. And we hadn't sung loud:

It's not Sigismund's fault that he is loved by all.
Poor Sigismund can't help it that he's gorgeous:
that such handsomeness exists is a miracle!
That night when she was sleeping off the cognac
I pinched her Leland passport, and wrote her
an apology-note: *I'll see you in Stamina strides one day.*
I'll post the pass back, soon. It's in a good cause. Your mate
Freddy B. When Kramer asks, please do sing very dumb.

I collected Hans next morning early with a port
of clothes for his hospital stay, toothpaste and comb
which he'd had none of the first time when I'd met him.
His mother was in tears, his sister defiant and glum.
She didn't call him Hanswurst this time. His Dad didn't appear.
Rudolf is at work. Oh my poor poor baby,
and she hated me, for doing their undodgeable dirty work for them.
I would have richly deserved hating. I got no Auf Wiedersehen,

Hans got a shorter goodbye than if they'd guessed my plans,
but if they'd guessed at that stage, I might have been eating
out of a jail tin plate. So: straight on the city subway
to the Stettiner Bahnhof, tickets for Herr Golightly
and his nephew Ludwig Altenkorn from Kassel.
His papers would take maybe a week to trace
and might be untraceable—but I'd give them two days.
You understand playing games?—A game! he clapped his hands.

In this game we're playing, your name is Lutz. No: Lutz.
Finally he cottoned on. *Lutzi, hurry up, what are you*
staring at? He turned away, to the holiday express
with few on it, being an autumn weekday, and said clearly
Ick seh mir dat Baby weenen an. I'm watching the baby cry.
In a pure Berlin accent. *Come on, get in,* I sighed.
If his letter had been in English Latin doctor-talk
I mightn't have understood it. German's mostly made of German.

The train made long smoke and fast street-ends
and we passed a troop of maybe a hundred SS
in tight step, wearing the black flat-top caps,
the peaked caps police were mad for since the War,
officer caps, Tommy caps, policemen's caps
not the stiff ski-caps the SA thugs had. An army
at war on its own people—but that's any police.
This army was out to police the world. I shuddered.

The train dinged and slowed, a few miles on. It went Buh!
and Buh! like poor Bulba Domeyko. Then, gradually, uproar
spread back along it. Heil! Heil! we were coming to a highway
level crossing. A motorcade of big open cars
and motorbikes with sidecars, bristling with SS and strappy guns
was stopped in front of an elephant. Waving its live rubber face
the beast was balancing, leg-chained and unhappy, on a foundered
flatbed trailer that was slewed across the roadway

and who was sitting in the middle car, and hauling
himself to his feet to give his drink-waiter bashed-child
salute to his public on the train? Adolf bloody Hitler,
in civvies and de luxe khaki trench coat, looking nervous
and very pissed off. His car had a spotlight on its rump
and his moist eyes glared with a look of I-want-to-be-lonely
and I-don't-die-to-grow. A bit like Arab Lawrence
but liverish and stubborner, not cracked by the weight he'd taken on.

The road cleared, the train sped up. We were heading for Stralsund.
I'd squibbed trying the frontiers with the papers we had. My notion
was to get to the Baltic, pinch a boat and sail to Denmark.
Being a sailor of course I could sail, so I thought.
Sail even at night. Hadn't I luffed and reefed with Sieverts?
We rolled into the city in the sunny evening, got a map
of Rügen at the station shop, sat in the water-park
feeding the ducks, walked on, did a recce of the harbour,

took our time over supper. The biggest brick church was lit up
so we went in, sat in a box of seats, heard the organ
climb out of little wee notes into enormous ones. The time
was getting close to where we'd be what police
are drawn to: loiterers. There were still holiday folk
and knee-wobbling drinkers round the streets
but no one round the harbour. *Remember, Hans,
don't stand up in the boat. Don't stand up. Can you swim?*—

I'm tired. Where's my Mama? I wanna go home,
is what comes out of him, loud; he can't keep his voice down,
unless you tell him to whisper. And tell him again, for each sentence.
I guessed he couldn't swim. All right. Don't capsize the boat
when you find one, Fred. Or two precious nackas will drown.
I found a bit of a skiff with its mainsail furled up
along the boom, and got both sails hoisted in a weak breeze
and off we set up the Strela Sound. It was easy,

so I thought: I was back in shallow-water, Myall Lakes work,
ten kilometres to the south end of Hiddensee Island, then fifty
to Danish Falster. If the breeze picked up a trifle and the stars
were the ones I thought they were, we could be safe by morning.
I was gently sad. I might never see Germany again,
poor Germany with its police-disease. No more nutmeg with meat,
no more sweet salt ribs. No red cabbage, or bock beer, or calf's brisket
stuffed with kidneys. Never never again a decent wurst.

No ploughed hilltops or great green tile-ovens, ducks'-down coverlets
or girls who knew how to plump them. I'd go home to corned beef
and scones and glad to get them, in the depression-time.
I'd go home and get old, beached in responsibility.
These here were my people, but too much so. Our Germanhood
was bleached manageable at the world's other end. No thatchers
or spiked thatcher's chairs in their work, no carpenters in buttony
sailors' rig. The detail was British at home, or rangy and corrugated.

Germany was my people but not my country, was the short of it.
Germany was my people who had lost the War
and I hadn't, so I couldn't cotton to their Adolf.
My Struggle was a body that wouldn't face atrocity, and vanished:
his dead body was his Kampf-book, that he'd closed my people in.
All the little lights, said Hans, looking back across the stern
under the sails. I was goose-winging them, holding
the jib out like pyjamas to run before the wind,

and watching out for shorelines. The loom of house-lights and stars
lit the water just enough. Don't you dare notice us, fishermen.
An hour or so and no more shore showing. The wind
started backing and filling and there was an ugly chop.
I was concentrating too much on stars and consoling Hans:
Mama said you were a good boy! when all of a jerk
the boom schwapped round and laid me out, unconscious,
in the bottom of the skiff. I woke up to the toe of a boot

and a hard voice saying *Who is He?* and Hans cowering,
making weedy noises; he didn't know how to do dignity.
Who's He? the bloke repeated. In German. That could be grim for us.
But at least I could talk to him, in his old-style corduroy pea-jacket.
He's my nephew, I said, *and we're lost. Where is this place?*
It looked low and muddy, then I saw it like come to attention,
the whole countryside, in one great garden, with forty-gallon jugs
and squared-off water, and naked stone people on blocks

weeping or pointing or shooting bow-and-arrows at the air.
At the top of a rise that looked made, criss-crossed with stairs
was this huge castle-house with a flag as weighty and broad
as a double bedspread hoisted in all crisp colours above it:
acorns and antlers, swords and right angles were on it,
and no hooked cross anywhere. Some men had gathered to
our head serang's silver whistle. Two had shotguns,
brown but noways rusty. We were marched up to the palace

and round the side of it. No grand front door for us
or, even more, for them. I asked again where we were
and was told the domain of the Dowager Countess zu Knull.
Along corridors and through rooms with carpets hung round the walls
we came to her, big-set and handsome in a greeny gown,
carving with a man's straight razor at a globe of something.
The understrapper-in-chief who'd found us on the shore
of the estate, I'll swear he dropped down on one knee:

Shipwrecked mariners, Translucent. I found them on the beach.
Hans' mouth was right open, taking in as much as his eyes,
and I pushed it shut for him. *I'm sorry for trespassing, Madam*,
I said. She replied *Did He see the aurora last night? Splendid
over the whole North, sheer cliffs of green light.* I wondered
who this 'He' was, the way they talked about you to you.
My nephew might have seen it. I was knocked out cold.
A few more questions, then she switched to good English

and questioned me in that. *Your German is southern, but*
barely regional. It is far better than your English,
which is that of a labourer. I will send you both home.
Then she spoke to the Factor, as the official who found us was called,
and we were marched off to the kitchens to be fed.
At least I'd got promoted to 'You'. Chlodwig-Wahnfriede
von Rauschnitz zu Knull: her granddaughter lives in Australia
and is a complete hippie. But she is a post-office pigeon

to the double eagle her gran was. The palace, for a start,
had no toilets or power; there were china pots and candles instead
like before the Great War. The whole barrack had this lavatory smell
and they said young peasant men came in their ribboned costume
on the day of their wedding for the old dame, if she felt frisky,
to start their honeymoon for them. It was a sort of blessing,
and they were shattered if she withheld it. All that
was done in a language the lower servants and peasants spoke

and she spoke to them in. *Where did she learn her English?*
I asked Zange the butler. *From a governess, and from lovers.*
Her rank don't go to school, he added for my ignorance.
I never caught sight of Her Translucence again
till the day I caught the coachman tormenting Hans with his whip:
Hopp, Dummerjan, hoppla! I caught him, pulled his coat up
over his head and thrashed him with that same thin leather stinger.
I'll kill you arsehole! he muffled out, rolling in the gravel

and I was called at tea-time to the Presence.
You defend the weak, Herr Golightly?
Where does it come from: I daresay from all the old centuries
of being under them, this holding your hat in your hands
over your privates when you are fronting the noblefolk,
then being wild with them and yourself for it, after?
I managed to notice and wrench my hands apart, letting go
of the hat they weren't holding. *I didn't set out to*, I said

but any man torments a bloke like Hans is scum—
she broke in to show who owned the talk: *If you wish it*
I will have the coachman flogged again. Or you may hang him.—
To hell with you, I thought. *I'd have to defend him then,*
I heard myself say. *He's the weak one, against you.*
She stepped back and went a greeny white, and said
We must not detain you. I will send your nephew home
to Kassel, and yourself to a shipping line which will hire you.—

Now there's a problem, I answered, and told her things
and finished up *So they'll have to hire Hans as well.*
I reckon he can swab decks or peel potatoes, or something.
He needn't be paid, even; so long as he has a berth.
I reckoned whoever she knew would jump at her command.
It was one difference between the Northern tribes, she said
in a different tone, *and Greece and Rome:*
They exposed their blighted children to predators in the wild:

we feared to hurt ours. It could bring a curse on us. Their tales
are full of such curses. You are a German! This Hitler is a Greek!
That thought wouldn't have struck me. The same night I found
Hans pulling himself in the pantry and the servants cheering.
They'd had to teach him. His consolation prize, tongue-biters' opera.
I'd have to teach him not to make it a public performance
or pick it off his clothes like a monkey, after. *Use this rag, Hans.*
Wipe him dry with that. I hope you bastards are satisfied.

That night or one soon after, I got up
long after midnight. It was pouring rain
on the sea and the land; the castle was a hollow cave
of gleams and passages, like every night. I was thirsty
but got lost looking for the kitchens. Voices drew me
to a huge like sitting-room with these rotted flags
hung from the rafters. Her Ladyship was in session
on a high seat, and wearing a laced green gown

of heavy stuff, and her hair in a silver string bag.
She had her hands on the head of a supreme sergeant-general
in Soviet rig and a bearded fellow in scarlet
and other men and women were seated facing her,
talking in turn. And in rhyme. It gave me a weird feeling.
A navy man, from some country's fleet, was reciting:
    We do not rape; we kill only men,
    scald and shatter and drown them, then

    rescue a few in moaning boats
    as masses more bob like fishing-floats—
An Air Force pilot stood up here and went on:
    We will not rape: we'll simply kill
    those who send young men to war:
    women and preachers, girls and teachers,
    the expert, the randy, the smart, the ill,
    all those who avoided the strafe before:

Men in the stratosphere, we silver Xs
will teach war equality of the sexes—
Then a soldier with tight buttoned pockets stood up:
It's death selects the fittest, not you,
civilian ladies. Be jealous of her.
She is the mother of good manners
but even her darlings she chops in two
and their muscles fly in a rose blur—

and we take it out on you.
The Cardinal in scarlet on Madam's breast spoke:
Two hundred million people
will be killed this century,
one half in arms, as soldiery.
The unarmed half police shall kill.
Such victories of the working class,
O such triumphs of the will.

Then Madam cried: What is this Master Race?
We have ruled Europe since Rome fell,
we nobles, the only Germans. All
you rest are a mingled peasantry.
(All stood up for this, and made a deep bow)
It will take a vast human sacrifice
to make you a folk-community.
Can you distinguish the bricks from the wall?

A woman jumped up, her hair was like flames:
Whine and scuttle from your blood web,
the boys' slaughter-game you blame women for,
and you'll mean nothing any more.
Life comes best down narrowest tubes:
you'll learn how narrow they can get.
Blame is on offer. Blame's in the air:
you think we will abstain from it?

Then all of them chanted Oh dear, oh dear,
we love that wartime atmosphere:
shouldery blouses, skin-tight trousers,
the Front is Meaning, the Front is here,
the Front is poetry, frightful and clear.
Bring it your rage and your shortfall,
be the cattle and the cull,
every death's the death of fear—

I sneaked away from their cabaret,
horrified. Behind me, an SS officer was singing
   Dig the pit in a wide green floor;
   for a thousand years we'll be metaphor.
   Weak is sweet but hard is true.
   Believe it. Working people do.—
I found our room at last, and all I wanted
was out of there. Hans woke and squawked *Can we*

go home now, Fredy? I've been a good damn cretin.—
Who called you that? But he sat picking his face
which he'd just taken up. Blood like from lice on his fingers.
It's hard for them out among sneaky pushed-around people,
the simple ones need us decent. Some do rise to them.
Is it the same day? he asked, looking out the window.
I guessed he meant is it always the same day?
Or is each day a new one? *Time it was a different one*, I said.

Her Translucence summoned me again, to say
we had a ship, out of some port I'd never heard of.
I wondered that she hadn't simply got me told.
Some queer good form to a guest? One that she'd put
among her servants. Among people she offered to hang.
Turned out I'd puzzled her. *Why, Mr Golightly, did you*
confide in me about your efforts to flee Germany?
I might have had you arrested and sent to Berlin.

There she had me. I thought, for the first time, about it
and got puzzled myself. And grinned, and told her so,
as if I still didn't believe in the danger. It hurt to say,
but don't ask me why: *I must have thought you were above that.*
Are we still in Germany here?—I live in the Ordensstaat.
From here to Portugal, no one pays for lodging or physic:
they go to the monasteries, donate to them if they have money,
are entertained cost free if not. Monk knights defend and expand

this polity, under the High and German Master.
Well I knew the oceans and most harbours, but land geography
was hazy in my head. I hadn't heard of her Order-State,
but that needn't mean much. Take the lady's word for it, Fred.
I severely doubted the free beds and feeding clear to Portugal:
I hadn't struck that. Though the German hospitals I'd been in
eighteen years back didn't charge me a penny, that was true.
They weren't monasteries, though. Not for some who had the energy.

Will you walk with me? she asked. *Why er gladly*, I stammered.
She pulled a long silk plait and spoke to a servant
and a chair was brought in, on two shafts. Men carried it
fore and aft. When she was in it, helped and wrapped
in a mighty bear-hide, off we went, me walking beside her
down corridors and landings and wide waterfall stairs.
Are you European, Mr Golightly?—
I suppose I'm white, Madam. I couldn't come at that Translucence

and she didn't force it on me. *Whom do you blame?*
Eve, perhaps? The holders of wealth? The Jews?
Blame for what? I was thinking, but my mouth
had answered *The murderers.*—*You're not European!*
she said, and looked at me with this sudden glad smile like a girl,
and no more high theatre for minutes. Then the creaky
chair came alongside a flock of seats in the sun
and fine-skinned old people on them, and she got back to nobling.

They were old ladies and generals and bankers
it seemed; they lived with her in the castle's apartments.
A sailor! How enviable! On what firm-land were you born?—
Stay at sea, stay off countries: too many die for countries
an old lady said as her crop-haired man swelled up
red round his white face-scar. I only knew her for that minute
but she gave me the best advice a man could get. But silly
and not do-able, like most advice. Madam lit from her chair

and hobbled, in pain and crooked, under big chestnut trees.
This came suddenly, she said. *I walked, I strode, I danced
then, within weeks, I crumbled. Here where we now are
I had sent my companion away, to be alone. I'd sat down
and I could not rise. It amazed me. Disobeyed by my bones!
Then I became afraid, but could not endure to cry out,
not on my own domain. Foolish pride, you see, Mr Golightly.*
What happened? The mares came, from their field just by;

*someone had left the gate ajar, and they came to me
and bent their heads down to me, till I understood to lift
my arms over their two necks. And be lifted up, and walked slowly
back through the trees, to where my servants saw and came running.
I confess my toes often trailed, as those two mares walked me.*
We were looking downhill to the sea and the gleam on it
like on a wet steel deck. *Terrible times are upon us*, she said.
More human sacrifice to make worse lies come true.

On the ship we got, where I taught Hans to peel potatoes
the skipper was a merry Dane who didn't seem to mind
us being pushed on him. And Haglund the supercargo
who was such a blondy redhead that when he rolled
a cigarette he seemed to be smoking his own hair,
knew a tale about her Ladyship, of an animal she kept
in the dungeons of her palace, one so fierce and strange
and horrible no expert could tell what it was. *Though*, she said

he is in a book.—In what book? they asked.—*Revelations!*
I hadn't heard that animal in my nights of her hospitality
and it got me thinking other scandals about her
might be moonshine too. But would she have let me hang the coachman?
I liked her free-lodgings realm clear to Portugal, but her midnight
cabaret haunted me, in later years. I dreamed of her once, naked
with a white scar from her hairline clear to her welcome-mat
and a face on either side of this healed line.

I had to watch out for Hans. It didn't matter
if the fellows sent him for kilos of compressed air;
they generally knew where to stop. If not, I told them.
We were only to the Kattegat, though, when I heard him
in the forrard hold saying *No that's rude, that's rude*
in a crying voice to the vinegar-mouthed second cook.
Who I hit. So hard in the face that I flattened
the bones of his features. He snuffled air and burbled quack

out through bunged-up purple. The ship's sawbones came sober
and reckoned there'd have to be delicate operations
to restore his looks. Big insurance, the boot for me and Hans,
but the skipper said *No insurance. Come here, you!*
and pulled the fellow's nose. He screamed as his face gruckled back
out to the shape it had been. *Insurance!* the skipper snorted
in his flu accent. *Any more fighd you both on shore.—*
I'll give that dough-cock a flotation test, the cook moaned at me

but the others heard him. *You do and you'll swim yourself.*
It wasn't me had to say it. I taught Hans to swab deck
Like this, watch me: I, the great Winnetou,
and don't throw up! Old Shatterhand wouldn't throw up.
He loved those Karl May stories: I had to read them to him,
and a letter from his mother how she loved him and that he
must do as I said. I was half ashamed to make that up.
I had to write it then to show him, and he treasured it.

We docked in Le Havre for engine work. I wrote to the Lenzings
how Hans was safe with me. Then we whipped to Paris to see Sam.
You've come to settle! But no: you're on your way home?
Dear God, it puts its claws on the innocent ones first, eh?
He said, shaking Hans' hand in this really elegant apartment
speaking Spanish to his wife Rachel and their two daughters
Ladino? No, I learned that in Queensland. Widely known there.
In the kitchen he ran there was even a duck-squeezing press

like a jack to screw the bird's juice out. And freezers, ocean-liner stoves
and cakes they serve in Heaven on special Tuesdays.
His offsider with the silver wine-dipper on a neck chain
made us nobly merry till Hans started poker-dealing
the Sèvres plates, dancing hop-hop Scheisse-pinke-heirassa.
You tried this stuff before, Hans? He mightn't have: they were Protestants.
That night in the apartment Sam cranked up the gramophone
for a record of the strangest high moaning worshipping singer.

He translated as the man intoned *B'rosh Ha-Shono: On the Day of New Year*
it is written, and on the Day of Atonement it is sealed:
how many shall pass from life, how many shall come into existence;
Who shall live, who shall die; who shall have a timely end,
who shall perish untimely; by water or fire, by sword or beasts
(*Joseph Shapiro*, Sam said. *Records by him are scarce as rubies:*)
who shall die by strangling, who by stoning.—Cheerful lad, I said.
Do you think it's all written?—I think we're coming to fearful pages.

You getting Hansel away equipped for Gretel is a start.
Millions more need to go. Then he added *I've also got some to leave*
your parents' Fatherland. Mad, though. Most Jews won't listen.
Run, from that corporal? We're Germans too. It'll return to normal.—
Aren't they really Germans, though? I asked. *Are blackfellers Australian?*
Sam asked me. *If you're different are you the same?*
That one reached right through me. *Never have just the one passport, son.*
Listen to Reb Shmuel. As if you fly bugger didn't know.

We tied up in Sydney the week before Christmas. I slipped
Hans ashore with me at three in the morning, hung around
Pyrmont till a café opened, then we crossed to the city.
No drays there any more, no Hansom cabs, but the new Bridge
looked terrific to me with the trams making welders' sparks on it.
I bought Christmas presents with the first Australian money
I'd seen in four years, sent a wire to Laura, and then
we were on the train, breathing cinders and oysters up the Hawkesbury.

Every train smelt industrial back then. *Is that Prussian*
lingo you're talking to that poor zany? an old chap asked.
Now don't get your feathers up! You'd be a German yourself?—
No I'm a pugilist! I snapped. *And he's my manager.*
Silence for a while, at that. I'd have been less shirty
if I hadn't been worried sick how Laura would take to our fosterling
that she couldn't even talk to. And how the world round us would treat him.
I'd written to warn her, but I might beat the letter home.

Even down the deep river gorges I'd been seeing lots of tents
just back from the line, with chimney pipes and scrap cookhouses,
like our Yankee hobo jungles, a bit, but with lots more women
and kiddies round them. *They couldn't pay their rent,*
the old man explained. *Terrible. You see their furniture*
stand on the street in the sun. Didn't you see that
where you've been? He was busting to know where I'd been
now he'd heard me talk Australian. I had seen the evictions

most of all in Germany. From a tram, I'll never forget,
in Fulda it was, I saw a woman keeping guard
on her family's belongings just suddenly drop on her knees
on the footpath, and gape, and keel over dead with starvation.
You knew that's what it was. And people edging up to pinch her goods
on the far side of the heap. Stuff they'd get pennies for.
Yet in Germany then you never saw tent-camps. Not allowed.
Somehow, in Europe, there's always a poorer mortared hole.

Hans didn't spoil my welcome home. It was mean of me
to think he might. Joe, who had got twice as tall,
couldn't get enough of Zeppelins, Hollywood, Nazis
and my welcome from Laura, that's lovely to remember, and private.
After a week, we worked out that with my ship's wages
—Hans hadn't got any—we'd last three to four months
in the house that Laura had bought with my big movie pays
high up in New Lambton. I wouldn't be able to go

on the road and leave Hans; she couldn't talk to him.
Joe said *I can*, and did, from babyhood with his grandma
and not too rusty yet. Hans stared for a while, then talked back
as if here was the real talk, that others seemed queer in refusing him.
Laura winced a bit, left out, but put a grown-up face on it.
I liked the house, and circled round and round in it
like a dog in long grass before he settles to sleep.
The nothing took away from my homecoming, but I played it

down when Laura asked. *I still feel flies on my face*
only when I look in the mirror! Not strange like the idea of owning
the things in a house I was in. Living in, not just staying.
The photos in frames on the sideboard were of us,
not of strangers. Of us with little Henry, or Cos,
with Golightly's tent show. Here was my share, I thought,
Joe with cricket cards *Here's Jardine. You heard about bodyline?*
Laura looking over Newcastle from the blue verandah,

Hans with his letter, or face down on his bed.
That year we had Christmas in our sort-of German style
like I gathered they'd had them the years I was away.
I mean we put up the pine-branch tree in the lounge room
and gathered round it after tea on Christmas eve
to sing and pass out presents. It turned out Hans knew two carols,
Silent Night and most of O Du Froehliche. But next morning
the presents he'd got were all ruined. The mug was broken,

the pyjamas ripped apart, the swimming trunks razored.
His face was unjointed, like a skin bag wobbling with passions
from fury to shame. *Stubborn hateful bad!* he shouted.
Is this how it's to be? A mad baby man in our house?
Laura rounded on me. Joe looked poisoned. Bless our happy Christmas.
Hartnäckig gehässig bös sobbed Hans, picking at his dinner
on a blue enamel plate in his room. I put my arm round him.
Not his fault he had to be lost a world away from home.

Not his fault he was bewildered, and wild at us and himself.
Bad man Hitler was going to cut you, Hanno,
down there in the rude parts. Make you like a sleepy old cat.—
Wicked man, the Hitler?—Wicked man! Have a happy Christmas.
Pray Mama and Papa have one too. You'll see them someday.
As a kid I used to love Christmas day visits: family
and others dropping in. That was twenty years behind me now
but behold, in the afternoon, we had one: Cosmo Morrison!

Well, he says.—*How did you know I was back?* I ask.
Merry Christmas, I add, and he says *Yes, a lot of that, to youse.*
We get him sitting down, because he's shy of Laura, and all elbows
and he admits he 'just had this feeling' I'd be home.
About Hans, he says *Well yes, if he's short in his brains*
he deserves all the more to keep everything that does work!
Only fair. He gets outside of a junk of Christmas cake
and I twig he's lonely, with nowhere much to go, and old suddenly.

Have you got a housekeeper, Cos?—Can't afford them now.
Work's so down, I live on lobsters and crabs
half the time. You'd skin a louse for its hide.—
I saw us having him to Christmas dinner in the future
and liked the idea. But it never happened.
They got this relief work, a couple of bob like a day
from the councils. The blokes can make a mile of road
last a year to build, with pick and shovels.

Laura's mind circled round Hans. *Most people*, she said,
if they do any at all, do ordinary-sized kindness.
Not my Fred. He smuggles a whole adult round the world
to—what? To draw a line between animals and people—
Well, Cos said, *a lot of the big guns forget that line*
and men crawl into hollow logs to die of hunger.
The depression's made steers of heaps more; you read it in their eyes.
Might take them another war to win their nuts back, he said.

So I should be proud of Fred?—You should.—Don't you know I am?
We lived along, watching the money trickle dry
in spite of all Laura's chooks and eggs and veges.
I looked for work round the city, anything at all,
never a dog's chance. And *That young bloke at your place,*
he don't seem to understand English. He a bit touched, is he?—
Yes. Pretends to talk a lingo of his own. He's not dangerous.
I could fob off neighbours' ignorance, but some day Hans'd crack it

for a smartie who picked his language. Then it'd be Goodnight nurse.
It got very clear we'd need to go bush to live
off the land. Fish and rabbits, a bit of garden:
you can't scrounge all that well in a suburb, though some did it.
Torsteins two doors up from us ate dogs. Ate every dog
they could catch within miles. Try the Depression yourself
before you blame them. Head of terrier in his jelly.
I thought of my old fishing camp up the Myall.

Laura shuddered at it. *I'm a town girl. But we'll be together.*
I can't see a better answer. I'll want a separate tent
or hut for us to sleep in. You were away all those years.
Then she said *About a third of working people*
are surplus now, aren't they? And it's people for work,
not work for people. We'd be better-mannered
just to drop dead. When work comes back, machines will do it.—
When work comes back, it'll be the machines culling workers.

[208]

It'll be called heroic. Some bits may be, culler against culler,
each one with his loaded culler-bar. I was full of that frisky
madness that's really rage. But what was I whingeing about?
Lovely climate, cover, the coppers not stopping you camping
if you kept off private land. And game and fish and room.
School would end for young Joe: no doctor-college for him
as if he'd wanted it. He'd leave school at fourteen like me
and start in the life class. His sorrow kept busting out in grins.

He'd taken to Hans, where I'd been dead scared he'd resent him.
Du Hansi komm schon! and off they'd go down the beach
or over to Sugarloaf Mountain and the farms out there.
In March I started going up on the old Coweambah
to Nelson Bay, because Bill Ripley the captain
gave free passage to out-of-work blokes. Then I'd bum
a ride on the droghers up the Myall and swim ashore
to build our camp. Starting with a hut and a galley

split out of ironbark from back on the ridges, that I'd carry,
and sheet iron I scrounged in the boat I kept planted there
in among a palm thicket. Some of my old stuff had lasted
there for ten years, but most of it had walked.
I caulked the hut walls, covered them with hessian bag
and cement-washed it, I cleaned out the freshwater well,
I made an oven from an oil drum set in antbed
and this time the mosquitoes never worried me at all.

Laura, she shed tears for her house she'd lose,
her bits of treasures, her pickled glass cabinet.
We advertised the place Low rental. Owners leaving for the country
and dole people mobbed it. We picked the Russells
because we got on with them straightaway. *Six bob a week*
is the dole now, said Ken Russell *Six bob a day we got*
when we was Diggers. Don't that tell you something? That day
I got, forwarded from Germany, a fat offer from the Reich Sport Bund.

That night before moving, I took all of us
to the talkies. The kangaroo newsreel led off
with this vibrant voice making heavy work of everything,
whether fun or dreadful. Japanese soldiers training was fun,
at the bandy run with long sharp rifles, but their bombing
into haze over cities in China, houses burning,
people shocked and dead, that horrified Hans, and he was right.
I took him out for a walk rather than deceive him.

No more of that for a long time. We dropped below luxury
till nearly '39, up there among the roos and herons,
living out of sugarbags. Odd letters would come care of Engels'
store, at the Bay. Yankee letters—one or two that caused words
and explaining from me. German letters with Hitler stamps.
Jost in the Wehrmacht: *We've got these new forage caps
the boys call Fotzen for their folds that fit snug round your head.*
Balz still at Zeppelins: *This place is running down.*

*A lot of men are gone that I never noticed were dark
or oily or hook-nosed, but it's slow ignition in my head.*
That one he never signed, but I knew it was Balthasar.
Leila wrote and thanked me for sending back her male side:
*I missed those parts of me—they thank you for their brush
with high society. Be careful what you post over here, parcels specially.
I love your bush idyll, but I'd go mad there in a week.
I dare you to borrow Leila next time, Fred, you tarzy man.*

Hans learned a bit of English gradually, swearwords first,
off the timber puntmen, kitchen English off Laura, bits
of beach and bush talk from Joe. They both ran wild,
never a shoe on them from Christmas to Christmas. When I'd score
a bit of work, or sell some fish that I'd smoked
we'd travel on the Cowie to what Laura called Civilisation
and window-shop, which I was good at for ten minutes.
Hans hugged Laura a lot and even got me jealous

but she said *Comfort is in every part of the skin.
You ought to go through the motions of that. It might bring you back.
The other is wonderful. I wouldn't be without the other
now you're home. I did for too long. But the touching—
what can I say that wouldn't make you sad?* I kept it quiet
from her that I'd forgotten most of touch; I had got used
to the inner man dealing with where I stopped and things started.
Only puffs at each end of me told me when lifting was a strain.

It was the old life of the Lakes all over again.
Same people, same fun, same peace. The magpies hadn't
learnt any new songs, crabs were just as clueless upside down
even though they knew life depended on making something work.
Hans came down from the Broadwater with Joe and a bag of bream
saying *Fuckin Käfer all spin roun and roun*—Christmas beetles,
Joe explained. *They were giving the slaty gums a pasting,
swarming in them, turning the leaves to this blood-scoury shit.*

These bream'll taste of them. And it did taste of their story.
When the foxes showed us a fowlhouse is a foxes' pantry,
we sent our chooks to live in a tree. Hans got so good
with the rubber catapult I made him that rabbits nearly learned
our veges were fatal. Enough didn't, though, and were our beef.
One smoky summer, there was a letter from Sam
about the German attaché bigwigs at the Pyramide.
They told me nations sometimes need annealing in fire

and I agreed with them, and told them how all creatures
were shapeless once, floppy and bowed over. It took Fire
to tighten and straighten them, so they could live and run
and hunt and find their names. Fire made them into real beings.
They got very short with me, asked me what tribe I came from.
Oh Sam, I thought, should I tell you how skin goes
to black sugar-brittle with the ghostly flames still on it?
All that day, with the smoke-scent through the trees, I thought

of the record he'd played me with the chanter Roitmann singing
Thou openest the book of records and it reads itself.
Every person's signature is in it. The great ram's horn is blown.
A gentle whisper is heard: the angels quaking with terror
declare The Day of Judgement is come!
They say if you don't read your memory for the words is better
and I always could remember words. *Let us tell how utterly holy*
this day is and how awe-inspiring, is how that song started.

Another song that started, at the end of '37,
was Laura getting pregnant again. *I feel like Sarah in the Bible,*
expecting in my old age. It made me, but not her, nervous
about living so far out, away from help. We all, the boys and I,
treated her like fine crystal, and we started shifting
back into the city when I talked her into spending the last month
at her parents'. They still kept me at dung-fork's length
and Hans at three lengths. In September, Louise Agnes was born.

BOOK 5

Lazarus Unstuck

In the middle of '39 we signed up with the Manpower,
Joe and I both. I'd managed to teach Hans
not to talk German around Laura or around strangers
which struck him half dumb but that was cover too.
As it turned out, the Manpower didn't check on him.
They gave us a number each, and said we'd hear from them
if and when war came. By then we knew it would.
Blokes were marrying wholesale. Any spinster could set her own terms.

As it came closer, I mourned how I'd forgot
how most things felt at all. Bag, stone, silk, skin, gravel, iron,
they all rubbed alike; fire was pale colours hopping
above brighter colours; water was a taste, a smell,
salt water another smell. Queer how I'd gone all the years
without breaking a main bone; I had some knubbly fingers
but that year the engine of a big International truck
kicked and broke my cranking arm. Not the right, thank God:

I heard my new elbows grind till they splinted them. Joe had
to work in my place; the lifting nearly killed him for a week
till he got the swing of it. And I got to carry the baby
for the first time ever, so far as she knew, Laura grinned.
In fact, I carried Louise to church
because she was baptised; because I felt the need.
It was *flectamus genua* and all the Latin coming back
propter magnam I'm living plaster, Lord, look! *gloriam tuam.*

In life there's nearly always at least one face
between us and God's face, I remember the priest saying.
We make sure there is, I guess, but he didn't say that.
The first of September when Hitler went into Poland
I told Hans the news. *Man should put a loudspeaker to his ear
and punish him with loud LOUD talking*, Hans replied,
going into stitches. He didn't get letters from Germany
and now if I did I might be in deep water.

Better off though than the Poles, as we watched German planes
angle down on them in the newsreels. You couldn't take Hans,
he'd panic and shout out. He'd ask me *Will there be blood?*
In November, Joe got called up for the militia:
*Never mind, Mum and Dad, it's only the chockos,
not overseas, not like the AIF.* In slouch hat and khaki slops
he set off on his bike for Singleton Camp,
and when he was out of sight his mother's smile drowned in sobs.

I met Bill Hines and Yall Sherritt in AIF uniform
strolling down Hunter Street in their own tobacco clouds.
Fred mate! You see we've got no sense. We live at Bonnie Hughie's.
He's the bull had our stall at Sydney Showground. Have a gasper.
You still don't? Grubbing stumps, prickly pear, cactoblaster beetles—
A soldier settler's a government rabbit digestion unit, Fred.
You been in America? You been in Germany? Keep that quiet.
War's nearly sure to make Fritz unpopular. No Light Horse this time.

They'd put their young days back on with their uniform.
So had Oyster Harris: *Ain't you bored of that home and beauty, Fred?*
You gonna be a slacker and take some Digger's job?
It seemed half the men I'd met years ago around the Lakes
were turning up in khaki and gaiters, all the timber men,
Maytoms and McDeans and Palmers. If only there'd be
war just against Hitler's thug army. Not the rest of Germany.
Wish in one hand. There was plenty of work, suddenly,

filling in for men enlisting. I was a night watchman,
a furniture polisher, a bouncer at the fights
and the sea breeze came up to our place with bellbirds chiming in it
and the ore ships sat out on the ocean, before the German raiders.
The war seemed to stop, after Poland. It was burning a long fuse,
and we had a usual Christmas, better, because now we had money.
The pudding was rich and dark as the Aga Khan
but I kept thinking what Joe had told me about

the Army's purpose they'd been taught: to close with and kill the enemy.
No buts about it. That's what the blokes were training for,
and making jokes to cover it, from others and themselves.
That's where the strappy not quite workers' rig
was marching them to. We kill because we die
was what the boys kept buried under recitations and nonsense.
They say we'll be mainly an infantry army again, Dad,
so most of us will be up the sharp end, if invasion comes.

Don't tell Mum this. Mum knew it. They all knew it.
That summer a strong notion took me to go home
to Dungog and make my peace with there. We made a day
and went up in the train with Hans and a picnic basket.
He loved it all, the Stockrington coal train at Hexham,
the Maitland swamps, cows picking their nose with their tongue
which he tried himself and couldn't. When the train pulled in
the quartzy platform gravel was like popcorn in the heat.

Walking up Dowling Street, with the new Royal Hotel full of hum
and wives sipping beers in cars and buggies outside,
I met Alec Le Lievre that I'd been at school with. He smiled
at Laura and Louise, studied Hans and decided not to ask
and told me *You know Miss Wilce? She's a hundred today.—*
Old Miss Wilce? She was old when I was a boy.—
Yes, round in Lord Street.—I remember they lived in Lord Street.
Twenty years and the place had me like creek water over a stone

that has rolled back down the bank. *Everyone's paying their respects,*
Alec suggested. So I nod to Laura and she grins
I'll look after him: we'll go shopping. Off she and Hans
and the stroller go, and Alec and I join a queue
down a dark lino hallway to the parlour. *Gooday, Freddy yes Boatcher.*
You been at sea? No I'm Cecil: brother Dick died in the black flu.—
and there's this woman I know, she looks like the apple
Eve left on the tree at the start of the world, and she's talking

perfect sense, her voice slipping into just
the odd carky heron note, about way back before my life,
before my granddad left Bavaria, how the naked blacks
were fascinated by the white people and would gather round
to study the simplest things: a woman washing clothes,
a man shoeing a horse. Or else they'd pretend not to see
the strangers at all. Things not in their stories shamed them.
There was no fighting. They were losing their world through their eyes.

I remember the Dunbar wreck, she said: when the sea came calm
the dead rose and were scattered on it, like cloth in the swells,
so the boatmen told us. That was the year of the big flood.
All old bad news, hers. Good news, and bad stuff prevented,
are in history too, but it mostly doesn't tell them.
Maybe they're Heaven's history. She didn't know me.
She was sixty-nine when I left school. As I went, she was telling
about the fire that had burnt out half Clarence Town when I was small.

I met one or two others I knew; they didn't mention war either,
but I had to go and see my father's grave:
I had a shameful feeling there might, with the war back on,
be more words on his stone than there should be, like scratched or painted.
I'm also ashamed to say I'd never been to his grave.
Turned out I didn't get then, either. He wasn't in that cemetery
and I couldn't well ask my mother where she'd laid him by.
I asked our relations after, and found he'd never got a stone.

So Dungog never noticed your feud with it? asked Laura
but she smiled and took my hand.
*I can imagine why your poor mother never gave
her husband a headstone. So can you. You just did
imagine exactly why. You know where the funeral was now.
Get them to take you there.* I had a firewood run
that took me out bush with Hans. It was no trouble to drive
round by Thurechts in our old cut-down Ford ute,

pick up aunt Elise who'd been at Dad's funeral, and go there.
It was a terrific day, autumn, magpies blowing through the trees
oodling and aardling among the harbour of crosses
and stubby columns and marble church doors in their ranks
and newer markers like stone school desks up on end.
Elise hunted round and wasn't quite sure at first. She settled
in the finish, though, on a grave with just a peg at the head.
That's Reinhard. Now I am sure. It was a day like today.

*Your mother wouldn't meet anyone, nor shake hands or nothing.
She wouldn't accept comfort. You had to just lead comforters away
gently as you could.* So my father was a hump in the ground
like a length of old furrow. With his back to where Mama had gone.
I would decorate his grave, but not till the war was fully over,
maybe years after it would finish. I'd know when.
I wasn't the boy any more, now I'd been to see him.
Hans was about, swishing gravestones with a leafy twig

and I stopped him, then realised there was no harm
but he wouldn't start again. Elise was looking old
among all those knee-high, sometimes waist-high churches.
This was about when the war's slow fuse hit the jelly:
Denmark and Norway fell to the Wehrmacht
then Holland, Belgium, France went under. With Adolf and Stalin
hand in glove, it meant police had things absolutely their way
from Brittany to Vladivostok. The papers were giddy with Dunkirk

but I thought of a trench half full of human blood
crossing two thirds of the world, getting soil-filled here and there
behind non-stop killings. Not many in Australia then, listening
to AIF Cheerios or the Youth Show on 2GB
seemed to think like that. But my living plaster made me think it:
trenches like the First War but packed with unarmed civilians;
them crying for mercy made a long saleyard noise with whipcracking
till you came close, and saw police up on the dirt fill

shooting into them, just for being down there, for the recoil,
to watch them stagger, jerk, rooster-jump or stand arrested,
trying to absorb the shot and live. And the shooters screamed laughing
Digest that one, Podge! That'll drain your bladder, Auntie!
To widow a pleader, stop a baby short, make frantic praying fail
would be just their glory, and the trenches were twisting
over the world like cut pressure hoses sprawling this way,
that way. One might easily switch towards Australia.

If Russians could do it, my own folk could. There or here.
If Turks could, so could both my own. I'd always known that
since the burning women. My skin was that knowledge inside out.
How few fit the template. How small the club to be in is,
out of all the trash and untidy elements. That's how police think
but narrowly watching the mortal harm you'd just done
in an instant, giggling at their struggle with it,
went even beyond police, and haunted me with horror.

England wrestling one end of the trench in the sky
through that springtime on the newsreels, and the sudden way
all British products except the King had vanished
followed me up the bush roads with their branches flying over.
I had to chop myself exhausted not to brood about the trench,
making stove-lengths out of the dry timber on farmers' places,
Hans helping load and making his little-kid jokes.
It's over the Other Side, men said. *It won't come here.*

In October that year, petrol was rationed, and old Ernie,
Laura's father, he caught a cold and died.
Her mother went completely off. I pitied her
even though she hated me as much as ever, and Hans worse:
A German idiot in my daughter's house, Mr Bircher—
she often still didn't call me Fred, as if I was
more a star boarder of her daughter's, a spark who might
still go away, so Laura could find a proper husband.

The old dame cried and cried, and only dried up with fury
when I came near. In November the little Nimbin
hit a mine off Newcastle. German mines lay out there
and who knew where else round the coast? The raider
Pinguin was loose in the Tasman, sinking more freighters
and I got papers from the Manpower to report
as a merchant seaman. I knew that was wrong. They weren't taking
my age, nor married men. *I did put down I was married!*—

It's a short run, Fred. We'll sort it out when you're back.
So it was home and pack the duffel. *This won't last, they reckon,*
and it's pay, now the winter wood's done. Hans, be good for Laura,
sei mir brav, gell? Laura and Louise had huge eyes.
Laura said *Well it's orders. It always starts with orders.*
Come back before I'm old. And Hans, he started crying
from all the feeling. In fact I was back in a month.
We just took the old Kooloona, blacked out, to Brisbane and Mackay

and you bet I kept my head down. No shore time, no pubs.
When I got back is when I walked into the band saw.
As a Christmas present to me the old lady, Laura's mother
had spilt her guts about Hans to the police and Welfare
and he was in the mental hospital.
There's no provision for mental defectives in the Act
Mr Beecher. But if we release him he'll go
into internment as a German i.e. enemy national.—

I told their official what I'd rescued Hans from, and showed him
what a Yank paper had reported: the T4 Programme,
Tiergartenstrasse 4, for killing off cretins and incurables.
We'd heard of the sterilisations, of course, but this!
You'd been in Berlin, Mr Beecher. Recently?
Since you abducted Hans there? No? Castrating a defective
guilty of sexual misconduct can be ordered here in some States.
Let your Hans beware the Tasmanian Chief Secretary!

he smiled as narrow as his Rhett Butler moustache
and said *He'll be safer as a mental patient with us*
than in internment. There he might be exchanged to Berlin
and, from what you show me, passed to the very Chiefest Secretary.
Abominable, all abominable. I was let visit Hans.
He was still in pyjamas although it was afternoon
and he cried to go home, to go in the ute again, where was Joe?
We keep them in pyjamas till they settle and stop clearing out,

this big nurse with a pumped-up bodice and steel key ring
told me, as Hans quailed from her, with dobs of gravy down his front.
Bring me home! Fredy! I'll be good. Bring me home!—
I didn't put you here, Hansi.—The Hitler put me here?—
Don't talk about the Hitler. Eh, Hans, remember, no Hitler.
Or they'll send you to him. Bastards. Mrs Riggs, she would!
the police-hearted bitch. Hitler's relations never die.
I can't undo what she's done, Fred. You know I didn't want it.

But—Laura struggled—*but it might be best, with you gone a lot.*
She knew that'd make me wild, and sat bowed under it,
then told me the clincher: she'd only narrowly stopped her ma
shelfing me too, as a signaller to Nazi ships. In that wartime
it would have worked. It had, on a few others. It still could
if ma thought that Laura's promise never
to speak to her again could be cried and slobbered away.
I was hanging by that thread. Bringing Hans home would snap it.

Well, I thought how to sell ma to Sir Peter
and useful ideas like that, till they sent me to sea again
to fume and grieve for Hans in his beautiful lake resort
of steel mesh and poor fellows who couldn't seal the porridge in their mouths.
Better than the hospital needle or the furniture lorry
with its exhaust feeding fumes to the hand-flappers locked inside it.
It took me to Manila to admit that Laura wasn't
all wrong. Her ma was, but not Laura. Nervous as a hawk

for two straight years that Hans might sit on, or drop,
or somehow break our baby Louise. I'd seen her
go white and pelt through the house and come back shaking
and never say what for. Some people are just terrified of ones
like Hitler's sister Paula—and lots more in his tribe, I'd heard.
Where we were going I hadn't been to before:
Shanghai. But I wasn't game even to mention Marlene
in case I'd sound too German. Though half our crew were Portuguesers.

I'd worked out if I got chipped, like officially,
for being German, I'd do my best to jump ship
in a neutral port. There'd be no pay in internment camp
to send to my family. For the moment, though,
Shanghai got me, fascinated me, took away my worries.
Ports, and the ocean between them,
were always my prayers, like that.
Shanghai stank like the Countess zu Knull's potty palace

but wonderful, richer, spicier and worse.
We were anchored off the French Concession,
way upriver. More people were packed into there
than I'd ever seen. More than Calcutta, or Batavia.
Talk was a roaring hum, and people were camping
fifty to a square of rag, penny cook-stalls flaring
with oil and smoke, and the cause of all that huddling
strutting through it with their slung swords: Jap officers

in khaki and jackboots, with the French johns eyeing them.
First day there, I wandered into this hurricane of pong
the onshore wind blew to us. There were these wheelbarrow vats
milling round by the hundreds, being haggled over then poured
into tanker barges, ripe and glopping.
La merde, said this Russian copper to me. *It is shit, for fertiliser.*
They buy from households, better price the richer you are
because the richer you eat, then they sell on to farmers.

You see man with bamboo staff? Imperial official from old times:
he dips and judges, you see? speed of material flowing down staff.
It tells him quality, whether is water added.
Vendors are ancient guild. Have their own dialect. Very—fescennine.
He seemed to know English from dictionaries. *Ilya Chaikov.*
Is my name. Service Politique, Police Française. We shook hands.
It was done before I thought. Me, shake hands with a copper!
One day my colleague beat up nightsoil barrowman. Mistake.

It is summer. They park vats round police station and lift lids.
Two hours, and cops surrender. More defeat for la gloire.
He was going off duty, so we went for a drink
up little streets with strings of writing like crackers
popping and flaring down every building and wall,
wide streets with beggars who went quiet like cicadas as we passed.
We sat in a place where very slim tight-packed women
danced with one another and looked us over.

Ilya told me their price. So low it shocked me.
Low? he grinned. *That is top. For that among poor you can buy*
child. Not just for short time, but to keep.
You can buy anything at all in Shanghai, he said then
and it took a while, but it sunk in. Anything at all.
We were drinking pastis, aniseedy strong stuff; water
went in to turn it milky. *Fuel of French empire*, he said,
but I was getting aniseedy myself. I talked to Yank sailors,

I remember getting cursed for saying I stayed clear of help
when I was in America. *We ain't cheap, buddy!*
Don't you say we're cheap! and going past the grand buildings
along the river front and whacking them with a cane
to make the money flow out of them. *Is wrong stick!*
and someone, a man in a white Foreign Legion cap,
shouting in German *Ei Amerikaner! Hey baby!*
Americans fuck babies! and Chinese parting like the sea.

Then I sobered up quick. A mad-drunk Nippon officer
was slashing his blade about, yelling *Uigh!* and *Kura!*
Police were round him at a distance; when he'd dash they'd run
back from him and in on him. Then two got him pinned and took his sword.
He came unglued at that. He sweated, he screamed, he ran
up to the men who had his two-handed man-harvester
and pleaded, bowing and bowing as they laughed at him.
He has killed a Chinese. Now lose sword, lose face:

my guide explained.—*He must cut his belly.*
Later he said *French Concession is Vichy. Ally of Japanese.*
We would get orders to give sword back. So we don't report.
He smiled a little smile. That was my first trip to China.
We got a going over at the Yangtse mouth
from a Jap gunboat, all papers and passports checked,
all tarpaulins lifted and looked under. A touch of blockade.
I grinned how the cops had made Jack-the-lad capital-punish himself.

None of the raiders sank us, coming home.
I brought Laura a coral and gold necklace from Shanghai
and she knocked me sideways by crying her eyes red over it.
Seemed I hadn't got her a present since the Twenties.
I know you don't care about little possessions and trinkets.
You could live out of a duffel bag. You might have forever.
That's why this is special. It was true. The Bolsheviks
could collectivise all ornaments tomorrow, for mine.

I went straight to see Hans. They told me with long faces
he wouldn't speak. They'd put him in a locked ward for it.
What's with you, Hanno? But he wouldn't look at me.
I made conversation, told him how I'd been away
to China where they wear quilt coats and sleep on stoves,
I told him I the great Winnetou commanded him
to talk to me. No go. Put them with the mad and they go mad,
I Muggins thought. Had I just brought him roundabout to his cutting?

Louise clung round my neck. What she liked best doing
was going to Mass with Daddy. The candles, the Lady,
the pretty soldered windows she called the Colour People.
It made me go more often, it even drew Laura
and that was dead touchy, because her mother's hate on me
was as much for Popery as Hunnery:
What rubbish is that? Grown men in petticoats bowing
and praying to Poor Amos. Who is Poor Amos?

I was going to front the Manpower to take me off
their crewing list, for being married. Laura thought and said *Don't
stir them up and remind them you exist.* Joe came home on leave
with like an oil of smoke in his skin, and a distance-judging look.
Hess flew to Scotland, the Wehrmacht took Athens, Max
Schmeling the boxer leaped on Crete with his parachute
and things were only middling. I saw from the Dungog paper
somebody sent me that a man named Jack Boots joined the Army.

I never heard he got hurt and I hope he didn't.
Then Hitler turned on Russia and the killing-trench doubled on itself.
For a day I felt my feet on the ground, my arms aching,
my—well. Laura got rushed and came up smiling—
then I vanished again. I was just the world around me till I looked
and could see myself, full rubber standing on air.
Along October I was ordered back to sea;
I thought of going bush, of ducking it; I protested

but if you don't crawl you don't get people speaking up for you.
*It'll give your missus a rest from your ugly dial, Buttocker!
Watch out for them Japs. There's something building up there.*
We were heading back to Shanghai, by way of Brisbane
where I sneaked ashore and put out feelers about Sir Peter.
Oh he's a back number now, the Breakfast Creek pub said:
*they get turned over. Didn't he die the other day?
I remember him. He auctioned a judge. He was an out-and-outer.*

We got through the Jap inspection boats—tougher than ever—
and into the Huangpu river. Swimming in the Huangpu,
Ilya reckoned, was French for getting questioned
by the coppers with a hose shoved down your throat.
I didn't meet up with him at first. We lay off the International
Settlement this time, with lightermen and bargemen
from over on the Pu Tung side discharging and reloading us.
And I met Sam. You could have knocked me down. I met Sam

walking along the Bund. *Ah Fred, my dear old Fred!*
We made a night of it, straight after. *I work in the French Concession;
still a bait-layer, my word, no new lurks, not at my age;
we live way up north, though, in the Jerusalem quarter
of the Japanese district. Japs hate the Chinese, not us Jews.
The French Concession has the Western palates, and it'll stay
because it's Vichy. For that very reason we daren't live there.
Every day I'm braced to run if I smell a whiff of German policy.*

Christ-killer slurs, they're routine, and I don't do much front-of-house.
He hunched over his coffee and didn't touch his cognac.
We left our run late. Millions left theirs too late.
Now Hitler's got our people yarded, for whatever he intends.
That's what I was up to, getting our people out of Europe
with some of their money to live on, if possible. The Nazis
take it all, you know. On the theory it's all loot from Aryans.
You remember our flat. I own it. But I don't draw rent.

Sam stared at the river. *I feel like Noah*, he said
safe on the Ark while all his fellow humans were drowning.
I've always felt that about my Dad's people. Now it's my mother's
people too. Both my worlds. He was rocking very slowly
back and forwards, like a beast that's stunned.
Sam, I said. But he went on *The white man's been aboard*
the Ark so long he thinks the deck is dry ground.
But my hosts the Japanese are going to board the Ark with vigour

to throw you overboard and eat up all your clean beasts.
Fred, if I were you I'd run for it. I wouldn't linger here.
For an answer I told him what I never had before
from the burning women onwards. Me in my living plaster.
You never knew how they'd take it, the ones I did tell.
Sam said *Well!* and looked shirty. He sat there fuming,
getting ahold of himself. *If you told that to one of your moderns*
who think any name they can give to a phenomenon

is its social superior, he finally told me, *they'd snub it*
into line with a term like Shock or Reaction
or Flight from Reality. To contain it and make it barren.
I think myself it's a story of law that you're carrying
for all places. You're wrong to call it the Nothing.
You should never accept any name for it, even from you.
Names don't last. When it ends, you'll have to tell it.
Meanwhile, he said, *I sit on my bunti here, useless.*

And he left me, shaking his head. I'd upset Sam!
I wished I'd never told him. I thought it might interest him,
be in his line. Well it was. When he got upset
he always got mysterious. He'd been through a lot.
He didn't need me to win something over him. If I was
reading him right. I might be right out in my reading him.
I still slept on board, and saw that our Captain was in
a tear about something that was stopping us clearing port.

Held to ransom by those Green Gang bastards! he spat out
to the mate as they passed me. I went ashore again
and the city was like cyclone weather. Something big coming.
I walked down the Bund and came to the Avenue
Edouard VII, where the French Concession border was.
They had a high barb wire barricade all along now
and just gateways through it. About a million Chinese
were arguing and pleading to get in, and not getting.

Already I'm talking like Ilya Chaikov. I got in
and he and I met up, and punished the beer.
Next morning we heard the International Settlement
was closed down, and the Yankee fleet sunk in Pearl Harbor
and Japan in the war. My ship would be impounded as British.
God help my shipmates. Not all of them got through
the starvation and bashings, as I found out four years later.
Meanwhile there was I in a clove hitch. Still free and cold sober,

holding on to my money, which luckily
I'd turned into francs the day before.
You aren't a person unless
you can meet the rent for being one. You can't own it outright.
There I was on an island walled in poor begging people
and I walked the lanes, and rue Wagner and rue Joffre
trying to work out my next move. Other sailors, a few,
had also jumped ship or made a home run from the Seamens Club

before the Japs got to it. Three or four French and neutral
ships were getting steam up to clear. I asked Ilya
but he smiled and said *A passport now, of right country,*
would cost a fortune. Green Gang has whole boxes full.
I have never had passport, myself. I have Stateless papers:
great luxury of not being national. My grandfather
marched Pskov to Khabarovsk on Tsar's pay, three rubles a year:
one for soap, one for sugar, one for woman to pleasure.

I knew where Sam worked, and forced myself to race there
and chance him still being dark on me. Of course he wasn't.
He just turned his kitchen over to his understrappers
and took me to his office. Wood-lined, with blue ribbons
and a big cane chair at his desk. He twiddled keys, dipped
and fished out an eagle-stamped booklet with a great big J
printed all through it. *Comedy isn't always funny, Fred.*
This man looked like you. He's in Eretz Israel now

on a—different passport that we got him. He was overjoyed
to be rid of this one. It'll get you safely past
Japanese, though. And if you strike Germans, ditch it.
Ditch it fast, I beg of you. Don't think that tricks will work.
Passports like this are going to be death, in Europe.
That's the rumour. I think you look enough like Max.
Max Baer: that's you. You've got the build for that name!
Go quick, old friend. God guide you. Don't let your steel rust, eh?

I tried round the ships, getting rowed about in a sampan
from one to the next. Jap gunboat wakes and launch wakes
threatened to swamp us. At last I scored on a Spaniard,
the San Felipe, bound for Manila. Goodbye big broad river
and out to the bigger one, past the old forts. The Japs
looked at my German passport and nodded. There was a wail
and Chinese stowaways were herded onto the poop deck,
lined up and mowed overboard with machine guns

in front of the lot of us. The Captain cursed and screamed *Guernica!*
with his officers holding him back and the head Jap eyeing him, calm
with this pinched inspector's mouth that could sentence him.
Then the men with the two red hills on their shirts left us
and we ploughed on, under fighter planes and cruisers' Aldis lamps,
me in a sweat of shame, ready every minute
to ditch one or other of my bloody passports. Manila
was GIs cranking ack-ack guns and goodbye San Felipe:

she was heading for Panama, I was in a lather for home,
the world was coming down, Guam, Hong Kong, the big Pom battleships,
the Japs were rounding up the Orient and islands like stockmen
and I was turning beer into indigestion at dock bars,
listening to people panic. *Hey sailor,* says this Yank
with a very grown up and restless-eyed looking wife,
Can you crew a yacht?—Motor? I ask.*—Sure, motor.—*
I reckon, I say, and remember to keep clipped and confident.

It was a sound boat, with wireless and two good diesels,
not too much draft. It'd roll, but sneak in close round islands.
The heart of it had a door, panelled in tropic wood, that opened
with a click like a bank safe on a luxury bed
and that's where Chuck Pitty the owner and his lady
pretty much stayed, while I and two Chinese and a Yorkshireman
worked the boat under a black Yank bos'un.
We cast off and island-hopped at night,

days we snuggled up to islands and slept a lot.
The Pittys kept watch then, and you heard them argue.
Damn right we gotta make it all the way to Australia!
You know what Japs do to white women—
I'm sure they don't waste quality, Chuck, she said to madden him
and he raved on, while she smoked. *Where's my where the hell's my*
goddam Barlow knife?—In Idaho, mayhap?
but the heat would sap the sarcasm out of her Algonquin manner

and trickle down her front, behind her buttons.
We were in beside a steep green island where the farms
went up and up in stairs like cattletracks at home
and the people looked exhausted any time of day
but the men came down to the shore and stood in the water
with their hoes in their hands just to stare at Mrs Pitty.
More and more of them. She smiled at them and shone
like a star being kind with its light, burning their hearts out.

I think if we'd been wrecked there, the women would have
taken her to meet their bolo knives. Ernie Glossop from Yorkshire
used to curse, on the very quiet, about her
stirring up the natives. He also hated it
when the Chinese blokes sneaked looks at her sidelong
in her working rig made of exercise and unbuttonings and cream.
In comics they stay the same figure right through the strife,
rounded and unscratched, to be died for. Arlene tried, I'll give her.

Who is our boss? I asked one night. *He made his money mining,*
Peng said who spoke good English. *Alaska, Idaho.*
Mrs Pitty is his second wife, his reward to himself, I think.
He is sorry the war came just now.—It's badly timed, I agreed,
for like private lives. Then we went quiet. The sky
was filling up with noise, planes groaning, ships' engines throbbing
and soon we were ghosting abaft of big silhouettes
just three nights before Christmas. Next day and next we kept running

south from Leyte with a Bulgar flag up. We'd rummaged in the locker
for a flag of convenience, Liberia maybe, and the Bulgar one
was the best he had. God knew if they were on our side;
we bent it on and hoisted it. I still bless the white green and red.
Flying boats looked us over. Pitty came out of their boudoir
and said we weren't to head down through the Indies and Ceram
but way east along the equator then cut south
around New Britain. He tipped there'd be fewer Japs that side

and wiped his salty cauli-and-carrot hair off his forehead.
*I love foreign travel, always did. Seems I damn near wore out
the world for new sights, till this. Running ahead of hellions is new.*
Peng answered *When one wears out the foreign sights, more travel
is possible by learning languages. We then go back to the countries
we've seen, and understand them.* He petered out under Pitty's savage look:
*Do you speak Jap? Do you understand the world from inside
those bastards' slanty-eyed little head-lopping poem-writing minds?*

Pitty wiped his mouth of froth, and Peng kept out of sight for hours.
He was a query. Good English in a Chinese working man? Either
the educated gent or the poor bent coolie, seems their custom.
He also didn't come from the Philippines, I gathered.
We started seeing Jap warships again, just as our oil ran low
and we cast about for some island where a mission
or plantation might spare us some. *Might even be oil left behind,
our employer said. Japs will be rounding up every white resident*

in the Pacific and the Indies. In this he could see clearer
than some we met where we tied up next: Kadad Island,
former Neu-Schwaben, as the kind old Catholic missionary
Father Vogt whispered to me. *My parishioners still speak of
marks when they mean money.* He had them fuel us from his tanks
because he wasn't leaving. *We are technically allies,
Nippon and I*, he laughed. *I am an old summer vest
and my home is New Schwaben. Don't you linger, though.*

As we ran south, a seaplane came over the horizon
ahead and straight at us. We looked, and realised, and ducked
and it gave us a shower of machine-gun slugs, then flew on.
We counted ourselves and bits. No one was hurt.
*There's something they don't want us to have seen
maybe*, Boss Pitty growled. *Or just damn cussedness more likely.*
The boat was getting heavy and losing way. Holes near the bow,
holes at the waterline, along the hull on both sides,

stringers snapped and sheathing loose. We kept taking water
faster than the pumps got rid of it. Pitty disappeared
into their love nest, slam! I began to see
what to do. I took our drums of reserve fuel below
forrard to the crew space—*We'll sleep on deck; we do already*—
and locked them in. Empty or full, they'd be buoyancy.
Wash Williams the bos'un didn't need to be told. He caught on,
stayed at the helm and let me play my games,

packing every space with buoyant stuff—not so much was, in the Forties—
jettisoning heavy and waterloggy stuff. Still we slowed and wallowed
and the water rose round the mountings of the engines
as we neared a high long island, searching for a place
to beach and fix the hull. Then Pitty opened the watertight
door of their cabin, not knowing the water stood
a foot above the door-sill. I looked up from the engine
I was building coffer-dams around: he crashed back on their bed

in a wave like Bondi Beach, and Arlene screamed and bounced
out and up on deck, wrapped in a silk sheet and babbling
as she turned into a public person. *Mrs Pitty*, Peng nodded
politely to her. And I woke up to how love had meant
their cabin air had buoyed us and saved us. By now we were sinking
with both engines dead, and had to swim for it, but not far.
Mrs P. had lost weight, but I'm grateful to her allure
for stopping the boss opening their door till that last moment.

I dried my wet dunnage and gave Arlene pants and a shirt
and we all traipsed off. At the end of every beach
was a black crocodile creek you had to wrestle inland to cross
then we saw a wharf and sheds. It was a plantation.
Pitty had the sense to stop us charging straight in.
You and me, Fred, we'll scout it. Rest of you sit tight.—
I look more like the locals, chief, said Wash. But Pitty said
All the better to deal with them if we strike Japs and get chopped.

We struck Japs. It was as bad as the burning women.
It stays with me like them. We got past the copra sheds
and slipped into this big garden of all bougainvillaea and trees.
It was cover to check the house from. Suddenly Japs came out
and went round the front. On the dirt under a flagpole
lay seven white people, bloodied and like sleeping. Father Vogt
was one of them, and he'd been split open with a sword
so you saw the halves of his heart and liver and organs.

Pitty's mouth was saying Buk! and I grabbed it
and held him till the Japs had boarded their patrol boat
and motored off. Then he overflowed, and leant on me
and overflowed again. I think our faces told the others
before we found the words. We buried the dead, and Arlene
surprised me by getting down in the graves to cross their
hands over their chests. Then we shovelled coral sand over them
and said what prayers we could think of, and added to them.

Arlene asked *Where were the women? Back there.*
There'd been none dead, with the men or anywhere about.
They must have been evacuäted, Ern answered, but he sounded
like he wanted convincing. He didn't like to imagine
what we all thought likely. Mrs Pitty had very much stopped
looking like she was indulging some big boys' game, and insisted
on taking her turn with the handcart we had supplies on,
rice and copra and tinned food from the house, and medicines,

jerking and bouncing on the vehicle track down the island.
It's all a blur, soon after this. A mosquito must have got me
and brought on malaria. I see myself staggering and falling
into shadows and trees, and the others supporting me along
and Louise with a flame out the top of her head like a candle
but this not being terrible, and then I came sane on this rickety
plantation boat they'd found, and Pitty cursing me:
You goddam Kraut spy bastard. We found your goddam Kraut passport!

I took it in, slowly. My heart turned edgeways with horror.
I was in so deadly a fix that I went to sleep again.
I kept waking up to it, and fainting
and each time it was still true. At sea with people who'd kill me
for something I'd never ever convince them was nonsense.
I guess that was a picture of those times altogether.
Pitty was blabbering about how they should put me overboard
till Arlene spoke up: *I couldn't bear a man*

who'd murdered someone right in front of my eyes
ever ever to touch me again. He saw she meant it.
I saw she meant it. The glamour lady saved my life, right there.
Saved it for the minute, for the trip ahead of us,
till civilisation. Then I'd be turned in and turned over.
As I improved, I tried to argue. The Chinese looked away
and Pitty worked himself up to *You're so cute*
you got the Japs to bump off that old Kraut missionary

because we'd seen you plotting with him! We're onto you, Mac.
My head shook like a boxer's. Gradually a coast loomed up.
It had to be Australian New Guinea—but no, it was Japanese New Guinea
and we learned that from great big shocker spouts
their mortars made in the sea. As our lot yelled and turned
the boat away, there'd be rustles in the air and a wide
flat BAM underwater. And one of those got us. The boat
just came apart. Glossop and I were on the part still floating

as another bomb got all those in the water. Killed them like fish
dynamited in a waterhole. I saw poor Arlene float past standing
just a foot under with this calm smoker's look on her face
and her eyes open. I reached, but she was dead, and then gone.
We floated away out on the tide, with Glossop making
truce plans for me: *We're in this together for now, lad.*
Of course you know I'll have to do my duty when we're seäved.
And I'd thought him a working man. *Wake up to yourself, Ernie!*

The tide took us in at night. We waded ashore and ran
for the edge of the bush. Black in there. Ernie wanted to take
the easier going under the beach palms. I wouldn't let him:
too easy to track us in the sand out there. We shoved and bogged
and got cut about, as I found by the blood all over me
in the morning. We slogged scrub till we dropped, near evening,
completely stuffed, and lay up in under lantana
that I knew by its cake-essence stink. When we woke up

the sun was away high, and Japs were camped on top of us.
We were in more strife than Speed Gordon. *Thy fookin allies,*
Glossop mouthed at me. We smelt their breakfast and starved
and when a line of them peed into the bushes, drops
of gold reached us, and dripped, and we had to take it.
We thought it was a forlorn conclusion that they'd find us.
They stayed two days. We lay there and wet ourselves
and slid our farts and froze the manure inside us—

and when they trooped off, making noise like twice as many,
and we were sure they weren't coming back, Ernie swore and cried
like a man passing a kidney stone, or a stone kidney.
My own liver brick cost me no pain. That day, we heard shooting
and Ern started looking like putty in the face
I'm burning goop, Fred lad. No more spy comics, he was sick.
I'd have to start carrying him. On the no rations we were getting.
Hunger I could feel. It crawled inside me so I could,

it cracked my mouth wide enough to drive a truck in, or my fist.
What direction to go? I had no idea, and Ernie
Glossop's ideas were turning to green cheese.
South ought to be right, but there were mountains that way.
Along the coast, we'd meet Japs. Natives, would they feed us or eat us?
Find a track, I thought, and follow it inland. It will go somewhere.
Because bush was like barbed green syrup you could swim in
a few hundred yards till you drowned. As jammed in daylight as in dark.

We must have gone a day or two, up this tunnel of track,
I was near out to it, trudging, with Ernie up as my jockey.
Suddenly there were men. Men made of the bush, it looked like,
of rain-slime and dirt with buckles and pouches in it.
Christ, it's Sinbad! one said, with a painted tin gun in his hands
and I woke up. *What do we learn from this Ron?*
I asked Mister Robilliard. My acrobat mate, with a Digger hat
rotting on his head. *Married-fashion, it's Fred!*

Seemed they were a long range commando lot. The shooting
we'd heard was of the Japs who'd peed on us. *Born for nothing,*
them cunts, one of the troop said, a squinny sour bloke
with a little nibbly face low down on his head like a lobster.
I scoffed tins of bully beef and they let me, because I was starving
and because I meant to carry my witness on
out to help. That would be up to me. *Did you happen*
to have a Chinese bloke with you? Ah. Married passion, Fred!

but I'm glad to see you, said Leftenant Robilliard.
Up and on, and soon we came to steep country
winding around and on up timber steps
chocked in the mud. They let me go first to get best
purchase on the rounds of tree-trunk, before their boots slicked
that staircase, and Glossop jerking, raving *Päätely Bridge!*
Päätely Bridge!—He'll have to be silenced, Ron said
and I had a bad feeling how they'd do it. *Shut up Jesus Ernie!*

Up and up, with Ernie down my back some of the time
like my old double man act, one upways, one down by the knees
and banging his head, till I'd haul him back. I strapped him
over one shoulder with a web belt in the finish. Up and up
and along the sky, then more up on more stairs.
To think I'd imagined Europe as the land of stairs!
Three flights up inside apartment houses. Nothing.
One day a noise hit us like split the plantation boat

and we went a backwards purler, tumbled it felt like a mile of
mud inside out, and was a hundred yards. The blokes stepped aside
for us, and crouched on up. Shooting and ping-scream of bullets
as I checked Ernie for punctures. None. Just grazes bleeding.
I lay beside him. So steep there it was as if a man
was leaning on the world, not lying on it.
The four o'clock rain came through the trees, so heavy
Ern started to float off down, and I had to moor him.

When the boys came back, one was missing
and Ron had got very serious. *We can't generally carry them*, he said.
I dropped down that I was dead weight on them, with Ern,
but no more got said. I think I was allowed points
for sleeping in the mud at night without a groundsheet
and not complaining. They moaned, all in jokes, but they moaned.
There's a sty in the sky where you die, and it's old New Guinea,
I think was the best one.

We came to a village, way up, but didn't walk in
and leave hobnail bootprints for the Japs to see. The people
brought out cold pork and heaps of boiled veg. They laughed a lot.
*Yu stap tokim maritpasin you tok tok tasol**
a lady said to Ron and her baby looked at him from the breast
while we all admired her other breast. They were the first people,
the only people I ever saw not wearing
any cloth in their clothes. Just grass and mat and bird plumes.

Two young fellows volunteered to carry Ern and spell me
because I was staggering. He went into a hammock
under a bamboo pole with cane loops bracing him
and off we went, miles down into a gorge
across a flood on knocking boulders and straight
into the sky again, the carriers singing *Pange lingua
gloriosi* in perfect time. *Corporis mysterium* which has got
a winding tune to it just perfect for climbing to the heavens.

It's a mad giant's teapot, that country, shit, steam and wet leaves;
you crawl up the spout and down. We were kept back one time
while the blokes did an ambush. It went on, road-drill and bang
for half a hour; I sneaked up to find out the results
and there were Jap bodies, and one of the commandos was down
cursing a shot knee. Two more were rigging a hand-grenade
on a long bamboo with a string. They sneaked it up under the bush
to a big stumphole, jerked the string, a hand came out but BOFF!

a man schoolboy-size rolled out screaming and tangling his guts
and one of them sniped him. His head sprayed, and I lost my fear of them.
Keep back when you're told Fred. Endanger us and I'll shoot you myself.
No grin from Ron with this. I picked up Ken Boyce their wounded man
and piggybacked him. We went for a day or so
before a big Nearly got us talking: he yanked my hair *Yaa!*
and stopped me stepping off a cliff. We would have busted
on frothing rocks half a mile down. We had a spell

* *You're always talking married-fashion (i.e. sex) but you do nothing but talk*

[234]

to celebrate. *I knew a man that could have gone over there*
and sucked himself on to the face and lipped himself down!
I was babbling. *I know you was in the circus with Ron,*
silly cunts the pair of yer. Remember I ain't got his training!
Next day he asked *What would you like to be?*—I told him:
Home, fart-dry and full of roast turkey.—*Well,* he said,
your shoulders under me should be dry but there's no turkeys.
Next day I got to why there weren't other wounded:

If you're fit enough and want a chance, you keep your weapon
and some bully and grenades. That's Ron, not HQ. None's talked yet.
He makes us finish Japs off, in spite of what they do, he added
and went quiet on that.
After weeks we came to wire and sentries
and said goodbye to Ron's lot, and got passed down the lines.
Freddy Baer I'll never forget what thee carried me and seäved me.
But I told thee from the start I have to report thee—

I looked away from Ernie, not to show my feelings.
All I had to do was be sure and miss the plane
we were both to go south on. Miss it by a hair and lose myself
in all the Army tangle of Port Moresby. I looked at his face,
starved hollow but pink from the shower, and shook his hand:
It's the manly thing, Ernie! Just when he smelt a rat I never heard.
He was never a quick thinker. I did curse at not going straight on south
but after hanging round the ORs messes for a day or two

and getting bombed, I found a ship in the harbour
and got made acting supercargo on her. An officer job on crew pay.
When we reached Cairns wharf, I saw men across it but took
no notice till one said *You won't get back aboard, Jack,*
if you go ashore: this is a picket line. I must have bridled
because he cursed me *Get it through your nut, Ironstein!*
Another man beside him chipped in Socialist politeness,
Comrade; this is a worker, remember that.

Scorn is for the class enemy. I had an idea I was being
buttered up for something, as I looked into that one's Mature look.
There was Hollywood there if ever I'd seen it, but I was
in a hurry to try and ring our neighbours at home
that had the phone on, and make a time to ring Laura.
I'd sent her a letter from Moresby to say I wasn't lost
but how were she and Joe and Louise and poor Hans?
No go. The phones were jammed with military stuff. Air Flash, Central.

I sent a wire, and a pub name to wire back to
then went to tell the pub. There was one on every corner
and soldiers skew-whiff in every one, roaring and shoving,
dancing arm in arm, bottle-shrapnel, monkey-yowls and recitations:
From four o'clock to eight o'clock with back and elbows bent,
the bucket jammed between me knees and toes dug in cement—
a sandy bloke was yelling at the door of one: *Goodbye fuckin' cows!*
You'd have thought the war was a gold rush. It was, in Cairns.

I went to a quieter back bar, and there was the fellow from the strike.
Sit down, Comrade!—I flinched at that name, for the killing trench
that ran out from it, but maybe he wouldn't know that, so
I sat my beer and myself down; we'd drink at a table like gentlemen.
We got to the strike, and he told me in his rugged sincere way
it was over wages and conditions. *The bosses can't be let use the war*
as a cover for winding back the workers' wages and conditions!—
No, I said. *But I'm sure the Party don't waste a smart bloke like you*

on ordinary Labor stuff, I said. *Wages and conditions!*
He bristled and did a good line in ruffled feathers. Then *No,*
of course there's more to it. There'd have to be, he judged, to snare me.
Defeat in New Guinea would discredit white colonialism—
he started to interest himself, and forget to pose. *Coming on top*
of the Depression, it would discredit the ruling class at home.
The people might feel emboldened to rise. What my hiders in Berlin
told me, how the Communists weren't allowed to help other Left parties

against Hitler made me ask: *What about invasion of home?*—
The worst times are the best times, eh, sailor? I looked at him
and suddenly understood why Stalin let Hitler take Germany,
and which toffs he learned from. When we got back there were no pickets
but soldiers with fixed bayonets, and the Skipper after my hide
to stow artillery aboard. Cannons like enormous kangaroos
chained on their timber pallets. Down the hold they went
and me after, to stow them. The Party bloke was screaming at soldiers.

I saw those kangas cough, too, on a shore under mountains.
No sooner we winched them up and ran them ashore
they got stoked, aimed and fired. Fighter planes hosed the plantation
at the end of their strip as they lifted off, and Jap
snipers fell out of the palm tree tops. I saw that.
The place was a bog with air like a rotting wash-house
and the sea like jelly. One of the young soldiers
I met on shore strapped with pouches was Mrs Morris's Henry,

I'll swear it was, but he didn't know that name at all:
My mum's name is Hester. Who are you anyway, fella?
Joe was fighting a mile from me, and I didn't know it.
I got home to Laura via Sydney, where we docked.
God I had the channels too, as sailors say,
late home by half a year, looking at Military Police again,
looking at GIs with women and Diggers with beer
and big Yanks in SP armbands who didn't take bets.

At home, the news was just middling. Laura's ma
had died at last—I learned to be respectful about that—Laura
had had work, back at Winns; ma had looked after Louise,
Newcastle had been shelled from a sub, and Sydney raided.
A man with a German name had snapped up a mansion and two houses
right on Sydney Harbour for three hundred pound the morning after
when half the toffs were doing a bolt.
The sea was fenced in barb wire and windows brown-papered over.

I went to see Hans. The place he was in I hated
like that leper-gaol I was stuck in on the Verweser River,
same drugs and rotting-flesh smell, same bars and locks, same sentence:
Expect to die here. For you, time has dried up.
A burly male nurse brought Hans, skulldragged him really
and I nearly hit the bugger.
What really stung though was that Hans
had to be forced to come. I'd abandoned him there, was how he saw it.

In spite of the cold breeze they had the window open
in the visitors room. Iron bars across them kept us safe
from the poor lunatics. There was a little jigging man
came past the window and said *Sell all you have
and give it to the poor!* I said *I haven't got much.—*
I will buy it! he shouted. *I am the Commercial Banking Company:*
I must have all your property! He'd gone as red as a goblet.
I am the fifth of May! I am full satisfaction.

I was just starting to work out what had happened him
in the Depression, most likely, when another man nurse in white
came round the corner. *Go back to your ward, McCudden,*
he snapped. The jigging fellow jumped, and defied him:
You will not close on me! I am the Sabbath made for man!
the white-coat stood with his hands on his hips. *Cry,* he ordered
in an even voice. *Cry, you jamrag.* And the mad fellow
shivered and broke. His face knotted and blubs gasped out of him

as he stood there in his ruin. The nurse watched him bawl.
I was up and holding the window bars. *That was a mongrel act,*
I said to the nurse fellow. He looked me up and down.
Fuck you, squire, he said. I snapped the fastenings of the bars
and dropped them out beside him. *Now, care to say that again?*
But he was no coward. *Come inside here and you'll be detained.*
As a patient, he said. *We often see that strong-man stuff from them.*
We just sedate them; the padded cells soak up their flash.

At least he melted the big freeze. Hans started bawling too,
stirred up with all the feeling. The nurse bloke grinned as if
he'd been chewing gold and got bits stuck in his teeth.
He wanted to make me see red and jump through that window.
Your Jerry imbecile has got a sweet little arse, he said,
I can see how you'd badly want him back. But really
he's happy as a sandboy. In here is a little Germany.—
Where do you drink? I asked, but he waved and walked off.

What bubbled out through Hans's crying, it rocked me
and I prayed it wasn't true. But they don't lie.
I told it to Laura and she said *We can't put up with that.*
We can't leave him in there, or we're as bad as they are.
It braced me up, that. I'd got close at times to wishing
I'd rescued somebody who could say Thanks mate, shake hands
and walk off out of your life straight after. When I told
Laura some of this, she said *Thanks Mr Baer!* in snorts of giggles.

She wanted to write letters, apply to Government big-guns.
She still thought we were respectable; ma's influence hanging over.
I painted her a picture: me in internment, her destitute,
the Welfare coming for Louise. *I spose at least she'd remember us,*
I said, laying it on. I was really burying ma, I think.
I've forgiven the poor old girl since, without noticing, as you do.
Laura thought some more and sent me to the Golightlys
which was miles better. Lula was liver-spotty old

but she summed it up: *So your feller can neither learn his lines*
nor be trusted to shut up, and belongs to Hitler?
Waste my time with an easy one, why don't yer?
She was getting on to it, and then we hit a wall:
I spoke about Leila being Leland and she froze.
Leila was a woman. If I was taken in by drag
over there in Germany, all the more fool me.
Leila wasn't in the country, she couldn't help me at all.

Well, a bloody fool was something I could feel.
Even her peeing standing up—but I swore I'd seen that.
I realised how much I'd wanted there to be someone
somewhere not trapped in just one half of life.
Shave every day, keep your clothes on, you're still trapped.
It seemed Leila thought the same. I'd noticed that practically
all the horrors done in my lifetime were by clean-shaven men
at the orders of clipped hairy-mouths. Golightlys' show wasn't travelling

for the duration. I wonder do you still
say that, up there in the future: the duration?
I was in Lula's bad books. And I had to find work.
We'd rented out the old Riggs' house that Laura inherited
up in Newcomen street, but that earned only wartime rent.
I got no more sailing orders, and didn't want them—
I'd drowned in '42, I discovered after the war.
I fixed up the ute to do some carrying, but

the petrol rationing hobbled me. Four gallons a month
for private, a bit more for commercial. Men with horse drays,
they were coining money. My salvation came the day
a nuggety bloke with a limp asked me in the pub
Fred, do you remember my nackas against your neck?
It was Ken Boyce, the commando I'd carried. I didn't
remember his nackas, but I said *Like a Mae West collar!*
He was classed Home Service now, and working in a fuel dump.

One thing and another, I got into black market petrol
and stayed in it till after the war. It meant we had
money to live, and to worry hard about Joe
since he'd stopped writing letters. Louise trotted off by herself
and lit candles for him. His mother dropped tears in her mending.
I try to find reasons why he's special and ought to be spared
but already there's millions of mothers' special boys dead.
He worshipped you. It's a pity you hardly noticed him.

That one sat. It was true, and I deserved it.
The best I could do was not make the same mistake twice.
I did like the helpless ones and went to light candles with Louise,
and during this I was a peacemaker, once at least.
Yank Marines were in town from the trains, yelling *Where's the action?*
Where's the good times in this burg? Going north they deserved them
some of the women reckoned. But Australian soldiers and sailors
not going north just then felt in their pockets,

found less money and ordinarier cigarettes
and got irritated. I was in a café in Darby street
with a couple of the fuel dump boys. We were eating little steaks
like you'd give the cat before the war. Marines swanked in
yelling *Service ol' buddy!* to the Greek, and the steaks they got
lapped over their plates, with tomatoes and eggs riding on them.
They do all right, for men who'll buy dressed pelican for chook
said one of our lot, loud. *What's your trouble, sonny?*

snaps the biggest Marine. The petrol sergeant stood up,
snatched that one's plate and gave him his own in its place:
That's more your weight. And the Marine amazed me:
he flicked out a knife. Him, a man big enough to bash up
four of the sergeant, and he brings out a knife.
The fuel man looked green but didn't dingo. *You don't do that,*
I said to the Yank. *In Australia they look down on you for that.—*
Gimme back my goddam steak, boy, or I'll spill your liver.

There was doubt on some of the other Yanks' faces, embarrassment
at their man. His head was specked pink, with sweat and whiskers
and I stepped up to him. *You've disgraced yourself,* I said.
How can these mates of yours trust you in battle now?
You're a fuck-up. Just as well they found out here.
And I snapped the knife off him. *Hey, Sweeney,* says one of his squad,
Siddown and eat your goddam little steak.
Hooray for Hollywood, I said to myself and liked myself.

The Sharpies Plate and tip-top swindling title
were won by my honest wife, though. One day at dinner
she asked me *How old would your little brother be who died?*
Forty-three, I said. *Why?—And Hans is what now? Thirty?*
Thirty-one?—So? I asked her.—*Well, why couldn't*
his disease have left him like Hans and talking mainly
his baby language? The light came on in my head
with a pop! like gas. She added *Their faces don't age as fast,*

I mean, if someone should think Hans looked too young—
You're a worldbeater, I said, kissing her. *An electric worldbeater!*
We'll go in like commandos, a canoe, lift him out of the ward—
Just wait your patience till I get your brother's birth certificate,
and then a ration card for him and an identity card;
that one's risky to do straight. I'll arrange it through a friend.
A day or two later, when she had all the cards we lived by then,
she said *Forget canoes. You'd wake his ward and they'd sing out*

worse than a fowlhouse. I'll go. They've never seen me.
There'd have to be papers—transfer form, doctor's certificate—
or else there'd be a manhunt for the Escaped Nazi Lunatic
that would come to our door, with soldiers, and carry me off with it.
They're short-staffed out there. All the experts are off treating
shellshock. How I know? I belong to this town, I do know
the people to ask, for any information. You'll have to
go to a man to get the forms we'll need. That's how

I met Kyle Bourke, who I liked and then for a bit didn't
because he seemed so close and easy with Laura.
How long have you known him? I was so casual.
Oh ever since school. She was so casual too.
But he had talent. He could draw print. What I mean,
the first time I saw him, in the basement of his bookshop
he handed me a sheet of newspaper. Columns, stories, wire photo:
I drew that, he said. I was puzzled, turned it over: blank

on the other side, but I thought no, they printed just one side—
I did. I drew that, he repeated. And wrote out some type on a pad
with Indian ink and a fine mapping pen. *Times Roman,*
ten point, well leaded. Can you tell it from the real stuff?
I can do you documents, passports, anything. I could do tenners but I don't.
My mouth just hung open. There were none of these Xeroxes then.
He called it drawing. *I do it freehand,* he said.
That newsprint page is my graduation piece, to convince clients.

Well, I'd often caused the feelings I now felt. He'd sold me.
He could lift his horse as high as I could lift mine.
You're Her bloke? You're lucky. No charge to Her.
What name does your man go by in there? We started planning,
doctor's certificate, transfer to clinic in Brisbane. The next day
I went back for it all, including a Queensland death certificate
dated months ahead. And Frank Boettcher's identity card:
These are the little hooks the Nazis catch Jews on, Kyle said,

I hope my kind of fellers are doing their duty in Europe.
The keepers never had a chance. Laura went to the asylum
in an Army Buick with Ken Boyce as MP driver-escort
to the German patient. In her cream costume, silk stockings, hat
she'd have bluffed a Field Marshal. She signed Hans out and swept him
away to the specialist head-doctors. Who were us. And the weeks
and months piled up over the adventure, with never a copper
to our door. It had worked. And going round with me

to roll forty-four gallon drums onto lorries and off
and be called Frank, and knock on the empties with a bolt
cleared the Bad Hospital out of Hans's mood. He took up
singing, in fact. He couldn't do music and words
at the same time, or learn verses at all; he sang just voice:
Ohhüümaanehn! by the hour if you let him *Aaradeez—*
Odd times an outsider would catch him at it, though I'd warned him
not to do it round people. *Yer offsider singing in tongues?*

a Gypsy bloke asked me up at Muswellbrook, and explained what that is:
the Holy Spirit singing through you, for once not harnessed to words
or any such cover-ups, was the way he put it.
As the venture to get Hans out faded, Laura's worry about Joe
ate at her again. I worried that I didn't worry
near enough. Was it that she'd kept him secret
from me for the three years, so he came as a shock of duty
to me, not as something shared? I wouldn't say that to her

and I dreaded the telegram just as much as she did,
I discovered when it came. Luckily I was at home that day,
because Laura held the envelope that could blow the old days away
and was crying and talking all together. She'd have et her heart out
till I came home to open it. I grabbed it and did
and Joe was alive, recovering in military hospital,
Greenslopes, Brisbane. Laura was dry-eyed and off
straightaway, packing her port. *Jesus, what will I find?*

They've given no details.—She didn't ask you, just went?
Some of the petrol blokes didn't much approve of me
not putting my foot down. But it never struck me she should
get my permission to go up to Brisbane for Joe.
Louise and Hans and I, we batched, and Lou stayed back
after school with the nuns. One evening she said a soldier
was butting up against a lady behind the school toilets.
Sobbing below the belt, was all that came into my head.

I didn't make a fuss, and Lou went off playing with her kitten.
Next doors came in, and skittered back from Hans a bit:
He's all right, I said. *My brother. He's been away. He's harmless.*
They had the phone and I was wanted on it. *Your brother?*
Laura was ringing from Brisbane. Joe was fine, don't worry,
a young strong fellow with a tin left foot, he'd get preference,
he could even dance again, as if he ever had in our bush camp—
then she told me what she thought of this comfort she'd been given.

Prepare yourself, love. Joe's not the boy he was. He's savage.
Lay in a lot of smokes. I pulled on some very long strings
to get cartons of Camel and Lucky Strike and Ardath.
Our yellowy ghost of a son
horrified me to look at him. And he seemed glad it did.
The atebrin tan, Dad. I'm not as fucking yellow as some,
and he limped to his room with a tin squeak in his left boot
and lay there smoking, a hundred, hundred and fifty a day.

Hans put his head round Joe's door and got screamed at
and didn't scream exactly back; but screamed, and smashed things.
I put him in the truck and drove him about, to calm him
and we sat at Broadmeadow and watched men coming off the train
with perspex Spitfires tied to their kitbags, for their kids.
There was a white Yank officer, spiffy as a Devil Doone comic
commanding a mob of Negro soldiers. He went off
and I listened to them, getting my Kentucky ear back:

Man you mama so fat she's on both sides of the family!—
You daddy so dumb he couldn't pass a blood test.
A couple of them drifted over. They'd summed Hans up without
even seeming to glance; his teary face and knotting fingers.
Sumption, a corporal said round at my side window
That's our officer's name. Captain Wilmott Sumption,
and we got onto names. The others were fanning and stretching
and wave-walking a pack of cards. *The devil's prayerbook, honey,*

and soon they had Hans out and showing him the suits.
By the time their captain came back with his stitching steps
they had the boy half taught poker. But Mr Sumption snarled
and they all formed up, and waved to us, and tramped off
singing *Chokecherry, chokecherry, makin' a stand:*
I got your little pokeberry eatin' from my hand.
Lord knows what that meant; but I still sing it sometimes.
This was late in a year named after a revolver calibre.

So was the next, when I turned fifty, and the war ended
but not the age of revolvers. Things were awful at home
with Joe screaming out in his sleep, or sitting in the dark
with the red muzzle of his cigarette brightening and darkening,
and calling me a coward every way, in silence, in words:
But that's your story, eh Dad? Slink away till what you find
at the end of your slink scares you into bolting for home?
It's hard to take. So I'd run away from it, to work,

to the newsreels, to Cos, who'd found a new love and got young again.
It beats that come-day-go-day-God-send-Sunday life, he said.
I tried to drop the newsreels, for their mixing of explosives and people,
those blotches of light way down under bombers. Cos wouldn't even
take the newspapers. He'd stopped years back. *Other people's trouble
is neither my business nor my enjoyment*, he said.
I can't get him to see, I explained. *And he could be right.*
The night my mother burned, it was mid-day and I'd pulled over

and we'd got out by this creek on the road to Merriwa.
You could see the mayflies quivering over the water. Hans
was unpacking our sandwiches, and all at once a force
was around me, pouring upwards and down,
hurting and swarming, and I was croaking out *Frank!*
and the names of schoolmates. It was a force of the past.
After a few minutes I was back in my no-feeling in the sun
with Hans staring at me, *You wasn't there*, he said in English.

I was uneasy all that day and night. Next day it was in the papers,
the fire-storm on Dresden. Then I knew what That had meant.
I drove back home and walked straight in to Joe's room:
Die Flieger haben Dresden in Brand gesetzt und deine Oma ist mit verbrannt.
The bombers have set Dresden afire and your Gran's been burned up in it,
is all I said to our poor son. He understood me.
Laura helped me with my head, that had tears and noise coming out,
not that they change much, but the instinct to cry must mean something.

After MacArthur took the war away, to the north,
our army was too big and too well supplied for the little
island fights it had men dying in to keep busy.
It was like a better-off country inside our dowdy country
and fellows like me, and Cos, and Ken Boyce and thousands more
were milking it for juice and all surplus, as it strutted round,
going to the races and driving trucks up and down,
resenting the Yanks. Blokes were getting out, or scheming to stay in.

Boyce sold his discharge, just to keep near the pumps, and the man
he sold it to went tearing off home to compete
at romance with a big maroon Italian on his fruit-block.
When the end came, we hardly noticed.
Bourkey kept drawing ration cards and coupons
openly at the high desk of his shop. Lot of men were off enjoying
a South Sea holiday, before they got their civvy suits
and took up the heavy chain once more, by say the pen end.

When the talk was full of deferred pay and war brides, though,
I, and not just me, was looking full on, in movies and papers
at the worldwide trench I'd known was there. Bulldozers were shoving
shit-sticking stiff-jointed thousands over into it, on the newsreels,
I couldn't stay away. The drivers in their flu masks
rolling the corpses up and in, the stubborn squinty-faced
German civilians being made to look, and to help,
and, a bit later, the barb wire and shower-heads and ovens.

I'd lived with it like always in the middle of my mind
but I hadn't imagined the starvation and the diseases.
I felt I was dead myself, and stank, and just couldn't rot away.
In the house, the family tiptoed around me.
Joe by that time he was on the mend
and wanted to come on the fuel truck. Laura twigged what had happened:
He changed when your mother died. I doubt he'll ever again
throw it up at you that he defended women.

Do you know for sure she's dead? Have you checked? Laura added.
Well I did know, but not like officially. I tried my relatives;
I wrote to the Air Force, and the British Occupation:
long waits for short letters. I got sent to the Red Cross
for a longer letter back but the same result. No Frau Sietz
in Dresden, in any refugee camp, in the world. No lady
who told a bush kid that in the great fires, birds
and hopping mice and prickly-swine came out to the humans to be safe.

As I started on my search, men hardly fatter than those bodies
being dozed into Europe were also coming back home
from the tropics up north. A planeload here, a ship there. Like
I met Oyster Harris between Cos and Mrs Cos, Elizabeth,
walking slow up Hunter Street like a skeleton tired out
from working in its grave-shorts.
Me, Fred? Couldn't kill me with a pick handle
but I won't spar with you this week. I got too much on.

A fit man with them said, after a bit of a silence,
I got a line on some Yank trucks to sell off.
You want to be in it? Cos is, and he vouches for you.
Well I did get into that and we saved a lot of three-tonners
from dumping in the sea. The fit man was Norrie Kurtz,
really Kerz, but who can say that? So he'd burnt it short.
He nearly got famous, different times. First day we reported
to collect a line of trucks, the Yanks hadn't left yet. They fed us

steaks and fluffed mash and ice cream like some hadn't tasted
since the Twenties, or ever. We were eating pure Hollywood,
and jamming more of it into ports and Gladstone bags, for our families.
Best movie they ever ate, too. *When we live like them*
says Norrie to me, *there's going to be vehicles almighty*
and nowhere to park them. I got some ideas about that.
But I was watching Laura and Betty Morrison not get along,
as they didn't, and sort of hoping the Lenzings

wouldn't answer my letter telling them Hans was alive
but yet would be alive themselves. I still do. They never answered.
I was sorry I couldn't do what my Dad used to when trouble
sparked up between any of those inside his love,
say between aunts and his smart wife: he'd halloo and sing
and prance and play the idiot till they stopped it.
He'd embarrass them out of it. No dignity if love was threatened,
he'd throw his own down and jump on it, even for a suggestion

say not to invite someone. *We shoot Moritz? I bags his whiskers and arse!*
Yahoo! And slap the trouserlegs. And keep on till it succeeded.
I hated strife and disagreement just as much
but between people I loved it made me stuffed and helpless.
Hans had this habit when he was feeling frisky
he'd tell you little jokes, cartoon ones, tell them to anybody:
A dog with his foot in a meat tin, dapper dapper!
and laugh to make you share it, and gulp if you wouldn't.

I grinned and told him that day, just to test Norrie's character,
Tell that one to Mr Kurtz. Well Mr Kurtz trumped me:
he laughed and answered *A cat with a window in her!*
and no one had had that much presence of mind before. Hans loved it.
I might have dodged knowing too much about the Atom Bomb
when it was first dropped on Hiroshima, that pretty port,
and on Nagasaki. I didn't take it in till on the pictures
they were showing a test, out in desert country,

this like wireless tower—and then the screen bulged white
with scrolls spreading wide from the bottom as it hoisted
like as if a billion beings were charging outwards, and it
towering straight above them under the boiling top cloud.
I heard myself say The Hermaphrodite! The Hermaphrodite,
almost out loud. I spose I meant war was now equal
for women and men. Now the front might even be safest.
I brooded on the white because I was a scar spirit.

I brooded, and the Nothing no-named inside me
started to thin away. I had patches of feeling
over the days. *You're scratching, Dad*, Joe said
looking aside from the wheel. *I've never seen that.*
I'd been thinking of the white of atrocity in the pictures,
the poor starvers of India, the big-kneed ones toppled into pits;
the cameras made even black pain silvery, and somehow
it all wound on to the sun-disc of the Bomb

like belt taking up on a wheel, or chain flowing off it.
But I refused escape or cure. I fought to stop sensation
as it crept on, because it came on vile wrong conditions.
I wouldn't be cured by others' pain and destruction:
I was better cursed than cured by the light of this new full burn.
I drove back touch, I prayed with a splintering heart
and no one could help, no one could be told it was happening
but I stayed clean and bodiless, for the right solution.

And lucky or blest that I did, because I'd have died
of the next that happened. We had an enormous fuel dump
out in the tea-tree. No big secret. Air Forces had flown over it
as it stacked and stacked up. I never liked its bare-rim piling.
It should have been planked up shipshape. Less a teetery balancing act.
We were there to load up. Joe pulled at an easy but key drum.
I yelled *Not that one!* but the slide had started,
the full forty-fours toppling and coming down on us,

as I threw Joe under me, Ampol with Plumes and Shells
crashed round us like a barrage, boom! the donner was Mobil,
wild horsepower trampled us and kicked us, I saw its round hooves.
As usual, pain might have meant I missed the reel of it
and got worse hurt staving off hurt.
Men dragged us out. Joe was white as paper
carrying a broken collarbone and a gear-stripped ankle. Me, I
was fine till a snapped prop spilt me. I was all rolled fractures,

bleeding inwards and outwards. They had a job to save me, they wasted
chloroform, I woke with a hangover of it. My arm was drinking
from a bottle, down like a wire. I was shored inside
like a collapsing mine, I was caulked and fothered
and wore a cap of pad on a skull re-glued like a jug.
I had faces round me looking down like a funeral:
Iowa smiled *Hey Fred!* Baz Thoroblood cried *Help me!*
You hid your talent in the end and stayed a little person,

said Marlene. *My talent hid me*, I told her back,
and Gefreiter Heimann lectured past me dry as fine print.
Slowly things got solider. The mealtime spoon, my iron bed,
the chair with present-day people in to see me,
the colours in the window from first bleary
to evening rosy, and the sodium nights.
It seemed I was in the Mater. Laura came every day
and I asked her what we were living on. *Don't worry, love.*

The black market had its ways.
The coppers can wait for their increase in cut, Ken Boyce said.
One day he brought in Ron Robilliard, who stood turning
his civvy hat around. *What do we?—Don't ask, Fred.
I know now what we learn. I'm sorry it made me
snap at you, up the swamp cliffs there.—*
You trained him good, Fred, Boyce grinned. *If we couldn't hit
chips in a fast creek, one bullet in each, we weren't good enough.—*

He trained me, I said. *In a different part of the circus.*
One day Hans was in, and the sunk fellow in the next bed
heard us talking German. He opened an eye, and another eye:
Deutsche, was? Sort of, but from here, not Germany,
I replied to him. *Volksdeutsch*, he said. *No*, I said.
And he closed up on me. No more from him that day.
A few days later it was: *Can you keep that idiot away?*
He gets on my nerves.—String your nerves across your arse

and play Heidenröslein on them!—Wit typical for the Red Front!
he said, and soon he started, Australia was this, it was that,
a fool's paradise, no depth here because no suffering. *My Division
lost more men killed than the whole Australian joke-Army.—*
Careless of them, I said. *You mean BHP Rod and Bar Division?*
He'd said he was injured there. Well he tried to rear up at that
and went green and sank back. I knew then it was safe to argue.
This joke-army won, away and at home, I said. *It saved its country.*

He shifted ground then, the Obstuf—that'd been his rank
in his glamorous police-army. He never told me his name.
He sniffed where I was weak, and told me bad stories instead:
One day we had to shoot old Jews who'd been Prussian Uhlans, he said
and sang a song: *Der Zygmunt Perl
                    was a true Hussar,
                    he fought for us,
                    for Germania,*

but now his head
lies mixed with feet
and his yellow star
Pour le Sémite—
It got to be like that in the room: friends and life in English,
secret Hell in German. *We'd melt snow water for those partisans.*
They'd hunch down: they knew what was coming. We'd arrange them
artistically, then drench them, and they'd freeze to white statues

until the spring. The Lovers. The Signpost. The Circle Jerk.
Laura would come in and the SS bloke would turn away from us
as we talked home or broken bones or flying saucers:
When one lands I'll believe it.—I think they're one of those things
you believe till they land. Or Norrie would sit down
and tell me his latest way to make cars shrivel
up small for parking. *You know how a cart tips up?*
Why shouldn't your car sit back on its rump when you leave it?

After they'd go, and the Sisters had done with me
I'd be half dreaming about cars stacked up like saucers
or Cos swelling his moustache to cool the tea in his cart
and the murmur would start again: *The Ivans liked to capture*
our boys in their white snow suits. They'd soak them in petrol
and let them run back to us, thinking maybe they weren't alight
till the fire would catch and tangle them. If they got right to us
they were dangerous and unhealable anyway; we'd shoot them coming.

Your comrade dressed in fire is not your comrade any more.—
Why did you go East? I asked him. *For the cruelty?—*
I went for the Führer, and the Fatherland and Europe.—
And brought ruin on them all.—I fought to halt that ruin.—
How old were you when you went to Russia?—Nineteen.—
So you're twenty-four now?—I'm older than you, Granpa.—
What brought you to Australia?—I wouldn't rot among
civilian rabble who'd failed our Führer. Let Ivan keep them.

Have you learned English?—I've learned enough to earn my bread.
Then he flapped his hand. *German is still spoken in Odessa:*
that's where I live. Ever hear of the Army Hole, Granpa?
That was partisan country, all swamp and bog between our Armies.
Folks from there caught a party of German nurses, and laid their bodies
out by the road after. They'd used an air compressor on them.
There were no civilians behind our lines in Russia.
Ivan agreed. He shot any who weren't known partisans.

You'll jump at the latest, Laura said. *The newsagent woman*
round the corner has put her eye on Hans. She asked me
where I'd been hiding that gorgeous big Palooka.
Now she's offered him work.—Paid work? I asked. *Doing what?—*
Fetching and carrying's the paid work.—Well, I said. *Hey, eh?—*
And next he's to live in, says Laura. *She got no one? She lose her fella?—*
Well, she's lost the Yanks.—I think I've seen her.—
Yes, Laura said, *she wears that blue button-through cleaner's dress.*

My rescue from the Russian Front was ordinary life like that
and a new bloke they moved into the room with a burnt leg
under a sort of trellis in his blankets. Big butcher-faced bloke,
he heard us talk at night. *Ar no,* he said, *bloody foreign language,*
I won't have that, not near me yez don't, arkle-barkle gibberidge,
as bad as Nelsons Bay, Gan Gan Army Camp, they got that full of yez.
The Sister bustled in: *Don't be slanging Fred, Mr Sloggett,*
he's my star patient: awful injuries, never moans. Nothing hurts him.

I worried a bit about the touch of police in Laura;
far-fetched, I spose, to see that in some sniffiness about
a button-through dress and a bit of the miraculous for Hans,
but police was a disease I had a nose for, always.
I held my trap, though, and listened to Mo on the wireless
and that same Hans came in, with a goofy new authority to him,
and called me a big Palooka. *I am a petrol,* he added
and all in English, then he dropped into German—

Don't talk German, mate. Mr Sloggett doesn't like it.
Hans puzzled and said *Mr Schlogget play with his tool.*
That did it. I had swearing at Hans and screaming from him
and the Obstuf murmuring *We shot a whole institute of idiots*
Ivan had left behind.—Now you're in Hell, I snapped at him
all peace ahead and no more atrocities for you.
It took me two years till I dropped down that he most likely
couldn't stop confessing his stories, of where the massed drums had led him.

Norrie came in the day I was to leave there
and told me his latest. *I found the word for it*
in a book: I call it the erectile motor car.
Turn the motor on and the car swells to full size,
get out and turn her off, and she collapses.—
And when you're in her and the motor like cuts out?—
O there'd be a delay on it collapsing.—
That was the day poor old Gandhi got shot, in India.

I went to confession just after I came home.
First time in years, again. Dark hair-oily phone box to God
with the gauzed speaking-grille. I didn't confess to the Nothing
this time. It wasn't a sin. Even if I'd done it.
Had I created it? I thought straight after that thought.
Was it something I'd made? If I had, I'd been the shirker
of the century. But it wasn't about my two-countries thing:
it was about something stronger. A way I couldn't let the world be.

Gradually old Norbert, Norrie, talked me round
to his inflatable-bodied motor car. It was the chassis that filled
with exhaust gas—you didn't sit in a gas bubble!
There'd be no more threat from collisions or capsizings,
you'd bounce off, or roll upright again. No accident ever worse
than a puncture. His narrow face with tufts of whiskers shone
like a church window, describing it. Blessed Norbert, pray for us.
I could have done our money on the horses and had less fun.

The rationing came off groceries. The black market life was going
the way of old uniform pants worn out on the building sites.
It seemed yesterday's Army had all turned into builders' labourers
so much of the world was getting fenced with palings and framed up.
I found I was carting more cement and roofing iron than petrol.
And yet it was a time of ghosts. I was up at Krambach
in the pub one day and a long bloke in the bar,
dairy-farmer by his strong white hands, he turned around

and suddenly went mad. *I smell Japs!* he screamed out
I smell Japs! and tore a bar stool up lengthways
to make a club. There was a scatter at the door
and two fellows in suits being hurried to a car by a third suit.
I glimpsed Japanese faces. The farmer exploded out the door
and sank his naily club a foot deep in the car's steel roof
before his mates secured him. *Cattle buyers from Japan*, someone said.
Jim was in Thailand. It's hard to switch off some blokes' memories.

This day, Cos and Betty and me and Laura were sitting
up in King Edward Park above the city. We each told a story.
Betty told how when she was a station cook
she had one boss who made her take the raisins
and sultanas out of any cakes that went stale
and use them again. He was deaf, but you got his attention
by saying Twenty-five quid, as soft as you liked, around him.
While she was there, her baby used to sit on a blanket

right near the kitchen door, on the homestead verandah.
One day Betty saw a wet circle round the baby's head
and she puzzled over it. A gleamy wet ring above the ears—
and then her blood ran cold because she knew what it was:
a python had tested to see whether it could fit over the baby.
They swallow big prey by drawing themselves over it
like a stocking. Apparently the child had been too big
or didn't keep still, or something had scared the snake in time.

Cos said: *I got this new bloke working for me.—*
I never saw him yet, I put in. *No, he heard you're German, like,*
so he ducks off when you're coming. He's a Slav, he reckons,
or maybe he's been a Slav. He goes back to Nelsons Bay camp
looking for German girls. Only Germans. I asked him about that
and he hummed and ha'ed, but I understood him to say
he can only perform, like, get a horn, with the frauleins.
Seems the Nazis were real buggers to him and his people.

And Laura's story: *Fred and I went on holidays to Sydney*
oh, twenty-odd years ago, when he was still on the dredge.
I'd got us tickets to a society ball through my school friend.
(*Got him to draw them,* I muttered. *You be quiet!* she blushed.)
Fred hired a dinner suit. There were a lot of men there still
done out in tail coats. Bumfreezers were just coming in.
A tall spiffy fellow, girls said he was a real jazzer
and I could see he was, he was spinning a little blonde thing

faster than a record, and then they spun right off. Vanished.
I noticed he was back for the dance after next. And then
there were odd snorts and giggles, as he turned in the dancing
and I noticed the one little change in his perfect get-up:
his tails were tucked in his trousers at the back.
I got the giggles myself and told Fred, but he didn't catch on.
You didn't, love. The man's editor of a big paper now. Ah, fun:
I could have enjoyed Hollywood! After that, I told some sort of story.

Norrie drove me in to town to get some petrol coupons
for Joe, who was starting as a Rawleighs traveller
in a brand new FJ Holden with the sandbags in the boot.
As we drove, old Norrie got on to the German excuses
as he sometimes did. *Cars, diesels, highways—we invented it all, Fred,*
got a grunt from me, and made me feel fifty-four years old.
And Röntgen inventing X-rays: do you reckon he might have saved
millions of lives, by now?—*Yeah, but not the same lives,* I said.

[252]

Kyle Bourke blew on our petrol-ration coupons and gave me them.
A sailor was here for you, Fred. The boys had sent him
He left a message for you from a Sam Moondeen.
My ears pointed at him. Sam hadn't written since the war.
I'd been worried. Where he lived or worked I'd no idea, to write to.
Seems your man was sailing to Australia with his family
and he gave this sailor his message, then that night
went overboard, jumped they think, out to sea off Gladstone.—

Give me his message.—'*Tell Fred that Noah couldn't bear*
to look at the ground' *or maybe* '*to look at the drowned*'.
The sailor wasn't sure which, exactly.—*When did this happen?*—
Oh weeks ago. They landed his family at Sydney
and the local Jews took them in. Your man from Shanghai was a Jew?
Bourke was looking at me, Norrie was looking at me:
Among other things he was a Jew. He was my best friend, I said
which was true but didn't sum it up. *He was my instructor*

I heard myself say, but knew they'd think I meant engineering.
Wording a gravestone is hard, and I wasn't near ready.
I'd have to see Rachel—and talk to her in what language?
My head was full of action, and not a thing I could do.
That's death. That's death, Sam would have said.
I went home numb in more than just my bark,
and Norrie saying *You know, one German in three*
died in the religious wars? Back in the seventeenth century?

That's hung over on us. You ought to read history, Fred.
Geez I wish I could speak German.—*You'd see the world all different,*
I managed to say. *You're better off reading books.*
I went home and lay on the bed and didn't go to work.
That is, I lay on the air and the bed legitimised it.
It was all leprosy again, rotting away inside me
and it asked: How good's your poem?
Can it make them alive again after dancing in the kerosene?

Can it help Sam swim into Heaven? Into Woodenbong, even?
That he called Nguthumbuyn, up there in the Border Ranges?
It's the white null spirit, that you can't imagine these things.
It's your deaf-body. Myself was talking to me,
the self that's the last between us and God, when others go.
With the family's living to earn, I had to snap out of this
after three days. I was going out to the Blitz wagon
and Hans's friend Mrs Zdenovich fronted me:

Is my sweetie over here? Tell him to come home for supper.
I like the way you pronounce my funny surname right:
mostly I get Za-Dennovik. You must've learnt off your brother,
he's so European, isn't he? With her smooth moist skin
going into her dress. I drove the rest of that week
and we went to bed with the fowls, like every family,
because of power blackouts; the great coal strikes were on.
That Friday evening I had to collect Louise

from her music lesson after school. Hans came up with me
and got a tennis racket and started hitting a ball
into the store space under the building opposite
from where I sat to wait. There was a crucifix
on the wall near me, and Jesus had his head turned hard
to one side, as if he was watching just one player
in Hans's tennis game; not Hans but the dark space that kept
returning his shots, mostly skew, so Hans had to chase them.

You have to pray with a whole heart, says my inner man to me,
and you haven't got one. *Can I get one?*
Forgive the Aborigines. *What have I got to forgive?*
They never hurt me! For being on our conscience.
I shook my head, and did. Forgiving feels like starting to.
That I spose I feel uneasy round you, I thought to them, shook my head
and started understanding. Hans served, and the ball came bounding back
like a happy pup. Forgive the Jews, my self said.

That one felt miles steep, stone-blocked and black as iron.
That's really not mine, the Hitler madness—No it's not, said my self.
It isn't on your head. But it's in your languages.
So I started that forgiveness, wincing, asking it as I gave it.
When I stopped asking it, cities stopped burning in my mind.
My efforts faded and went inwards. I was let rest
and come back to Hans searching under the building for his ball.
Then my self said Forgive women. *Those burning?* All women, it said.

Something tore on me, like bandage coming off scab and hair,
the white tearing off me like linen. And I knew what was coming:
Forgive God, my self said.
I shuddered at that one. Judging Him and sensing life eternal,
said my self, are different hearts. You want a single heart, to pray.
Choose one and drop one. I looked inside them both
and only one of them allowed prayer, so I chose it,
and my prayer was prayed and sent, already as I chose it.

Nothing happened that evening. Next morning I woke under weight.
Our bedclothes were on me, warming me to just above the perfect
heat I must have been at for thirty-four years.
The bedspread was covered with like caterpillars, the clock was icy,
stinging like a memory of cowtime buckets before dawn.
My thighs weren't glassy under my silk hands any more
but with pores and hairs. Memory stormed back from far, to cover
over the null time, so fast that I had only like that day

of pure rediscovering. How water dries and milk dries on,
how cold starts at knees and shoulders, where flesh isn't thick,
how a kicked toe delays its pain for a second, and then pounces—
but it was closing over, all my lone secret story.
Every thing I got turned at once into something I'd got back
except the pains I don't know that many boys feel,
rheuma and the witches' shot, sciatica. And aches, aches
in bones that had gone away still unbroken, when I was twenty.

I learned that week, in love and swears, that the earlier
times I'd been back had not been full returns,
just ghostly half-measures, memory dreaming flesh at half gravity.
Now I was sore and heavy and bogged in chairs. I lifted
nothing but my long frame, with my wrists; I walked hard stomps,
I extended all the way in itch and muscle-twist and cloth-rub
from the head I'd lived in to the feet that had been my far limits,
and from the first I knew no counter-prayer, no horror, nothing

would bring my null-body back. It was gone forever.
The limelight goes off me with it. We went on living:
Joe got married next year, which filled his dimples with grins.
Lou went to high school. I backed Norrie when I'd make extra cash
and some people picked I was different. *Not up in your point-shoes,
Fred?* as Ron asked me, getting back into his, from the war.
Later on we travelled—I paid to sleep!—and people died
of old age. But there's too much in life: you can't describe it.